THE RAPE OF LUCRETIA *and the Founding of Republics*

The Rape of Lucretia
and the Founding of Republics

Readings *in*
Livy, Machiavelli,
and Rousseau

Melissa M. Matthes

The Pennsylvania State University Press
University Park, Pennsylvania

Library of Congress Cataloging-in-Publication Data

Matthes, Melissa M., 1964–
The rape of Lucretia and the founding of republics:
readings in Livy, Machiavelli, and Rousseau / Melissa M. Matthes.
p. cm.
Includes bibliographical references and index.
ISBN 0-271-02054-7 (cloth : alk. paper)—
ISBN 0-271-02055-5 (paper : alk. paper)
1. Feminist theory—Political aspects. 2. Republicanism.
3. Republics. 4. Lucretia—In literature. I. Title.

HQ1190 .M378 2000
321.8′6′01—dc21 99-059008

Printed in the United States of America
Published by
The Pennsylvania State University Press,
University Park, PA 16802-1003

It is the policy of The Pennsylvania State University
Press to use acid-free paper for the first printing of
all clothbound books. Publications on uncoated
stock satisfy the minimum requirements of American
National Standard for Information Sciences—
Permanence of Paper for Printed Library Materials,
ANSI Z39.48–1992.

for **DMT**

CONTENTS

	Acknowledgments	ix
1	A Conversation Between Republicanism and Feminism	1
2	Livy and the Repetition of Republican Foundations	23
3	*La Mandragola* and the Seduction of Lucrezia	51
4	The Seriously Comedic, or Why Machiavelli's Lucrezia Is Not Livy's Virtuous Roman	77
5	The Paradox of Rousseau's Politics and the Return to the Founding	99
6	*Nouvelle Héloïse* and the Supplement of Sexual Difference	117
7	Concluding Remarks	155
	Bibliography	175
	Index	185

ACKNOWLEDGMENTS

When I was in graduate school, one of my friends asserted that all graduate work is autobiographical. By this she meant that the topics about which we choose to write reveal something fundamental but deeply unconscious about who we are. So, of course, we spent some quite ponderous moments (it was graduate school, after all) and some other rather silly moments (again, it was graduate school) trying to discern what each of our colleague's dissertation topics revealed about its author.

Now, with this book complete, the question of whether one's work is always autobiographical returns in another register. And, not surprisingly, the answer remains for me a resounding yes—not because something psychologically fundamental is revealed here, but because it would not have reached completion without all of those people who have been and remain fundamental to my identity as a scholar and teacher.

So this "autobiography" acknowledges and thanks my mentors, Wendy Brown, Peter Euben, Donna Haraway, Jack Schaar, Kurt Tauber, and Mark Taylor; my graduate school buddies, Kate DeGroot, Catherine Holland, Valerie Ross, and Miquel Vatter; and my current colleagues, Charles Buttersworth and Katie King. Also, I would like to embrace the memory of two of my friends in this autobiography: Paige Baty, who taught me the intellectual pleasures of finding my own way, and Meaghan Price, an undergraduate at the University of Maryland, who inspired me to give my best to teaching.

Also, for believing in my scholarship and helping it to take its current published form, I would like to thank Sandy Thatcher at Penn State Press, as well as Bruce Smith at Allegheny College, who read and re-read this manscript with tireless attention and insight.

I would also like to thank the History of Consciousness Program at the University of California, Santa Cruz, and the University of Maryland for their generous financial support of this project.

1

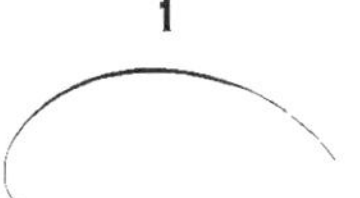

A Conversation Between Republicanism and Feminism

One of the distinctive features of republics is their concern with the common good. Significantly, this common good is not given, predetermined or static. Rather, constituting the "common good" is itself the very fiber of republican politics; republican political life is spent creating and contesting what that "common good" means.

Furthermore, because republics privilege civil rather than blood relations, bonds within republics are fragile; citizens are joined together only by a spirit of fraternity, rather than by the force of an ancestral inheritance. Consequently, the maintenance of republican stability depends, in part, on the crafting and subsequent remembrance of a shared tradition. Nonetheless, the authority of this tradition must not itself become so ossified or hegemonic that it thwarts the very political action that is vital to republics. Thus, republics struggle, always, to achieve a balance between the constitution of citizen identities that are performative and protean and the cultivation of strong civic bonds forged through the recollection of a common and cooperatively generated tradition.

Republics celebrate public life—speech, performance, appearance and reputation, which are pivotal both to their founding and to their maintenance. In no other political community is the relation between speech and politics more integral to that community's political identity than in republics. Republican actors understand themselves to be in *conversation* with a tradition of republicanism through which they conceive their origins. Machiavelli captures this moment of being in conversation with one's republican ancestors when at the end of a day of playing cards and chatting with the local merchants, he dons the garb of the ancients and receives their wisdom: "I am not ashamed to speak with them and to ask them the reasons for their actions."[1]

1. "To Francesco Vettori: 10 December 1513," in *The Letters of Machiavelli,* ed. and trans. Allan Gilbert (Chicago: University of Chicago Press, 1988), 142.

While speech is essential, republican citizenship is also, as this example illuminates, a visually and theatrically constituted epistemological field. As Machiavelli notes, "I take off the day's clothing, covered with mud and dust, and I put on garments regal and courtly; and reclothed appropriately, I enter the ancient courts of ancient men."[2] Republican politics is performative; it is dramatic, requiring both actors and spectators who are continuously exchanging roles. Republican politics is the *process* of contesting meaning and creating identity in public. Here politics is clearly about the creation of meaning, rather than the search for truth.[3] Indeed, often the performance of the truth is more important than the truth itself.

Despite their garrulous and theatrical qualities, republican politics are also traditional;[4] Machiavelli is, after all, consulting with the ancients. There is always both a nuanced texture and a specific context to republican conversations and their performance. In other words, these performances are not random play but are rather the stylized repetition of specific acts. It is these very repetitions that constitute the republic rather than simply represent it. This is, as Paul Ricoeur notes, "a quite strange brand of imitation which comprises and constructs the very thing it imitates!"[5] Indeed, the founding bonds of republics are often generated through the repetition of stories for which there are no stable originals.

This relation between the original and the repetition and between the real and representation is a frequent source of contestation in republican politics. For example, the "we" of the republic is constituted and maintained by a process of seeing and being seen by others; it is a process of repetitive re-presentation in the realm of appearances: "The reality of the world is guaranteed by the presence of others, by its appearing to all."[6] Fundamental to republics is this bond that joins each to the other in public fraternity through appearance, speech and action. Nonetheless, as important as this realm of appearance before others is to the security of the republic, there is also concurrently a desire to minimize, if not eliminate, dependence

2. Ibid.

3. Norman Jacobson, *Pride and Solace: The Functions and Limits of Political Theory* (New York: Methuen, 1978).

4. See J. G. A. Pocock's *The Machiavellian Moment: Florentine Political Thought and the Atlantic Republic Tradition* (Princeton: Princeton University Press, 1975) for a discussion of the tradition of republicanism.

5. Paul Ricoeur, *Freud and Philosophy,* trans. Denis Savage (New Haven: Yale University Press, 1970), 11.

6. Hannah Arendt, *The Human Condition* (Chicago: University of Chicago Press, 1958), 199.

upon others. Thus, republican actors contend with the recognition of an identity constituted through representation with and before others, as well as with an anxiety of the contingency that this reliance upon others suggests; it is a struggle, perhaps, most aptly captured in the republican language of *virtù* and *fortuna*. Furthermore, this struggle with autonomy and dependence, with sameness and difference, with public appearance and subjective essence complicates republican *virtù* as more than masculine heroics.

Thus, the republic is deeply gendered. Split at its inception into public and private spheres that mimic the constitution of sexual difference, republics are notoriously decried for their foundational subordination of women.[7] And yet the feminine and femininity, if not women, continually overstep the boundaries of this denial; and the effects of this ongoing quarrel are manifest, partially, in a male anxiety that plagues the fragile fraternal bond as it struggles with, and equivocates between, incorporation and renunciation of the feminine.

Most dramatically this negotiation, this struggle with the feminine other, is evident at the founding of the republic. It is then, with the violence of inauguration, when the boundaries are temporarily fixed and presumably stable, that that which must be banished or denied in order for the political community to begin is most visible. Not surprisingly then, the stories that explain and constitute the genesis of republics, their "founding stories," are also often the stories of women, specifically of women's sexual violation and of men's intercession with femininity and feminine powers.

At its genesis, what must later be absent and silent—what is most destabilizing to, and vulnerable about, the incipient republic—is most exposed. What is manifest, most obviously, is the violence and deception at the very origin of the polity, but also, and perhaps more important, the radical contingency of the republican claim to political power as well as

7. There is a plethora of feminist work pertinent specifically to this issue. For a critique of the public/private split in general, see Jean Bethke Elshtain, *Public Man/Private Woman: Women in Social and Political Thought* (Princeton: Princeton University Press, 1981); for critiques of the split of the public and private spheres in classical literature, see Adrienne Rich, "Conditions for Work: The Common World of Women," in *On Lies, Secrets, and Silence: Selected Prose* (New York: Norton, 1979), and Nancy Hartsock, "The Erotic Dimension and the Homeric Ideal," in *Money, Sex and Power: Toward a Feminist Historical Materialism* (New York: Longman, 1983); and for a historical critique of the eighteenth-century banishment of women to the private realm of republican motherhood, see Joan Landes, *Women and the Public Sphere in the Age of the French Revolution* (Ithaca: Cornell University Press, 1988).

the fragility of the bond among republican actors who are united, in part, because of their own failed masculinity.

It is here, at the founding, that a feminist political theorist can discover, reveal and re-create how the parameters of the republic, indeed, of the political itself, are negotiated and defined. And that is what this particular investigation will pursue, not only the rather obvious gendering of the public and private spheres in republics, but also the more subtle gendering of the very foundations of republicanism—the intersection of speech and politics, of the origin and its repetitions, and of specularity and citizenship. In other words, the gendering and theatricality of republican politics itself.

Toward that end, this book explores Livy's, Machiavelli's and Rousseau's thinking about republics, primarily through detailed meditations on the story they each repeat of the founding of the republic.[8] That story of the rape of Lucretia and the founding of the Roman republic is reproduced by each theorist in a way that illuminates not only their conception of political founding but also their formulation of republican politics itself. Indeed, this book will argue that each rendition, re-presentation, and recollection of the story of Lucretia seeks to spur the very republic that its retelling appears merely to describe.

I. The Rape of Lucretia

The earliest accounts of the rape of Lucretia are found in Livy's *Ab Urbe Condita* and Ovid's *Fasti*. Renditions appear again in the Italian and English Renaissance. In Italy, in addition to Niccolo Machiavelli's satirical retelling of the rape in his comedy *La Mandragola*, other popular versions included Saint Augustine's interpretation in *The City of God*; Coluccio Salutati's rhetorical treatise as Chancellor of Florence, *Declamatio Lucretia*, and Giovanni Boccaccio's didactic rendition in *Concerning Famous Women*. And these are only the written accounts; there were numerous pictorial and other artistic representations of Lucretia and her plight, including a three-dimensional float of Lucretia paraded at the third wedding ceremony of her namesake, Lucretia Borgia. Lucretia's story assumed political significance again in the

8. Although I will give an in-depth analysis of what is considered the "original" dramatic retelling of Lucretia's story in Livy's *Early History of Rome*, the focus of this analysis will be on Machiavelli's and Rousseau's renditions. I will use Livy's account as a means to suggest broadly the significance of the story and as a way to locate Machiavelli's and Rousseau's retellings of it.

eighteenth century, primarily in France,[9] when it was recounted, not only in Jean-Jacques Rousseau's unfinished tragic rendition, "La Mort de Lucrèce," but reinterpreted by Voltaire in his tragedy *Brutus*.

Paradoxically, the tale itself does not seem to have the makings of transhistorical interest. It is, after all, only a story about a woman, and then a story, rather common under patriarchy, of a woman who is raped and then commits suicide after her "disgrace." Yet the story recurs across time and across Europe. Why? It is only by recognizing that each resurgence of the Lucretia story is linked to intense interest in the founding of a republic that the significance of the tale and its repetitions develops.

The variations in the historical incarnations of the story are intriguing, especially the logic that seems to necessitate the rape of a woman in order to found a republic. Why is sexual violation of a woman found at the republican origin; that is, why are republics, rather than tyrannies or monarchies, established as a result of the rape of a woman? How does that fact reconfigure one's consequent understanding of republican *virtù*? How does rape secure a fraternal bond? What values and principles are being concurrently destroyed (e.g., tyranny and domestic security) and established (e.g., fraternity and sex-right) by these violent beginnings? And finally, how are gender roles and hierarchies inaugurated by these particular origin stories? What is "female honor" when a woman's suicide is the catalyst for republican freedom? What is "male honor" when sexual violence unites strangers?

Interestingly, both Sigmund Freud in *Totem and Taboo* and Norman O. Brown in his rereading of Freud in *Love's Body* offer compelling analyses for why there is this constellation of sexual violence, republican foundings and gender hierarchy.[10] Both of these thinkers suggest that the creation of the bonds of fraternity are deeply embedded in formations of sexual difference. Freud argues that the killing of the father that inaugurates the equality of citizen-brothers is motivated, in part, by the desire for shared sexual access to women. Norman O. Brown asserts that women traditionally enjoy more

9. During the founding of the Dutch republic in the eighteenth century, there were also several theatrical renditions of Lucretia's story. See *The Dutch Republic in the Eighteenth Century: Decline, Enlightenment and Revolution*, ed. Margaret Jacob and Wijnand W. Mijnhardt (Ithaca: Cornell University Press, 1992).

10. Indeed, Norman O. Brown asserts, "Without an understanding of the seamy side of sexuality there is no understanding of politics" (*Love's Body* [New York: Vintage Books, 1966], 11). Sigmund Freud, *Totem and Taboo: Some Points of Agreement Between the Mental Lives of Savages and Neurotics* (London: Routledge, 1961).

autonomy in fraternal republics than under customary patriarchal monarchies because the separation of spheres leaves women to be "mistresses of their own domains."[11]

Nonetheless, the renditions and repetitions of the story of the rape of Lucretia in the republican tradition suggest that the constitution of sexual difference is not quite as finished or stable as these two theoretical accounts would seem to augur. Although the story of the rape of Lucretia is ostensibly an account of how the republic is founded over a woman's dead body, there is also a way in which the specter of Lucretia's raped body continues to haunt the new republic. In the trajectory of republican history, Lucretia's story, as itself historical object, is both recalled and repeated, and then forgotten and denied. Lucretia's raped body as well as her story remain taboo throughout the life of the republic because her sexual violation reminds her male kin of their own failed masculinity (they could not safeguard her) *and* of their own continued desires for sexual conquest (each would like to have the sexual and political power of the tyrant/rapist). Thus, there is in these republican renditions a recognized contagion between the recollection of the story of Lucretia's rape and the temptation that her violation represents. Indeed, although republicans do not themselves rape Lucretia, they found their citizenry on the recollection of the temptation that the spectacle of her violation recalls.

This founding story confounds the frequent feminist interpretation of republics as fundamentally misogynist in their rigid distinction between the public and private spheres. For example, Adrienne Rich critiques republics for their denial of the body and of necessity.[12] Yet Lucretia's story highlights how in this instance, rather than simply denying the body, a kind of authority is ascribed to the materiality of Lucretia's female body. Moreover, the labor of this female body fulfills not a biological need, but a cultural one. Male authority is constituted by, and repeatedly made contingent on, this external validation.

As Luce Irigaray has observed, the formation of the political often occurs through, and is dependent upon, the feminine.[13] Here, the female body is the means by which a spectacle is constructed, a spectacle that inaugurates a political community founded upon seeing and being seen, as the transhistorical retellings of this story demonstrate. It is the spectacle

11. Ibid., 13.

12. Rich, *On Lies, Secrets, and Silences*.

13. Luce Irigaray, *The Sex Which Is Not One*, trans. Catherine Porter (Ithaca: Cornell University Press, 1985).

of Lucretia's body, both literally and metaphorically, that helps to constitute the political "we." Although the display of Lucretia's body appears to suggest the passivity of the female body (i.e., the display of the dead woman for the male gaze), the spectacle of Lucretia's rape and suicide also ignites political action; her violation and suicide spurs a political founding. Her suicide thus becomes a form of female power, a kind of "ennobling violation."[14] Through her suicide, Lucretia determines how her body and life will be read.

II. REPUBLICAN FOUNDINGS

To found a republic is to recognize, implicitly, that politics is social. First, the very notion of a founding suggests the creation of something that does not naturally exist; "to found" denotes deliberately crafting that which does not simply evolve from what existed previously. Moreover, to found a republic is to forge an association or community built upon civic rather than blood relations. As such, a republic is a creation of history, with a recognized beginning and, presumably, an end.

As a result, among republicans there is a suspicion that political life is an aberration in nature, an artifice, and thus continually at risk from the vicissitudes of all things human.[15] That the republican ideal acknowledged the fact of its own mortality is symbolized, as J. G. A. Pocock notes, "by its choice of hero as the unsuccessful rebel Brutus."[16] From the perspective of this book, the repetition of the story of the rape and suicide of Lucretia is further evidence of republican anxiety regarding its own demise. Republican politics is understood by its citizens as the "art of the possible" and as therefore necessarily contingent.

Through the founding of a republic, a political "we" is constituted. A republic does not recognize a preexisting identity but instead creates one. And in this creation, one of the virtues of republicanism is manifest—its concern with the construction and maintenance of a common good. At its core, republicanism has a conception of what citizens share; to be political in a republic is to be attentive to interests other than one's own.

14. Gayatri Spivak, "Can the Subaltern Speak?" in *Marxism and Interpretation* (Urbana: University of Illinois Press, 1988).

15. See, for example, Bruce James Smith, *Politics and Remembrance: Republican Themes In Machiavelli, Burke and Tocqueville* (Princeton: Princeton University Press, 1985) and J. G. A. Pocock, *The Machiavellian Moment*.

16. Pocock, *The Machiavellian Moment*, 51.

Thus republican political identity is achieved in action, rather than existing as a given. In political action the doing, the performance, is crucial. And the common good is generated by this ability to be performed. Citizens "do not act because of what they already are, their actions do not express a prior, stable identity; they presuppose an unstable, multiple self that seeks its, at best, episodic self realization in action and in the identity that is its reward."[17]

Because this performance is contingent on the recognition and reception of others, republican politics is, consequently, also focused on what kind of citizens, as well as what kind of politics, this process produces. For example, Jean-Jacques Rousseau, quite anxious about a political process in which citizen identity is constituted through the spectatorship of others, focuses much of his political thinking on describing and controlling the perceived dangers of this identity constitution.

Republicanism, then, is more than a form of government; it is a way of thinking and talking about political things. As Hannah Arendt has eloquently argued, political action in republics is not simply about the performance of a specific deed; it is also the performance of that deed before one's fellow citizens, and their subsequent response to, and narration of, that deed.[18] As important as the deed itself are the stories told about it; how deeds are narrated and how they are remembered is a form of republican political action. As a result, "republics generally have been noisy places, home to oration and dialogue."[19]

The stories that republics tell are more than literary superstructure; these stories are integral to the construction of the republic's political identity. Stories not only memorialize the important deeds and moments in the republic's history, but they also actually help to constitute those moments as memorable, as important. The stories and their retellings are the creation as well as the remembrance of a shared past. The stories' repetitions are a manifestation of the need for the continuous renewal of the bonds that form the republic.

The pivotal moment most frequently memorialized in the republic's history is the story of its founding. A return to the foundation unites the citizens across time and space—a reminder both of the temporality of the

17. Bonnie Honig, "Toward an Agonistic Feminism: Hannah Arendt and the Politics of Identity," in *Feminists Theorize the Political*, ed. Judith Butler and Joan M. Scott (New York: Routledge, 1992), 220.

18. Arendt, *The Human Condition*.

19. Smith, *Politics and Remembrance*, 8.

republic and of its continuity. Furthermore, the oft-repeated tale of the founding links each republic that memorializes the tale to those republics that have preceded it. The story serves as a form of continuity with the past; it is a hedge against the deterioration of time, repeated in the hope of renovation and renewal.

The covenant of the republic has often been this principle of echo:[20] repetitions collectively recalled. Memory thus serves as a form of action in republics. Indeed, as Arendt argues, actions only live on in the narratives of those who perform them and the narratives of those who understand, interpret and *recall* them. What is done is defined by what is said about it.

Yet the repetition of this origin story must not become, as Arendt worries, "a decisive principle" that forestalls politics with "its homogeneity of past and origin."[21] Republican politics requires an element of the undetermined in order to preserve the viability of actions collectively achieved. The founding story of the rape of Lucretia closes spaces in republican politics but opens others, in part, because it is frequently told in dramatic form. The story, as theatre, is concrete yet open to reconceptualization, rooted yet unfinished. As theatre, the story is susceptible to rearrangement, reinterpretation, recreation and recovery.

The story of the rape of Lucretia also recalls the violence of beginnings. The violence at the foundation is a recognition that the inauguration of politics necessitates that which the maintenance of republican politics itself cannot permit—the exclusion of the contingent. Foundings, paradoxically, often seem to violate the most basic principles of the political communities they seek to inaugurate. Hence, there is an ambivalent relation to founding: on the one hand, there are the oft-repeated retellings of the founding in order to secure the fraternal bonds; and on the other hand, there is the desire to erase the moment of origin, as both Machiavelli and Rousseau detail. This desire to forget is also a desire to forestall the temptations that recollection may incite. Thus, the story of the rape of Lucretia is simultaneously recalled and then denied and forgotten.

III. REPUBLICAN SPECULARITY

Part of what it means to be a republican citizen, as noted above, is to perform for others. The "we" of the republic is constituted by the mutual

20. Ibid., 19.

21. Hannah Arendt, *On Revolution* (New York: Viking Press, 1963), 174.

recognition of each by the other. Fraternity is, in part, the acknowledgment of strangers as brothers. And this bond is itself partially safeguarded by seeing and being seen by others. One is constituted as a citizen by the gaze of the other. Each performs, then, for the other and with the knowledge of being seen. This confers three important qualities on republican citizenship: (1) a sociability of citizenship: one is not a citizen unless one acts in public *and* is seen to be acting by others; (2) a reciprocity of citizenship: one's actions are always performed with the knowledge that one is being looked at and therefore are adjusted accordingly—that is, the look of the other changes the act itself; and (3) the recognition of the power and responsibility of the spectator/audience. Because of this sociability and reciprocity, republican political actors must learn not only how to act but how to look.

Given this implicit reliance of each upon the other, the cultivation of judgment is paramount to the production of republican citizenship. Judgment is foregrounded because the very constitution of citizens is dependent on the estimation and interpretation of others. Hence, we witness the concern in republican theory with the problem of representation, framed in both Machiavelli and Rousseau as a concern with appearances and authenticity, respectively.

One of the consequences of the second quality of republican citizenship, the knowledge of always being looked at, propels Rousseau's relentless concern with authenticity—the fear that the knowledge of the look of the other prohibits self-transparency and generates dissimulation, vanity and *amour-propre.* For Machiavelli, however, this knowledge and necessity of the other is what legitimizes his manipulation of appearance in a drive to achieve the common good. However, for Machiavelli, it is the third quality, the power of looking, that primarily informs his formulation of political judgment. The successful political actor must learn what to look at, how to look, as well as how to discriminate between the real and the representation. Indeed, aptly deploying the power of looking, as well as manipulating the gaze, is pivotal to Machiavellian *virtù.*

These performances, these ceremonies of reciprocity and the interpretation of such actions are not metaphors for political activity, they are politics itself. These performances constitute the reality of the republic; they are its self-portrayal and enactment. Inherent in this self-portrayal is a fundamental dilemma for republicanism—the very mechanism for constituting identity/citizenship is deeply gendered.

This is an argument that the public gaze is not only an action and a mode of vision, but also always a matter of sexual difference. A rather rigid interpretation of specularity is that the gaze is necessarily masculine and the object is inherently feminized. My analysis, instead, is an examination of the ways in which masculinity is itself constituted by being looked at, by the seduction of the gaze in republican politics. For example, Machiavelli aptly articulates the stunning power of being looked at and the ability to manipulate appearance in *The Prince*. His is a conception of power in which he who successfully makes himself the object of the gaze has the most power.

Importantly, to be a member of a republic necessitates that one be not only a subject but an object as well, that one simultaneously inhabit both "masculine" and "feminine" positions. One is constituted by being looked at, by the performance one gives *and* by the judgment and narration one makes by looking at others. Together, looking and being looked at are crucial to the notion of the "common good."

It is an irony of republican politics that at his most masculine moment of action, the republican citizen is simultaneously "feminized" by the gaze of the other. It is no surprise, then, that republics are such fragile communities, continually threatened by each member's desire to position himself as the despot, the sole spectator who sees all and yet remains unmoved by being seen. The ingenious theoretical moves republican thinkers will make to limit this perceived danger is often at the very core of their political thinking. This ingenuity is perhaps most compellingly exemplified by Rousseau.

As I will argue throughout this book, both Machiavelli and Rousseau have distinct strategies for coping with their anxiety about this perceived vulnerability of republican specularity. Each will alternately suggest either complete domination or accommodation of the gaze of one's fellow citizens. Machiavelli indulges in being the object of the gaze, controlling but enjoying the feminized masquerade; while Rousseau denies himself this pleasure and tries to conceive of political life without the debilitating gaze of an imperial other. Interestingly, Machiavelli seems to revel in the power of looking, while Rousseau remains preoccupied with the disempowerment of being looked at. (Even so, Rousseau struggles with, and often gives in to, the temptation of "playing to" and performing for the audience.)

This ambivalent relation to the gaze of the other is further manifested by the ambivalence that male citizens (and republican thinkers) have toward constructions of the feminine. In both Machiavelli's and Rousseau's thinking there is a contradictory desire for either complete domination of the feminine (witness Machiavelli's oft-cited denunciation of Fortuna) or for the complete incorporation of the feminine in a tamed and domesticated form (witness Rousseau's now much-belabored construction of republican motherhood). What is most important, however, is that both the denunciation and the incorporation take specifically republican—that is, "theatrical"—forms in the work of both thinkers.

Performative citizenship highlights the fact that there is no fixed, stable identity. There is no preexisting citizenry, only the continually created and renewed bonds of that unstable construct, the collective "we." As a consequence, this performance is not an imitation; here, the representation is the real. Clifford Geertz makes this observation about a Balinese theatre state in which the polity's essential manifestation rests in its self-portrayal; its action is an acting out.[22] A similar observation can be made about the republics that both Machiavelli and Rousseau imagine. The acting out is the action of politics. Hence, the founding story is more than political ideology; it is both the form and the structure of republican politics.

What I am arguing against here is the misconception that this theatricality of republican politics is simply "an artifice, more or less cunning, more or less illusional, designed to facilitate the aims of the ruler . . . the instrument of powers concealed beneath it or towering over it. Its relation to the real business of politics . . . is extrinsic."[23] Instead, my aim is to think through the ways in which republican politics itself is intrinsically and substantively theatrical. This theatrical power does not disguise the "real" operation of power but is itself both constitutive of, and a deployment of, that power.

Consequently, one of the juxtapositions that I focus on in the following chapters is the interplay between reality and appearance, between authenticity and falsity. For what theatricality suggests is that there is no real, no authentic, no singular truth; instead, there is only the repetition of the performance, which itself enacts a slippage between fact and fiction, between the real and the representation. In theatre there is no first time, no original; there is only recurrence and reproduction. Theatricality is not so much an imitation of reality as an action itself.

22. Clifford Geertz, *Negara: The Theatre State in Nineteenth-Century Bali* (Princeton: Princeton University Press, 1980).

23. Ibid., 122.

If politics is about the process of creating meaning rather than representing truth, then the status of truth itself is implicitly challenged in the theatricality of republican politics. If politics is performative, then truth becomes suspect as just another performative moment. This suspicion takes concrete form in the political thinking of both Machiavelli and Rousseau.

Machiavelli is quick to dismiss adherence to the truth in the pursuit of political power. What constitutes the real in Machiavellian terms is a negotiation between *fortuna* and *virtù*, not a preexisting category to which one strives to correspond. For Machiavelli, performance is primary; appearance alone will often suffice.

Similarly, and perhaps surprisingly to conservative readings of his work, Rousseau can also be read as challenging the distinction between authenticity and falsity. Particularly in his later work, when he loses confidence in the reader's (spectator's) ability to read accurately (interpret) his words (actions), Rousseau relies on a rather Machiavellian manipulation and orchestration of "truth." The increasing didacticism of his dialogues (usually prefaces justifying his writing of a particular work) is a manifestation not only of Rousseau's skepticism about whether truth-telling is possible, but of his invention of, rather than search for, that truth. Rousseau invents the real, the true, in the *guise* of the natural, the transparent and the authentic. While Machiavelli is not worried about the loss of the real or even about keeping his machinations secret, Rousseau relentlessly tries to disguise what he has discovered, that there is no real, or at least not one sufficient to his purposes.

Finally, the distinction between the real and appearance is itself gendered. First, the distinction is gendered in the most obvious way, because appearance is often associated in each thinker's work with women and with femininity. In Machiavelli, appearance is associated with the feminine Fortuna. Although the judgment of (masculine) *virtù* is required to interpret and intercept the power of Fortuna, the political actor must also learn how to orchestrate (feminine) *appearance* in order to succeed. Machiavelli details how to read appearances, how not to be misled by Fortuna, *and*, importantly, how to mislead others. Politics requires, then, knowing how and when to assume the position of the actor (the masculine role of *virtù*) and how and when to assume the role of object (the feminized role of Fortuna/appearance).

In Rousseau, women are also associated with appearance. Sophie, Rousseau's ideal woman, is an imitation without an original: a simulacrum, a sheer invention. She disrupts the boundary between the real and the representational. In this instance, what counts as the real is as imagined as the imitation. For Rousseau the split between the real and the representation slips as Rousseau uncovers that the real is itself unstable.

IV. POLITICAL THEORY AND FEMINISM

With this conception of republics and republican foundings in mind, this book is imagined as a conversation between the tradition of republicanism and the narratives of feminist theory. As such, it is also more broadly a conversation between the tradition of political theory and feminism. Feminists have often debated the possible relations that feminism can have to the legacy of political theory. Some have argued that because of the tradition's concern with the public *as* the political, women's interests and experiences, specifically those understood as "private" (i.e., mothering and reproduction and the gendered division of labor) have necessarily been excluded from the canon of political theory.[24] In these formulations, women become the Other against whom the tradition defines itself. As a result, all one can do as a feminist is stand outside, excluded, looking in, noting the ways in which one's questions and concerns fundamentally violate the historic parameters.

Others have argued that to engage the culture of political theory on its own terms is to run the risk of appropriation and of the potential reinscription of that exclusionary tradition.[25] Arguing that the authority of masculinity is deeply embedded in the language and construction of the legacy itself, these theorists assert that "femininity" has been reduced to an endless re-presentation and mirroring of masculinity. In this formulation, sexual difference, indeed, "woman," exists as a category prior to its articulation, and it exists in a way that the tradition of political theory can never "get right." The focus is on *what* woman signifies in the tradition of political theory rather than on *how* she signifies.[26]

24. See Mary O'Brien, *The Politics of Reproduction* (Boston: Routledge, 1981), and Hartsock, *Money, Sex and Power*.

25. See *New French Feminisms: An Anthology*, ed. Elaine Marks and Isabelle de Courtivron (Amherst: University of Massachusetts Press, 1980); specifically, see Julia Kristeva and Luce Irigaray in this volume.

26. For a compelling critique of this model of political theory as a voracious vulture of women's culture, see Linda Zirilli's "Resignifying the Woman Question in Political Theory," in *Signifying Woman: Culture and Chaos in Rousseau, Burke, and Mill* (Ithaca: Cornell University Press, 1994).

In contrast, this work will insist, as others have,[27] that there is an alternative that allows for a feminist mediation without either the need for an autonomous culture of women's interests or one that risks the danger of appropriation when reengaging the tradition. This is a conception in which there is no autonomous externality named "women's interests" that is not integral to defining what counts as "the political." Indeed, this book will argue that the delineation of sexual difference is itself both constituted by, and constitutive of, formulations of political and specifically republican formulations.

The focus of this book will be on how the signification of woman helps to produce republican politics as well as on how the signification of republican politics produces woman. Neither category will be presumed to exist prior to the articulation of the other. Although political theory is "not the inventor of this category [i.e., woman], it does code it in ways that are neither unique and independent of, nor simply reducible to other practices defining the meaning of women in society."[28] Political theory becomes, in this conception, part of the historical constitution of sexual difference. The focus of this analysis will be less on *what* woman signifies in republican political foundings and more on *how* she signifies and on how her signification makes possible specific formulations of politics and political life.

This book will argue further that because of the mutually constitutive relation between "woman" and "politics," masculinity has not yet managed finally and fully to co-opt the productivity of power. Although the category of woman is socially constituted and defined within the tradition of political theory, it has not been wholly evacuated of all its disruptive autonomy and political resistance. While there is not a female "essence" that evades social construction, the signification of woman and sexual difference itself cannot be readily contained and restrained—the process of signifying woman, indeed of signifying politics itself, always exceeds what is within the easy grasp of the political theorist.

* * *

In his introduction to *Politics and Vision: Continuity and Innovation in Western Political Thought*, Sheldon Wolin asserts that "of all the constraints on the

27. See, for example, Wendy Brown, *Manhood and Politics: A Feminist Reading in Political Theory* (Totowa, N.J.: Rowman and Littlefield, 1988); Christine Di Stefano, *Configurations of Masculinity: A Feminist Perspective on Modern Political Theory* (Ithaca: Cornell University Press, 1991); and Hanna Pitkin, *Fortune Is a Woman: Gender and Politics in the Thought of Niccolo Machiavelli* (Berkeley: University of California Press, 1984).

28. Zirilli, "Resignifying the Woman Question," 140.

political philosopher's freedom to speculate, none has been so great as the tradition of political philosophy itself."[29] As evidence, Wolin cites the tenacity of a tradition in which the terms of the debate have been set, refined and transmitted as cultural legacy. Nonetheless, while recognizing the constraints, Wolin also heralds the advantages of this heritage. The tradition, he argues, gives the political theorist a sense of traveling in a familiar world where the landscape has already been explored. It enables communication between contemporaries by serving as a convenient shorthand among them. Further, the tradition contributes to the endless task of accommodating new political experience to the existing scheme of things, thus producing the appearance of continuity. Political thinking becomes, then, not so much a tradition of discovery as one of meaning created over time.[30]

Yet, these "advantages" loom as monolithic obstacles to the feminist theorist first approaching the canonical terrain of political theory. The landscape is not familiar to her; no place in it marks visibly where she has been; the communication among contemporaries is often one in which her concerns and experiences are difficult to articulate in the vernacular of political theory; and her sense of continuity with the past is decidedly disrupted when what she considers political turns out not to have been transmitted or preserved by convention.

Nonetheless, for the feminist political theorist the innovations that conventional theorists have made to the tradition itself are illuminating. As Wolin notes, one of the formative elements of political thinking is innovation.[31] Although the tradition of political theory has privileged that which is public, universal and masculine, it has also simultaneously and continuously contested the parameters for defining the political. And these contestations, as Wolin notes, take form not through assertions of unprecedented originality or novelty, but through rearranged constellations of meaning. For example, what makes Machiavelli's and Rousseau's work "original," according to this model, lies less in what they newly create than in what they reject or omit in their thinking and in what they emphasize or recover. This reconfiguring is what Wolin applauds as the displacement of

29. Sheldon Wolin, *Politics and Vision: Continuity and Innovation in Western Political Thought* (Boston: Little, Brown, 1960), 22.

30. Ibid., 23.

31. This is a good reason, then, for feminists to look to foundings, which are themselves quintessential innovations.

a unifying assumption that throws a system of ideas out of balance; this is the innovation of political theory. Subordinate ideas become prominent, while primary ideas recede into secondary importance.[32]

And here, finally, is a method that the feminist theorist can deploy. By bringing what has been in the background of traditional political theory to the foreground, by showing how such background elements have been constitutive of the foreground, the feminist theorist can often fundamentally alter what has been preserved and understood as a conventional given.

This is not to dismiss, however, the importance of very legitimate criticisms of this political tradition. Political theory is not so monolithic that it can consume and subsume all antagonistic engagements with it. Rather, mine is an argument that the questions and engagements of feminist political theory are not alien or extraneous to the tradition of political theory but are part of the legacy of innovation central to the tradition itself.

Feminist political theory is not the adding of women to the stir of the political tradition, nor is it the discounting of that tradition for its neglect of women; rather, the originality of much contemporary feminist political theory, like the originality of both Machiavelli and Rousseau, lies in what it emphasizes or recovers. Using the founding story of the rape of Lucretia as a guiding trope, this work engages both with the theorists concerned with the origins of republics who have neglected this pivotal story, as well as with those feminist theorists who have derided republics for their inegalitarian public/private split and masculinist *virtù*. Feminist political theory, such as the project of this book, is still reminiscent of the journey Sheldon Wolin invokes of transversing a familiar landscape, but this feminist journey is genealogical rather than linear. It is a journey that examines *how* the familiar landscape was produced: What features were highlighted and marked for easy recognition by the previous travelers? It is a journey that explores what the shorthand of the tradition occludes: What aspects of political life can the signs and symbols of the tradition not translate or, at least, not translate adequately? It is also a journey that revisits, as this book will, the sites where the contests over the parameters of politics were fought: What were the features of those contests, and how did the victors try to stabilize the dissension? The feminist sojourn in political theory is a genealogical one that surveys the moments and places the tradition has not yet visited or perhaps taken sufficiently into account.

32. Wolin, *Politics and Vision*, 25.

If one takes seriously the theoretical crisis of "the death of the subject," the devaluation of universal claims, the limitations of transhistorical narratives and the various ruptures in representation, *and* if one recognizes Nietzsche's assertion that in times of crisis every culture tends to turn to its "others," to become feminized (in the sense of having to face its limitations, gaps and deficiencies), then political theory, at this moment of theoretical crisis, must (and should) turn to its feminized other in order to understand itself: "It is as if the modern subject, the split subject, discovers the feminine layer of his own thought just as he loses the mastery he used to assume as his own. He discovers his gender specificity as a loss of the former universal value that was attributed to the masculine gender. Under the impact of feminist criticism, in fact, the complicity between the masculine and the universal is unveiled and rejected."[33] This feminized other is then recognized, not as outside the tradition, but as pivotal to its very constitution. Feminist political theory offers a genealogy of the production of truth, of politics and of masculinity inside the boundaries of political theory. It is a genealogy that illuminates, as well, the effects of a tradition that ignores crucial elements of its own constitution. Rereading the canon of political theory for its negotiation and contestation with the feminine is a way to break apart the perception of the tradition as monolithic, exclusionary and masculinist: in other words, as quintessentially modern. Instead, from a feminist perspective, the tradition can begin to interrogate itself, to speak its silences and to expose its gaps.

I want to be careful, here. I am not suggesting that the categories *masculinity* and *femininity* have some transhistorical essence. Rather, this duality and its contents are constituted by historically specific vectors of social, economic and political power. Furthermore, what is packed into the category of femininity in the republican tradition of founding narratives are those qualities and activities that are most destabilizing to the representation and security of masculine identity. These denied and subordinated attributes, paradoxically, are what actually create and preserve the very possibility for masculinity. Republican masculinity requires the feminine, the banished other, in order to found itself and in order to know and recognize itself. The intention, in part, of this book is to reveal what Luce Irigaray, calls the grammar of gender[34]—that is, to interrogate the conditions and

33. Rosi Braidotti, *Patterns of Discourse: A Study of Women in Contemporary Philosophy* (Cambridge: Polity, 1991), 10.

34. Irigaray, *This Sex Which Is Not One.*

mechanisms through which the categories of masculinity and femininity are themselves delineated.

This is not to deny that femininity is repeatedly denigrated and subordinated in these constructions of republics but rather to highlight that the articulation of the boundary between masculinity and femininity is itself a source of repeated political contestation. This analysis will read the oft-repeated founding story of the rape of Lucretia as a symptom, in the Freudian sense; a manifestation of a repression that fails. Any symptom articulates something that is so dangerous to the health of the psyche that it must be repressed but yet is so strong, so seductive in its desire, that it can not be fully denied. Duplicitous by nature, a symptom tries to maintain a balance of sorts, but it does so by obliquely pointing to that which threatens to disturb the order.[35] The historical retellings of the rape of Lucretia illustrate, in part, the failure of politics to deny the feminine; the retellings articulate the inability, finally, for politics to be only about a stable and secured masculinity.

The story of the rape of Lucretia simultaneously resonates in three registers. First, the performance of the story constitutes not only the boundaries between the public and private spheres, but more important, the boundaries of sexual difference itself; the very constitution of republican masculinity is enacted in the story. Second, the repeated performances of the story are a manifestation of the anxiety about that newly constituted masculinity and the fragility of the incipient political community, the republic, which is secured by it. Third, since the story is often performed as theatre, particularly in the two examples that are the primary focus of this book, the performative repetition of the story highlights constitutive elements of republics.

What will preoccupy the following chapters, overall, is not only the similarities in the telling of these founding stories, but also, and significantly, the differences among the historical renditions of the story. Obviously, the Lucretia story told by Machiavelli in the Italian Renaissance and the one repeated by Rousseau during the French Enlightenment cannot be conflated simply as republican founding stories with the same transhistorical purpose and agenda. Although there are important similarities in the way these stories function in republican politics, this analysis will be

35. Elisabeth Bronfen, *Over Her Dead Body: Death, Femininity and the Aesthetic* (New York: Routledge, 1992), x.

attentive to the ways that the retellings and performances of the story of Lucretia are historically specific, enacting particular conceptions of sexual difference as well as distinct productions of republics and republican politics. Ultimately, this examination of the retellings of the rape of Lucretia will illuminate aspects of Livy's, Machiavelli's and Rousseau's political thought that would have remained unexamined, perhaps undertheorized, without attention to this founding story. For example, a more nuanced view of Machiavelli's "economy of violence"[36] becomes possible through attention to the strategy of seduction in *La Mandragola*, Machiavelli's rendition of the story of the rape of Lucretia. Or, in another instance, Rousseau's interpretation of Lucretia's rape shifts the terms of the debate regarding authenticity and republican *virtù* to conceptions of the real and the problems of representation in republican life.

Consequently, it is not the purpose of this juxtaposition of Livy, Machiavelli and Rousseau to develop a unified theory of republican truth, specularity or citizenship. Lucretia's story is not used to unify Western republics under her rubric, but rather to launch an examination of three conceptions of republicanism—Livy's, Machiavelli's and Rousseau's—from the perspective of this founding story.

V. Overview

Each of the remaining chapters of this book (with the exception of the conclusion) details a specific historical and ostensibly republican version of the Lucretia story. Chapter 2, "Livy and the Repetition of Republican Foundations," focuses on Livy's version in *Ab Urbe Condita*. Chapter 3, "*La Mandragola* and the Seduction of Lucrezia," and Chapter 4, "The Seriously Comedic: Why Machiavelli's Lucrezia Is Not Livy's Virtuous Roman," each address *La Mandragola*, Machiavelli's reinterpretation of the tale. Rousseau's two versions, "La Mort de Lucrèce" and *Nouvelle Héloïse,* are considered in Chapter 5, "The Paradox of Rousseau's Politics and the Return to the Founding," and Chapter 6, "*Nouvelle Héloïse* and the Supplement of Sexual Difference." Each rendition is considered in light of how it elucidates aspects of each storyteller/theorist's conception of republican foundings, as well as his political theory more generally. Often each version is also juxtaposed with other accounts of the story popular at the time. For example, in the chapters

36. Wolin, *Politics and Vision*.

on Machiavelli's reinterpretation, not only is Machiavelli's version contrasted with Livy's (the one with which he is most obviously engaged), but it is also compared to Augustine's and Coluccio Salutati's versions, both of which Machiavelli is rather deliberately satirizing.

Livy's story of the rape of Lucretia in *Ab Urbe Condita* (*The Early History of Rome*) sets the context for my analysis of both Machiavelli's and Rousseau's versions. By juxtaposing the sexually violent, ultimately fatal story of Lucretia's rape with its sanitized, desexualized mirror image, the story of Brutus at the oracle, I use Livy's narrative to illuminate how Lucretia's rape and suicide can simultaneously remind republicans of the bonds that unite them and serve as a symptom of their failed masculinity. This focus on a failed masculinity is manifest also in Machiavelli's comedy, with its cuckolded husbands and duplicitous "happy ending," as well as in both of Rousseau's accounts when the "theorist of authenticity" resorts to the machinations of femininity in order to maintain "natural manhood."

Also given close attention in these chapters is an analysis of the significance of the status of Lucretia's rape in each version. While she is violently raped in Livy's version, in Machiavelli's play she assents to her seduction. In one of Rousseau's accounts, "La Mort de Lucrèce," the status of the rape is incompletely narrated but is complicated by an overdetermined scenario of love and power. And in the other Rousseau version, *Nouvelle Héloïse*, there is no rape, only fornication and the temptation of adultery. These recastings of the crime and its seeming indeterminacy play an important role in thinking through each theorist's formulation of republican political action.

My concluding chapter briefly examines what the genealogical approach of this book has illuminated about the "origin" of the republican tradition as articulated through this story. Although the primary focus of the book has been on the distinctiveness of each version of the story of the rape of Lucretia, in this concluding chapter, I speculate as to why this particular tale has been so energetically repeated and reinterpreted by these republican theorists. This chapter also tells another story: this one of the relation this project has imagined between republican theory and feminism and why in the end there might not be any fully compelling single reason for these repetitions, only better narratives to be told of the relation among femininity, masculinity and political foundings.

2

Livy and the Repetition of Republican Foundations

Among the stories told about Lucretia, the one usually perceived as the original in the tradition of republican political theory and the one to which both Niccolo Machiavelli and Jean-Jacques Rousseau specifically refer is Titus Livy's account in *Ab Urbe Condita*. Nonetheless, despite its genealogical primacy for this project, the story is itself a repetition and amalgamation of earlier cult legends. Classical scholars credit the influx of myths from Ardea into ancient Rome as the earliest sources for the story.[1] Yet even more significant for this analysis is that even within Livy's own first pentad, Lucretia's story is itself a repetition. Her plight is foreshadowed by the rape and death of the vestal virgin Rhea Silvia, who gives birth to the twin founders, Romulus and Remus, as well as echoed later by the slaughter of Verginia, whose violation prompts the restoration of republican institutions in the third book.

Other founding stories are duplicated in *The Early History* as well. The story of the founding Etruscan Tarquin, Lucomo Tarquinii, and his ambitious wife Tanaquil, who assists him in becoming king of Rome, is repeated in the account of Lucius Tarquin and his wife Tullia, whose maniacal ambition for her husband to become king drives her to patricide. Indeed, the stories so closely resemble one another that they seem merely variations of the same tale.

Not confined to the genesis and retellings of the story of Lucretia, repetition is thus both a methodological and a theoretical touchstone for Livy's history. Through repetition Livy defines not only the scope and meaning of his historical project but also the process of the Roman

1. Ettore Pais, *Ancient Legends of Roman History*, trans. Mario Cosenza (New York: Dodd, Mead and Co., 1905), 185–203.

founding itself. These repetitions are not the marks of careless scholarship[2] but rather an integral part of Livy's formulation of history and its role in political life.

This chapter is primarily dedicated to a close reading of Livy's version of the story of Lucretia as a narrative that articulates the pivotal relation between sexual violence and republican political foundings. Why are the stories of women's sexual violence simultaneously recalled and then buried in Livy's history? Is the repetition of these narratives of sexual violence contrived, oddly, to induce forgetfulness? By multiplying the stories of women's sexual violence, do the women and their sexual violation begin to vanish? Is sexual violence the one aspect of the founding that must not be recalled, the element that, although it stabilizes the origin and permits movement forward, also recalls the chaos of the founding? What has sexual violence secured that would be threatened by its revelation?

* * *

The story of the rape of Lucretia and the founding of the republic as Livy tells it in Book 1 of *The Early History of Rome* is as follows:

One day several men, among them Collatinus, Lucretia's husband, were drinking in the quarters of Sextus Tarquinius, the son of the then-ruling tyrant. Soon the subject of wives arose, and each man bragged that his wife was the most virtuous. Collatinus interrupted the rivalry urging, "What need is there of words when in a few hours we can prove beyond doubt the incomparable superiority of my Lucretia?" With this the men galloped off to Rome, where they found all of the other men's wives luxuriously enjoying themselves in their husband's absence while only Lucretia was found modestly dressed and "hard at work by lamplight upon her spinning."[3]

During the subsequent dinner, Tarquin was inflamed with lust by Lucretia's beauty and proven chastity. Several nights later he burst into Lucretia's bedroom, demanding she submit to him. Even when he threatened her with death, Lucretia refused. Finally, he reviled her: "If death will not move you, dishonor shall. I shall kill you first, then cut the throat of a slave and lay his naked body by your side. Will they not believe that you

2. Some scholars have dismissed the obvious repetitions as Livy's failure to recognize, because of his use of several sources, when he was retelling the same story. See, for example, Pais, *Ancient Legends of Roman History,* and P. G. Walsh, *Livy: His Historical Aims and Methods* (Cambridge: Cambridge University Press, 1970).

3. Titus Livy, *The Early History of Rome,* trans. Aubrey de Selincourt (New York: Penguin Books, 1978), 1.57, 98. Textual citations will be to this edition.

have been caught in adultery with a servant—and paid the price?" (99). With this threat, Lucretia yielded.

The following day she called her father, her husband, and Brutus, a family friend, around her. She recounted the rape and demanded revenge. She would testify to her innocence, she asserted, by killing herself: "My heart is innocent, and death will be my witness" (99). Her family tried to dissuade her, arguing vehemently that only her body, not her honor had been violated, that without intention there could be no guilt. Refusing to listen, Lucretia plunged a dagger into her heart.

While her husband and father were lost in grief, Brutus pulled the dagger from Lucretia's breast and urged the men to join together to drive the despotic Tarquins from Rome. Roman men rallied around Brutus's call for vengeance, and Rome was subsequently liberated and Brutus named the founding father of the republic.

I. AN EXEGESIS OF THE NARRATIVE

Perhaps this violence at the foundation could be dismissed as simply the necessity of any beginning, the violence imperative for the constitution of authority. As Niccolo Machiavelli asserts centuries later, innovations necessitate violence; and most certainly a republic is a dramatic innovation to a previously tyrannical state. Nonetheless, this narrative of sexual violence, present often at the republican foundings that look to Rome as their model, seems to be constitutive of the republic itself.

According to Livy, rape was among the "first steps to be taken in the founding of the mightiest empire the world has ever known": "The Vestal Virgin (Rhea Silva) was raped and gave birth to twin boys. Mars, she declared, was their father—perhaps she believed it, perhaps she was merely hoping to palliate her guilt. Whatever the truth of the matter, neither gods nor men could save her or her babes from the savage hands of the king" (37–38). The rest of the story is well known; the boys were ordered by the king to be drowned but were fortuitously found by a she-wolf and nursed by her until found by a herdsman whose wife Larentia raised them to adulthood.[4] These boys then grew up to become Romulus and Remus, founders of Rome.

4. Livy notes at the end of this popular story that some believe that the origin of this fable was "the fact that Larentia was a common whore and was called Wolf by the shepherds." He makes no other comments on the story's veracity.

The rape of Rhea Silvia highlights not only the premise that there is often violence at beginnings but also that specifically *sexual* violence may be integral to the Roman founding. In the beginning it is a woman's sexual violation that inaugurates the process of foundings. Moreover, there is the suggestion that Romulus and Remus are not of divine birth—as Livy's rather intrusive "perhaps she believed it, perhaps she was merely hoping to palliate her guilt" implies. The casting of this suspicion on the Vestal Virgin's credibility is, in part, Livy's attempt to make Romulus a figure with whom his contemporaries could more readily identify as mortal rather than divine. In this recasting of Romulus, Livy reiterates his conception of history as mimetic, as the source for imitation. However, although Romulus is held up as a figure for emulation, Rhea is disappeared from history: "The mother was bound and flung into prison."[5] Nothing is known of her fate. What is known, however, is that the traditional punishment for vestal virgins who breached their code of virginity was to be buried alive at the Collantine Gate.[6] Thus, Rhea, the virgin mother, lies under the foundation. She, like Lucretia, is the foundation that makes the founding possible.

Another alternative might be to read the founding/rape story of Lucretia (and of Rhea Silvia)[7] as simply the consequence of a familial vendetta. In other words, because the woman of one community has been violated by a transgressor from another, the men of the violated woman's community seek revenge by conquering the rapist. Yet the complications and political consequences of the story defy this facile reading. First, men other than the kin of the raped woman are ignited to rebellion by the rape. The most telling example is Brutus himself. Although Brutus has a long-standing personal vendetta against the Tarquins—they murdered both his father and brother—the murder of his relatives does not stir him to action. The rape of Lucretia more than ten years later, however, has the power to enflame him, as a "true Roman."[8] Moreover, this vengeance is not of the eye-for-an-eye, tooth-for-a-tooth variety. Collatinus, Lucretia's husband, does not want to rape Tarquin women, nor does Brutus seem bent on

5. Livy 1.4, 38.

6. Michael Serres, *Rome: The Book of Foundations*, trans. Felicia McCarren (Stanford: Stanford University Press, 1991), 68.

7. N.B.: Rhea Silvia was made a vestal virgin by her uncle, Amulius, after he murdered her brothers in order to ensure his right to the throne. Although Amulius claimed that he made Rhea a vestal virgin in order to honor her, it was actually done, as Livy notes, in order to preclude the possibility of her continuing her father's line (Livy 1.3, 37).

8. Ibid., 100.

murder. Rather, what it means to avenge Lucretia's rape is not simply to drive the tyrants from Rome but to establish a republic.

Second, this explanation of the story as the culmination of a familial vendetta does not reveal the so-called logic of the narrative, that is, why a *republic*, rather than a tyranny or monarchy, is established as a result of Lucretia's rape. Presumably, after the exile of the Tarquins, another tyranny could have been established; however, the story of Lucretia's rape/suicide seems, again, to spawn the founding specifically of a republic.

According to feminists Carole Pateman, Gayle Rubin, and others,[9] under patriarchy the ability to control the exchange of women is important because it guarantees the certainty of paternity. In other words, it is important that women do not have sexual intercourse with men to whom they do not legitimately "belong" so that the men to whom they do belong can be assured that the offspring are theirs. Paternity, as Pateman notes, has to be "discovered or invented. Unlike maternity, paternity is merely a social fact, a human invention."[10] Consequently, at its most fundamental level, rape jeopardizes the organization of paternal rights.

Under tyranny, as Tarquin's rape establishes, there is no legitimate control or exchange of women. All women belong, in effect, to the tyrant. Consequently, there can only be one legitimate father, and he is the tyrant. Yet Tarquin's rape of Lucretia is more than the exercise of his patriarchal power; it is also the wielding of his political power. Sextus, as son of the tyrant, hopes to establish his right of succession through the rape.[11] Lucretia's rape is a patriarchal repetition; just as Rhea's rape gave birth to a line of monarchs, Sextus, through his rape of Lucretia, is seeking to maintain that lineage. He is reenacting a founding claim to authority.

Both political and patriarchal powers are collapsed under tyranny. Patriarchal power, the ability to guarantee the certainty of paternity, is, in part, what authorizes political power. In accordance with the traditional

9. See, for example, Carole Pateman, *The Sexual Contract* (Stanford: Stanford University Press, 1988); Gayle Rubin, "The Traffic in Women," in *Toward an Anthropology of Women*, ed. Rayna R. Reiter (New York: New Monthly Review Press, 1995); and Mary O'Brien, *The Politics of Reproduction* (Boston: Routledge, 1981).

10. Pateman, *The Sexual Contract*, 35.

11. Although kingship was not a matter of lineage in Rome at the time Livy was writing his history, Tarquin's rape can be understood as a manifestation of how he claims the authority of kingship belonging to his father. Here it is important to recall that Livy is telling a mythological story with the intent of offering an exemplum for the refounding of the republic. My analysis is reading the story as such, as Livy's *theory* of foundings, not Roman history.

definition of patriarchy, power is located in fatherhood: "Classical patriarchal argument was that sons were born into subjection to their fathers and therefore into political subjection. Political right was natural and not conventional, no consent or contract was involved and political power was paternal, having its origin in the procreative power of the father."[12] And the reign of the Tarquins begins with a confounding of patriarchal rights, thus highlighting early in Livy's narrative the danger of fusing patriarchal and political power. The first Tarquin, Lucomo, is the sole inheritor of his father's property as a result of the premature death of his older brother, Arruns. However, Lucomo's father does not realize, when he bequeaths his patriarchal privileges, that Arruns's wife is pregnant at the time of his son's death. This child should be the rightful heir. From the beginning, then, the Tarquins are usurpers. The legitimate heir, Egerius ("the needy one") grows up to become the father of Collatinus, Lucretia's husband. Thus, Sextus's rape of Lucretia is designed, in part, to prevent the legitimate paternity of the Collatine line, a lineage thwarted from the onset of the Tarquin reign.

Lucretia's husband, then, is both literally and metaphorically the son in subjection to Tarquin's paternal as well as obvious political power. Tarquin rapes Lucretia not only for her beauty but also for her chastity. To violate Lucretia is in effect to violate her father and husband, to exert power over them, to demonstrate forcibly that they cannot control their women, cannot guarantee paternity and therefore cannot assume political authority/power. The founding of the republic, which Lucretia's rape ignites, is meant to change all that, however. The founding is the opportunity for the sons, the future republican citizens, to assume political authority without fathers and without guaranteed paternity. Lucretia's suicide ensures that she does not give birth to another line of tyrants. Rather, in the republic the sons will give birth to themselves. As a result of Lucretia's suicide, Collatinus is one of the early (although eventually expelled) republican leaders. Republican men understand cogently the danger of political power organized patriarchically, and thus they change the economy in which political power circulates. They will not rely on guaranteed paternity to secure political power. Rather, in the republic they will become their own fathers.

In the story immediately preceding Lucretia's, two of Tarquin's sons, Titus and Arruns, along with Brutus, are sent by the king to consult the

12. Pateman, *The Sexual Contract,* 24.

oracle at Delphi. After finishing the king's business at the oracle, the sons pose the question of who will succeed their father to the throne. The oracle's cryptic answer is "He who shall be the first to kiss his mother shall hold in Rome supreme authority."[13] Titus and Arruns decide to keep the prophecy secret and draw lots to determine which of them would, on their return, kiss his mother. However, Brutus, feigning clumsiness, falls to the ground and "his lips touched the Earth—the mother of all things" (97).

This story is a potent illustration of the loss of paternal power in the transition to the republic. The tyrant father will not be able to bequeath his power to his legitimate sons. Rather, the transmission of patriarchal and political power is disrupted by the illegitimate son's deceptive kiss of Mother Earth. Brutus, through his kiss, conceives the republic without the father.

This story of Brutus and the foreshadowed founding is at some level the sanitized, desexualized mirror image of the sexually violent, ultimately fatal story of Lucretia's rape. This doubling begins to expose the significance of the rape of a woman to the founding of the republic. The juxtaposition highlights, for example, both the insignificance of particular women—that is, the Tarquins' mother and Lucretia herself—while simultaneously heralding the pervasiveness of "feminine power" through the symbol of the Mother Earth and the desire to avenge Lucretia's lost innocence. Here the symbols and metaphors of women and femininity are more real than their bodies. The oracle's answer to the Tarquins' question desexualizes women; the kiss is not for a flesh and blood woman but rather for her symbolic replacement, the Earth. Nonetheless, the kiss is fruitful (i.e., giving birth to the republic), thus maintaining images of maternity and motherhood. The "dangerous" elements of woman's autonomous sexuality are tamed, while her generative potential is released. Brutus, through his kiss, conceives the Republic—the perfect emblem and fantasy of male solo procreation. Brutus has become both his own mother and his own father—the guarantee of paternity is self-generated.

This preface to the Lucretia story makes explicit the relation between the founding of the republic and metaphors of birth and motherhood. The story demonstrates the generative power of the male—his kiss initiates the republic. In a male assumption of the powers of the woman/mother, autonomous female sexuality and transgression under tyranny have been

13. Livy 1.57, 97.

displaced. The reproductive powers of women are appropriated in this republican birthing.

The transition to republicanism is an implicit challenge to patriarchal rule, traditionally conceived. The sons rebel and seize political rights, which they then share equally among themselves. All men, not just fathers, can now generate political life and political right: "Political creativity belongs not to paternity but to masculinity."[14] The bond among men is fraternal rather than paternal. Power is lateral, not hierarchical. And with the loss of paternal authority, masculinity assumes increased significance. Being a man, not a father, authorizes political right. How that masculinity/manhood is defined and maintained, however, will rest, in part, on the movement and exchange of Lucretia's body.

And this is the critical aspect of the story that Brutus's solo creation neglects—the very material role Lucretia's body plays in the story of the founding. Although the fantasy is of solo procreation, it is a "real woman"—not the metaphorical Earth Mother—who is pivotal to the narrative. In multiple ways, Lucretia's body controls the narrative unfolding; in fact, her body generates the narrative. As Mieke Bal argues in another context regarding the biblical Book of Judges, "The story is not told; it is done." In other words, through the rape and suicide of Lucretia, the founding of the republic is enacted. Once Lucretia becomes the answer to the brag of which man's wife is the most virtuous, "the only communicative function left open to her, as object, is to become speech, in body language."[15] This she does by literally taking in the seed of the tyrant Tarquin and then expunging it through her suicide. Her body contains the tyranny, both literally and metaphorically. While for a man, his words have effect, for a woman, only her body does.

Furthermore, Lucretia must die, literally forfeiting her body, in Livy's version, in order to testify to her innocence, her explicit motivation for committing suicide: "Never shall Lucretia provide a precedent for unchaste women to escape what they deserve."[16] Apparently, Lucretia's alive body cannot speak; her dead body, however, speaks volumes.[17] Indeed, as Elisabeth

14. Pateman, *The Sexual Contract,* 36.

15. Mieke Bal, "The Rape of Narrative and the Narrative of Rape: Speech Acts and Body Language in Judges," in *Literature and the Body: Essays on Populations and Persons,* ed. Elaine Scarry (Baltimore: Johns Hopkins University Press, 1988), 27.

16. Livy 1.57, 99.

17. Consider the ways in which this is still true, particularly in rape cases. Recall the rape trials involving the Central Park jogger and the St. John's University student—in which the

Bronfen notes, "knowledge gained through a dead female body is ultimately analytic"; that is, knowledge achieved from a female corpse is contained and self-referential. Derived from a single point of view (i.e., that of the alive male observer), this knowledge is not fecund; that is, it is not conceived in union with a speaking female, nor for that matter even an alive one. His perspectival knowledge is simply archived in her dead body. This is knowledge for and about the male gaze—his masculinity and his survival: "Over the dead woman's corpse, his status as subject will have been secured."[18] Thus, although female reproductive powers are displaced in the republican birthing, the female body, as corpse, is still integral to the formation of male identity.

Lucretia must die, then, for two reasons: first, because she is at risk of being pregnant with a monstrosity—the offspring of the tyrant.[19] The lineage of tyrants must be thwarted; the republic requires that the sons give birth to themselves in order to defy paternal power. And, second, she must die because her violation marks the failure of masculinity, specifically of her male kin to protect her. She reveals their failure to be men.

With her death, however, Lucretia becomes the female *pharmakon*; she is both the source of disruption and of the return to order. Simultaneously the sign of what ails the community and its remedy, Lucretia is a paradoxical figure. Her rape both ensures the bond among the republican brothers and highlights the fragility of that bond. On the one hand, her rape codifies the bond because it is a reminder of the tyrant's violation of the men's political rights and of their lack of political authority. The men band together against the usurpation of their power by the tyrannical father.

---

nearly-dead body of the Central Park jogger who, being so badly beaten could not testify on her own behalf, was a better witness to her rape than the St. John's student who, while not beaten and therefore able to give her own account of her experience, was unable to persuade the court of her violation. The respective juries decided that the Central Park jogger was raped, while the St. John's University student was not.

18. Elisabeth Bronfen, *Over Her Dead Body: Death, Femininity and the Aesthetic* (New York: Routledge, 1992), 101.

19. Interestingly, in Greek tragedy a woman's suicide by hanging was associated with marriage—or rather, with an excessive valuation of the status of a bride—while suicide that shed blood, like Lucretia's, was associated with maternity through which a wife, in her heroic pains of childbirth, found complete fulfillment (Nicole Loraux, *Tragic Ways of Killing a Woman*, trans. Anthony Forster [Cambridge: Harvard University Press, 1987]), 10. Although it is difficult to demonstrate that Livy too is deploying this formulation, some evidence would suggest that Lucretia kills herself not only to protect her husband's honor (because she is now violated chattel) but also because of the threat of pregnancy.

On the other hand, Lucretia's violation is also the talisman of what haunts the fraternal bond—the phantom of a failed masculinity. Her desecration is the vestige of a bravado that could display Lucretia's innocence but not preserve it. It was, after all, her own husband's bragging that precipitated her rape. Consequently, in the republic, notions of masculinity rather than certainty of paternity assume heightened political significance. Republics demand that their citizens be men within the parameters of a politically defined masculinity.

With the separation of political and patriarchal power in the republic, public and private spheres are strictly delineated. Issues of paternity are confined to the private sphere, and public life becomes the purview of men, the world of Brutus and his solo parthenogenesis. Nonetheless, there remains a tension among republican citizens about the possibility of a resurrected tyrant, of the return of the father and his patriarchal privileges. Each republican citizen is perceived as potentially reinstating the tyrant. Each recalls that the patriarchal father was not only feared but envied. This trepidation is fueled in part by the memory of their own "effeminacy"—a weakness so profound that the *virtù* of a woman was required to restore their manhood.

Livy notes these heightened suspicions in the beginning of Book 2: "I cannot help wondering, myself, whether the precautions taken at this time to safeguard liberty even in the smallest details were not excessive: a notable instance concerned one of the consuls, Tarquinius Collatinus, whose sole offense was the fact that his name—Tarquin—was universally detested."[20] Livy argues throughout Book 2 that the primary threat to the early republic is internal discord, specifically the instability of the men themselves. True patriotism, he insists, takes time: "It is founded upon respect for the family and love of the soil. Premature liberty of this kind [i.e., republican] would have been a disaster" (106). Men require a particular maturity before they are fit for republican liberty. Only after certain conditions of manhood are achieved are they fit for republicanism; thus, for Livy, a republic represents political adulthood.[21]

This apprehension about the ability of men to be republicans is partially kindled by the homosociality[22] of the republic. Male citizens must

20. Livy 2.1, 106.

21. "For it was that government which, as it were, nursed our strength and enabled us ultimately to produce sound fruit from liberty, as only a politically adult nation can" (ibid., 105).

22. I use the term *homosociality* here rather than *homosexuality* because the fear is not of sexuality between men but of passivity and dependence among them. In the Roman Republic,

rely on each other for the success and health of the state:[23] in a republic, fraternity is more than a noble sentiment, it is a political imperative. Yet, this homosocial basis for community seems oddly to threaten the very rudiments of the republic; it is a dependence with shades of the effeminacy the men suffered under tyranny. Now rather than being dependent upon the father, they are dependent upon one another.

Consequently, in Livy's version, Lucretia's body is used to mediate the rivalry and fear that plagues the security of the republic: "Reigning everywhere, although prohibited in practice, homosexuality is played out through the bodies of women, matter or sign and heterosexuality has been up to now just an alibi for the smooth workings of man's relations with himself, of relations among men."[24] Lucretia's body defuses the homosocial elements of the republic and testifies to male aggression. Her body is the passive terrain that certifies masculine autonomy. Assuring the citizens that their interdependence is not passive submission to one another, her body signals guaranteed access to, and control of, women. Lucretia's corpse preserves femininity within the republican economy, although it is a femininity without any of the power women are represented as wielding under patriarchal tyranny. For example, Livy tells several stories of the diabolical power women wield under tyranny; indeed, he describes how women are themselves the cause of tyranny. In the five-act tragedy of the reign of the Tarquins, tyrannical women ignite and maintain the despotic monarchy, while the virtues of a chaste republican woman destroys the tyranny and spurs the founding of the republic.[25]

---

homosexuality was neither illegal nor socially scorned. What was derided, however, was male passivity in sexual relationships. Sexual passivity was associated with political impotence in both republican and imperial Rome. See John Boswell's *Christianity, Social Tolerance and Homosexuality* (Chicago: University of Chicago Press, 1980).

23. Paul Rahe, *Republics Ancient and Modern: Classical Republicanism and the American Revolution* (Chapel Hill: University of North Carolina Press, 1992), chap. 4.

24. Luce Irigaray, "Women on the Market," in *The Sex Which Is Not One*, trans. Catherine Porter (Ithaca: Cornell University Press, 1985), 172.

25. It is noteworthy that in Latin there are two words for female, *femina* and *mulier*, just as there are two words for men, *vir* and *homo*. *Femina* and *vir* were used to signify the upper classes, while *mulier* and *homo* applied to everyone else. Since aristocratic life centered upon loyalty and service to the Republic, *femina* and *vir* became identified with its virtues, especially patriotism, frugality, generosity and defense of the Senate and the conservative state religion. Conversely, *mulier* and *homo*, because of their use to indicate members of the lower order, came to connote foreign vices, avarice, luxury, association with the mob and conspiracy. Thus, the women of the Tarquin reign are referred to throughout as *mulier*, while Lucretia is referred to only as *femina* (Franceso Santoro L'Hoir, *The Rhetoric of Gender Terms: 'Man', 'Woman' and the Portrayal of Character in Latin Prose* [Leiden: E. J. Brill, 1992], 2–5).

In fact, the reign of the Tarquins begins with the maniacal ambition of a woman. Lucomo, who will become the first foreign king of Rome, leaves Tarquinii at the urging of his aristocratic wife, Tanaquil, to seek his fortune in Rome. During their journey she boldly interprets an omen of an eagle taking and then replacing the cap on Lucomo's head as a sign that the crown of Rome will eventually be his. Tanaquil's reading of the prophecy marks not only her ambition but also her status as a foreign usurper. In Rome the reading of auguries was confined to men, and amateurs did not divine without the assistance of a professional seer;[26] that Tanaquil assumes this role is itself an omen of her future trespasses. Moreover, when Lucomo dies, it is Tanaquil who decides his successor; she chooses not one of her own sons but Servius, whom she had raised as if he were her son. Thus, her tyrannical power violates even the patriarchal right of paternal succession; she usurps political as well as patriarchal power when she does not permit her husband's children to succeed him.

Succeeding Tanaquil's dominion is another woman, Tullia, who marries one of Lucomo's sons and is herself the daughter of Servius. Her ambition is to restore her husband's patriarchal rights as the former king's son. Thus, she sets in motion a plot to assassinate her own father: "It was the woman," Livy notes, "who took the first step along the road to crime."[27] Although seemingly restoring patriarchal succession, Tullia obviously violates patriarchal authority by killing her own father. And Livy is quite explicit as to Tullia's model: "To Tullia the thought of Tanaquil's success was torture. She was determined to emulate it" (1.47, 86). Part of the danger of tyranny and the women who prosper under it, then, is that they perpetuate themselves as models for each other. Thus, Livy's republican Lucretia must disrupt this mimetic lure of tyrannical women; she must be represented in a way that both recalls to women their female *virtù*[28] and restores to men the masculinity they have forfeited under tyranny.

By winning the initial "best wife contest" when she is found at her spinning,[29] Lucretia sets the parameters for female republican *virtù*: an ideal

26. Robert M. Ogilvie, *A Commentary on Livy: Books 1–5* (Oxford: Clarendon Press, 1965), 144.

27. Livy 1.46, 85.

28. Although *virtù* is usually applied only to men (the word being etymologically derived from *vir*), I am deliberately cultivating a conception of female *virtù* in order to suggest that the qualities and virtues of Lucretia are political; that is, her virtues are necessary for the fulfillment of the political sphere, not mere "domestic virtues" for the preservation of the family. See also L'Hoir, *The Rhetoric of Gender Terms*.

29. So much was spinning considered a symbol of female republican virtue that Augustus

republican woman is sequestered in the *domus*, renounces the entertaining company of others and is fulfilled by household work. Later, by thwarting the satisfaction of Sextus's patriarchal ambitions through her suicide, Lucretia repudiates the power offered women under tyranny.[30] Disrupting the collapse of patriarchal and political power, Lucretia's suicidal renunciation inaugurates a fundamental aspect of the republic—the autonomy of political power.

Her gesture also reflects a new economy in which women and their bodies will be replaced by *representations* of women and their bodies. This is one of the ways in which republics seek to contain the disruption of feminine power. Confined to the private sphere, republican women achieve more political potency as representations than as reality. For example, the symbolic display of Lucretia's body after her suicide motivates the Roman citizenry against the despotic monarch and models the future for republican women. Lucretia's corpse is a representation of meaning elsewhere, signaling women's role in the future republic as silent signifiers who are the carriers of culture and cultural value, but are not participants or makers of it.

In Livy's history, female republican *virtù*, unlike male *virtù*, requires that women become the compliant template for the projection of male representations. What women symbolize is more important than what they are; their *seeming* replaces their *being*. Hence, Lucretia kills herself so that she will be perceived as innocent. It is not sufficient that she *is* innocent. Lucretia's *virtù* is performative, not a manifestation of what she is, not a giving necessarily of her form to matter; rather, her virtù is a demonstration for others. Her suicide is a performance for a particular audience. Lucretia understands how her sexual violation will be understood and consequently orchestrates her death in such a way as to ensure that her violation will be read the way she wants.[31] She does not kill herself because she believes

---

actively encouraged his wives and daughters to learn to spin, presumably in order to cast a "republican" aura on his reign.

30. This is made explicit in the version of Dionysius of Halicarnassus, in which Sextus tries to seduce Lucretia with promises of power. "For," he said, "if you will consent to gratify me, I will make you my wife and with me you shall reign, for the present, over the city my father has given me, and, after his death, over the Romans, the Latins, the Tyrrhenians, and all the other nations he rules; for I know that I shall succeed to my father's kingdom, as is right, since I am his eldest son" (*The Roman Antiquities*, trans. Earnest Cary [Cambridge: Harvard University Press, 1961], 2:475).

31. Gayatri Spivak notes the profound irony of women's attempts to locate their free will in suicide: "This text [i.e., story of self-immolation] articulates the difficult task of rewriting its own

herself guilty, as Augustine will argue centuries later,[32] but because her reputation is more important than her self-knowledge. She cares not only that she is innocent but that she is *perceived* as innocent; in this way, she exemplifies Livy's conception of female *virtù*. As a republican woman, what she makes is less significant than what is made of her. In Livy's republic, women are the real who must become representations.

In addition, inside Livy's history the Lucretia story itself confounds the real and the representational. The story is found on the cusp of myth and history, thus simultaneously establishing and resisting the line between the real and the representation. Like the story of Romulus, the narrative of Lucretia's life is designed to have effect in the Augustan present. It is a theatrical tragedy staged with the elements of Ciceronian oratory to recall Roman citizens to a past greatness. Livy does not look to contemporary historical events to inspire republican *virtù,* but rather he crafts a representation, a myth, which has more potency than verifiable historical reality.

In Livy's republic, then, the rape and suicide of Lucretia celebrates female *virtù* that is not a threat to masculinity but is rather the very possibility for the achievement of male *virtù*. Femininity is reduced to a representation, a mirror for men and their relations with each other. Lucretia's corpse is a mirror into which men gaze and see themselves. Reflecting only the images men impose upon it, the female corpse at the founding, at the origin of history, serves as a source for unity among men. Forbidding dialogue with the Other, it is the source for stability, the only term that literally stays still at the otherwise chaotic founding. Consequently, a mirror (a female corpse) that reduces femininity to a reflection of sameness is the source of authority at the founding.

It is noteworthy that traditionally in fifth-century Rome nothing was said about women at their burial. Indeed, having praise given at a woman's funeral was a privilege, as Livy notes, that women were not accorded until 386 B.C.E., and even then it was granted only to a limited number of women: "When it was found that there was not enough gold in the treasury to pay the Gauls the agreed sum [for the temple of Jupiter], contribution from the women had been accepted, to avoid touching what was

---

conditions of impossibility as the conditions of its possibility" ("Can the Subaltern Speak?" in *Marxism and the Interpretation of Culture* [Urbana: University of Illinois Press, 1988], 285). In other words, Lucretia's suicide cannot be read simply. Her suicide reinscribes her subordination while simultaneously seeking to displace it.

32. See Chapter 3 for a discussion of Augustine's account of Lucretia.

consecrated. The women who had contributed were formally thanked and were further granted the privilege, hitherto confined to men, of having laudatory orations pronounced at their funerals."[33] At noble male Roman burials, on the other hand, the man's body was carried by members of the nobility into the forum, where amid mourners wearing the clothes and death masks of the deceased ancestors, a son or a close relative pronounced an encomium (*laudatio funerbris*). The eulogy began with the life events of the deceased and included the exploits of the other dead ancestors represented at the gathering. These orations were preserved and eventually became an important source for history.[34]

Lucretia's burial, however, recalls the silence attendant at women's funerals. Although her body is carried into the forum, it is the display of her corpse, not her life deeds, that inspires wonder; no words are spoken of her heroic suicide or of her *virtù*. Rather, what Brutus cries while Lucretia's body is displayed is that "it is time for deeds not tears"; Lucretia is barely mourned. In fact, after Lucretia dies, Brutus quickly withdraws the knife from her body and passes it from Collatinus to Lucretius and then to Valerius.[35] This ritual bonding through the transfer of what Livy describes as the "knife dripping with blood" (*culturum manantem cruore*) begins the restoration of masculinity. The blood from a woman's corpse and the knife of her suicide become the tools for restoring masculinity.

Here is an apt demonstration, again, of the complementary relation between the *display* of a woman's body and the *effects* of a man's words. With Lucretia's body and Brutus's words, the Romans are incited to action: "Lucretia's body was carried from the house into the public square. Crowds gathered, as crowds will to gape and wonder—and the sight was unexpected enough and horrible enough to attract them . . . and when Brutus cried out that it was time for deeds not tears, and urged them, like true Romans, to take up arms against the tyrants who had dared to treat them as a vanquished enemy, not a *man* amongst them could resist the call."[36] This is a poignant illustration of the power of the spectacle of Lucretia's suicide. As spectacle, women are mirrors of value for men; the specularity of women's bodies make social and cultural life possible: "In order to serve

33. Livy 5.51, 396–397.

34. Andrew Lintott, "Roman Historians," in *The Roman World*, ed. John Boardman, Jasper Griffin, and Oswyn Murray (Oxford: Oxford University Press, 1986), 227.

35. Livy 1.59, 99.

36. Ibid., 100; emphasis mine.

as such, they [women] give up their bodies to men as the supporting material of specularization, of speculation. They yield up to him their natural and social values as a locus of imprints, marks and mirage for his activity."[37] In other words, woman, as spectacle, helps to constitute male identity; Lucretia's suicide is the material from which republican citizenship is fashioned. Her female corpse is the means by which a spectacle is constructed—a spectacle that inaugurates a political community founded upon seeing and being seen. It is the spectacle of the female body, both literally and metaphorically, that constitutes the initial political "we."

Reduced from real otherness to representational sameness as well as confined to the private sphere, femininity is then valued only as a commodity signifying relations between and among men. Femininity is no longer an autonomous threat: "Femininity [becomes] a role, an image, a value, imposed upon women by male systems of representation."[38] The real is lost in the representation. Or, at least, that is what the subordination of the feminine to the private sphere is intended to enact. What happens, however, is that femininity continues to overstep this confinement, which must then be repeatedly enacted. And, this is another dimension of Lucretia's plight.

Although Lucretia's suicide reduces her to her body and to representational sameness as corpse, her decision to suffer the rape in order to be able to speak her own truth simultaneously defies a pivotal aspect of her prescribed cultural role. She steps outside her cultural role as body when she speaks of her violation: "The female herself must never control reproductions whether of cultural systems or of human beings. She must never see, and certainly never speak about, what she learns from her position."[39] The story of Lucretia's rape details, on the one hand, the desire to reduce Lucretia to a nonspeaking, nonsignifying body *and*, on the other hand, the simultaneous recognition and deployment of the fact that bodies do indeed speak and thus resist and destabilize unitary interpretations. By retelling her rape, Lucretia has revealed the cultural secret of male impotence; it is a transgression for which she accepts death. When her father and husband try to convince her not to commit suicide, she chides them that they can decide only what shall be done to Sextus, but that she will decide what is

37. Irigaray, "Women on the Market," in *The Sex Which Is Not One,* 177.

38. Irigaray, "The Power of Discourse," in ibid., 84.

39. Patricia Joplin, "Ritual Work on Human Flesh: Livy's Lucretia and the Rape of the Body Politic," *Helios* 17 (Spring 1990): 58.

appropriate for herself. She defies her role as passive representation. Although she demands revenge, she does not trust her kin's ability to secure it: "He it is who last night came as my enemy disguised as my guest, and took his pleasure of me. That pleasure will be my death—and his, too, *if you are men*."[40] That conditional "if" stresses her skepticism and is a challenge for her male kin to fulfill. Yet it is this challenge that works to inaugurate their republican masculinity. Lucretia's suicide is generative; her kin manage successfully to avenge her rape *and* to found the republic. In some odd way, Lucretia's suicide has taught them how to be men.

Of course, it is tempting to read Lucretia's suicide as an implicit submission to patriarchy, as her desire to protect her husband's honor as well as her own; she judges herself guilty by the terms of patriarchy, despite her resistance. Yet, Lucretia's speech after her rape[41] demonstrates, oddly, that she was not completely passive. Although she is ultimately reduced to her body, Lucretia decides what the display of her body will mean. She chooses to submit to the rape rather than to have her dead body read as guilty of adultery with a slave. She testifies to her innocence, in part disclosing the cultural secret of the autonomy of female generative powers as well as her own kin's failed masculinity. Lucretia's revenge is in both her speaking of her violation and in her suicide: "By undoing her own body, she undoes the gender construction which places her in an inferior position. . . . Paradoxically, she can do so only by re-emphasizing the body in an act of disembodiment."[42] In other words, in Livy's founding narrative, female *virtù* is articulated through the very medium that seems most to deny women's agency—their corporeality.

This ambiguity, however, illuminates Livy's complicated conception of *fortuna/fatum*.[43] Although Livy believes that Rome is bound to succeed (i.e., fated by the gods), he also wants to demonstrate that Rome's success is due to the behavior of her citizens. Thus, on the one hand, Livy presupposes Roman fate (*fatum*)—the Stoic conception of determinism with its element of divine control. Yet, on the other hand, he wants to highlight

40. Livy 1.59, 99; emphasis mine.

41. It is noteworthy that only in Livy's version of the Lucretia story is there a record of Lucretia's words describing the rape. In Ovid's version the narrator refers to the rape that Lucretia is reportedly too modest to recount.

42. Bronfen, *Over Her Dead Body*, 143.

43. Often the words *fatum* and *fortuna* are collapsed in Livy's extant work. See D. S. Levene, *Religion in Livy* (Leiden: E. J. Brill, 1993), for a discussion of the history of Livy's use of these concepts.

the significance of Roman *virtù* and the importance of individual conduct. The elements of free will are necessary for the historian who crafts his history in order to spur the return of his contemporaries to greatness. Consequently, Lucretia's rape and her deployment of that which has condemned her personifies Livy's conception of *fortuna/fatum*. Lucretia is destined for destruction, a victim of a fate she cannot control and did not choose, but she demonstrates the superiority of her *virtù* and exercises her autonomy within that destiny by choosing what her rape and death will signify. Despite the inevitability of Roman greatness (and republicanism) in which Livy believes, he nonetheless affords Lucretia some measure of autonomy in order to remind his readers that individual conduct matters. Even within a prescribed fate there is opportunity for the performance of *virtù*.

II. Livy's Conception of Foundings

Livy began to compose his history between 31 and 27 B.C.E., near the end of, or shortly after, a period of sustained disorder (the Roman Civil Wars) and when Augustus's celebrated transferal of the republic from his own power to that of the Senate in 27 B.C.E. had made refoundation a matter of the highest political priority.[44] The structure of Livy's narrative as a whole implies that Roman identity and greatness may be preserved indefinitely through successive reenactments of a historical cycle that is exemplified in the first half of Roman history.[45] In other words, Livy's history not only tells the stories of the founding, but is itself meant both structurally and theoretically to reenact that founding. The reformulations of the founding stories related in the first pentad suggest that the founding is both repeatable and a process, not a one-time innovation.

This potentially recurring cycle is unprecedented in the historiographic tradition prior to Livy, and it ascribes to Rome a unique place in the history of nations. Although historians like Thucydides and Herodotus had a notion of recurrent history, Livy's formulation is distinct in two regards: first, he focuses on the repeated rise and decline of a single nation rather than on a succession of leaders or nations; and second, he centers his history less on averting decline and more on the possibilities for rebirth.[46]

44. Gary B. Miles, "Maiores, Conditores, and Livy's Perspective on the Past," *Transactions of the American Philological Association* 118 (1988): 210.

45. Gary B. Miles, "The Cycle of Roman History in Livy's First Pentad," *American Journal of Philology* 107 (Spring 1986): 1–33.

46. Ibid.

Not surprisingly, Livy also reconceives the role of the founder (*conditor*) as one who not only saves the city from destruction but who also *renews* specific loyalties that are embodied in the original acts of foundation.[47] The founder is not only a savior but also someone who restores the bonds of the community. The founder does not so much originate the community as restore it to its former self. Paradoxically, in Livy, the *conditor* often is both the source of the decline of the community and its restoration; he is a *pharmakon*—both poison and cure: "Livy shows us simultaneously the thing and its shadow: the origin, the murder, and its re-covering."[48]

Livy's history thus introduces the idea of the founding as process rather than as a unitary moment. In his first pentad there are multiple foundings—the founding by Romulus and Remus, the republican founding by Brutus after the rape of Lucretia and the refounding after the Gallic sack of Rome. The founding is developmental. No founding is itself original; each refers to the previous one, repeating it and, in the first pentad, adding to it. Gary Miles lists the founders of the first pentad as: Romulus, the original founder of the city; Numa, who first elaborated the institutions of public religion; Servius Tullius, who organized the citizens into a formal hierarchy of merit; all the kings, except Tarquinius Superbus, who increased the size of the city (2.1.2); Appius Claudius, the decemvir who presided over the first compilation of written law at Rome (3.58.2); Augustus, honored as *templorum omnium restituorem ac conditorem* (4.20.7); Furius Camillus, who saved the city from total conquest by the Gauls and both the city and her gods from abandonment by disaffected citizens (5.49.7–8); and Brutus, whose expulsion of the last king of Rome initiated a new era of Roman liberty (8.34.3).[49] Thus, each origin refers to another; the beginning itself demands a beginning. The origin repeats itself, much as Livy's own history does.

Conceiving of history as recurrent rather than linear, Livy is not lost in a nostalgia of past Roman greatness. Rather, his history is a testament that Rome had previously experienced and recovered from decline. "History was not a straight progression from black to white" for Livy, "but a chequered patchwork in which good and evil had always been interwoven."[50] From the beginning good and evil are enmeshed.

In the beginning not only is there violence, but there is duality, an

47. Ibid., 30–32.

48. Serres, *Rome: The Book of Foundations*, 233.

49. Miles, "Maiores, Conditores, and Livy's Perspective on the Past."

50. Ogilvie, *Commentary on Livy*, 24.

inherent contest—two sets of two brothers, Aeneas and Antenor and/or Romulus and Remus, as well as two stories of *hostis ad hospitalis*. There are two contesting founding stories, the Trojan story, which heralds Aeneas as the father of Rome, and the Roman story, which credits Romulus with its origination. Livy adroitly sought to reconcile the two, thus putting at the origin of Rome a divergence. In Livy's version, Aeneas does not found Rome, but Romulus and Remus are descendants of his son Ascanius, who did set out to begin a new settlement. The return to the origin, the retelling of the founding, reveals a bifurcation, a double, the two-faced god of beginnings, Janus. The founding is thus unstable, itself a genealogy of possibilities.

For Livy the founding is not a pristine moment of principled wholeness. But rather the first sentence of the story narrates a tale of destruction: "It is generally accepted that after the fall of Troy the Greeks kept up hostilities against all the Trojans except Aeneas and Antenor."[51] In the beginning is violence: fratricide, rape and suicide. Yet it is a violence that defines and limits, that creates foundation rather than begets more violence, and incites reciprocity. It is a violence that creates unity at an origin that begins with duality; oddly, it is also a brutality that generates authority.

Classicists have noted, for example, that Livy does not apologize for the rape of the Sabine women, as Cicero does.[52] Cicero is careful to point out that these were well-born and highly educated women who were ruthlessly violated. Livy, on the other hand, describes how the women are seduced by the sweet talk of their rapists and eventually fall in love with them: "They [the Romans] spoke honeyed words and vowed that it was passionate love which had prompted their offense. No plea can better touch a woman's heart."[53] For Livy the rape of the Sabine women is part of the necessary violence of the process of founding. It is a prerequisite for the grandeur of Rome. The story exemplifies how founding violence creates foundation as well as stabilizes and sets the limits for what will become Rome. The women, as objects of violence, ultimately contain the violence. When their fathers and brothers seek revenge for their violation, the women thwart the battle, begging their fathers not to kill their own grandchildren.

51. Livy 1.1, 34.

52. Ogilvie, *Commentary on Livy*, 65. Cicero calls Romulus's plan for the capture of the women "subagreste" (rather boorish).

53. Livy 1.9, 44.

The account of the Sabine women is also the first of several renditions in the first pentad of *hostis pro hospite* (an enemy in the place of a guest); that is, the movement from violation of the guest-host ethic to the return of hospitality, of the affection due guests. The Romans initially violate the guest-host code when they invite the Sabines to the games of Neptunus Equestor and then steal their daughters and sisters. However, the women, as the objects of that violation, restore the ethic. This guest-host duty and its violation is pivotal to the process of the founding, to setting the boundaries and limits of republican Rome.

The Tarquins are themselves invited guests (Etruscans) who then become enemies of their host, Rome.[54] In the story of Lucretia, Sextus, her rapist, is an invited guest who becomes an enemy. The rape, then, is a reenactment of the larger political relation the Tarquins have with the Romans—foreigners who usurp the throne while promising friendship. The rape is a repetition that defines the parameters of the republic's foundation.

Like the Sabine women, Lucretia both arouses the violence and restores order. As hostess, she is a *pharmakon*—her presence both invites the desecration of the guest-host ethic and helps to restore it. As female victim, she is herself the condition that enables foundation; yet she is not permitted to share in that which she enables. She is what is covered over, entombed in the foundation, as it were. For Lucretia, this is both literally and metaphorically true.

Lucretia kills herself after her violation, spurring the founding of the Roman republic. Nonetheless, her sacrifice is not memorialized among the virtues of the republic. Women are not accorded a privileged role in the new republic in honor of Lucretia. Rather, women are returned to their role as hostesses, as matrons of the *domus*—the very role that ignited Lucretia's violation. The sexual violation of women is retold in the process of the foundings but is never overcome. It is a story whose moral truth is assumed, left unchallenged and uninterrogated.

How and why is sexual violence a necessary part of the founding? Livy offers no answers, no speculations. So while the process of founding

54. Indeed, the reign of the Tarquins is marked by the repeated violation of the guest-host ethic. Prior to the rape of Lucretia, Sextus had feigned a dispute with his father in order to cajole the people of Gabii to befriend him. He went to Gabii as a guest, claiming allegiance by being an enemy of their enemy, Tarquinius Superbus. The ploy, of course, was simply one to facilitate the Tarquin conquest of the city.

is recalled and repeated as an exemplar of moral virtue, the rape of the Sabine women, the rape and suicide of Lucretia, the slaughter of Verginia—in other words, the role of women as themselves founders, as *pharmakons* who make possible the very movement of history—is neglected and forgotten. The sexual violence that makes possible the very foundation of Rome is buried within it. What makes Rome viable must itself be overcome and denied.

The repetition of the founding thus not only serves the purposes of recollection, but its repetition also makes possible the movement of history. The stories of the first pentad, of the founding, seek to delineate the boundary between myth and history. And once these mythical foundations are covered over, it is possible to move from legend to history. Myth makes history possible, although it is a genealogical heritage that history attempts to deny.[55] Perhaps stories of sexual violence, specifically the story of the rape and suicide of Lucretia, are similarly situated—they are recalled as myths that stabilize the Roman foundation but are simultaneously erased as evocations that threaten the very male republican citizens they have helped to beget.

III. Livy as Historical Dramatist

Methodologically, Livy's history is itself a repetition. In writing his history, Livy did not consult any primary documents or do original archival research. Instead, he relied on the histories produced by others, namely Polybius, Licinius Macer and Valerius Antias, even when primary sources were available for his consultation.[56] Indeed, in the Preface to his history Livy acknowledges that his work is not original: "Countless others have written on this theme and it may be that I shall pass unnoticed amongst them."[57] Noting Livy's dependence on previous historians is not intended to cast aspersions on his reliability, as some have, but rather to note what being an historian meant for Livy and to develop an understanding of his conception of the past and its role in political life.

Livy was among the first Romans to devote himself solely to writing history. All other historians had held either political or military positions before they turned to history. Only Livy, in dedicating his life to the

55. Serres, *Rome: The Book of Foundations,* 168.

56. Ogilvie, *Commentary on Livy,* 5–16.

57. Ibid.

writing of Rome's history, insisted that history writing could be one's main political activity. Others had felt a need to apologize for their turn to history after a more public political life. Livy, on the other hand, unabashedly justified his retreat to history as a escape from the turbulence of political life: "I shall find antiquity a rewarding study, if only because, while I am absorbed in it, I shall be able to turn my eyes from the troubles which for so long have tormented the modern world."[58]

Livy's escapism did not mean that he did not conceive of his history as serving a political purpose, however. Rather, he hoped that his history would help Rome recover her greatness: "The study of history is the best medicine for a sick mind; for in history you have a record of the infinite variety of human experience plainly set out for all to see; and in that record you can find for yourself and your country both examples and warnings; fine things to take as models, base things, rotten through and through, to avoid."[59] Thus, Livy's ambition is to facilitate the resurrection of Roman greatness. Contemplation of the past may show how to recover a former excellence as well as how to avoid potential blunders; it is a sentiment that both Machiavelli and Rousseau will endorse centuries later.

Although Livy finds history writing a private haven, he hopes his history will do more than provide a mental refuge from the present. Livy wants to write a history, as will both Machiavelli and Rousseau, that will spur imitation and incite political action, not one whose narrative effect is catharsis or passivity. Livy's history is designed to serve as a source for emulation, as itself a template for repetition.

Conceiving of his history as a model for action, Livy makes his history literary rather than annalistic; that is, although his history is still largely chronological (in the tradition of the annalists), his attention is narrative, not temporal. Moreover, his focus is on individuals rather than communities, on psychology rather than economic or military forces, and on dramatic coherence rather than historical accuracy: "I invite the reader's attention to the much more serious consideration of the kind of lives our ancestors lived, of who were the men, and what the means, both in politics and war, by which Rome's power was first acquired and subsequently expanded."[60] Because of this emphasis, Livy often casts historical events as moral episodes in order to illuminate a particular truth. Nonetheless, it is

58. Livy 1.1, 33.
59. Livy 1.1, 34.
60. Livy, Preface, 34.

in the construction of the episodes themselves that Livy takes the greatest pains and liberties for achieving compelling moral drama.

Applying Aristotle's dramatic techniques regarding the unity of time and place, Livy often collapses several historical episodes into one and locates the action in one place rather than several. For example, in his account of Coriolanus, he omits altogether two pairs of consuls and conflates two separate campaigns into one (2.34–40); the result is, as Robert Ogilvie notes, "historical nonsense, but tense reading."[61] Also, in two of the other renditions of Lucretia's story contemporary with Livy's (Ovid's version in *Fasti* and Dionysius of Halicarnassus's in *Roman Antiquities*), there are frequent scene changes and incidental characters. Although these other historical versions offer more details, neither is as dramatic as Livy's. In fact, so much do some of his episodes resemble the five-part format of tragedies that scholars have occasionally believed that Livy was rewriting plays.[62] Indeed, Livy covers the reign of the Tarquins in five main acts: (i) the execution of the trouble maker and critic, Turnus Herdonius; (ii) the overthrow of Gabii as a result of Sextus's deception; (iii) city affairs and the secularization of all places of worship; (iv) the consultation of the Delphic Oracle; and (v) the rape and suicide of Lucretia. For Livy the history of the Tarquins is, in part, a tragedy with a moral: the triumph of *pudicitia* (chastity, virtue) over *superbia* (haughtiness, insolence).[63]

Contributing to this formulation of Livy's history as theatre is his use of speeches not only to offer psychological insights into a character but also to heighten dramatic tension. Influenced both by the historian Thucydides and by the techniques of Greek drama, Livy punctuates climactic moments with speeches. For example, in Book 1 when Horatius kills the last Curati, Livy writes: "What followed cannot be called a fight. 'I have killed two already, to avenge my brothers' ghosts. I offer the last to settle our quarrel, that Rome may be mistress of Alba.' With these proud words he plunged his sword with a downward stroke into the throat of his enemy, now too weak to sustain his shield, and then stripped him where he lay."[64] The episode of the Curati and Horati concludes with the speech of Horatius's father defending his son from capital punishment for rashly killing his own sister. The speeches serve a twofold purpose. First, they make the figures of Roman history appear as actors rather than as objects of history,

61. Ogilvie, *Commentary on Livy*, 18.

62. Ibid., 196.

63. Ibid.

64. Livy 1.26, 61.

thus structurally illuminating Livy's belief that humanity, not nature or the gods, makes history. There is also an absence of discussion of social and economic forces in Livy's history as well as a refusal to rely completely on explanations of fate. Second, through the use of speeches, history becomes "philosophy teaching by example."[65] Speeches are the moral exemplar for emulation. They encapsulate a theory ready for either reenactment or repulsion.

Further adding to the theatrical elements of his history, Livy often recounts events from the perspective of the spectators as well as from the position of the vanquished rather than the victorious. Narrating events from the position of the spectator invites the reader to be involved in the history, to place him- or herself directly into history. The spectator's viewpoint also affords the Romans the opportunity to observe themselves from the perspective of those upon whom they have acted. By adding spectacle to his narrative history, Livy grants the Romans a discursive space in which to imagine themselves as both actors and spectators. Moreover, his emphasis on the psychological aspects of conflict—the courage, anguish and so forth, of the combatants—permits Livy to ignore the technical devices used in battle.[66] Politically, this confirms his preference for peace rather than war as the route to Roman greatness; while theoretically, this facility with psychological observation highlights his affinity for tragedy. Livy's purpose was not merely to instruct and edify but also to affect his readers with that "pity and fear" to which so many Hellenistic historians aspired.[67]

Theatre was not an integral part of Livy's history merely to entertain his reader; indeed, he insists that his purpose is *not* to charm: "Nothing can be thought to be further from my intention at the beginning of this work than to diverge unduly from the true order of events and by introducing various embellishments to attempt to provide my readers with enjoyable digressions."[68] Rather, Livy's theatrical elements were pivotal to his understanding of how historical memory was constituted.

In Augustan Rome, under the influence of Ciceronian oratory, memory itself was considered an art form. First and foremost, memory was

65. Walsh, *Livy: His Historical Aims and Methods,* 273.

66. P. G. Walsh notes, "All the battle accounts are frighteningly dull variations on an identical theme. First the Romans, through the enemy's numerical superiority or through surprise, fall into difficulties, then, through the extraordinary bravery or cleverness of their leaders, they gain the upper hand, and finally kill 40,000 or 35,000 of the enemy, or occasionally fewer" (ibid., 158–59).

67. Ibid., 177.

68. Livy, *Rome and Italy,* trans. Betty Radice (New York: Penguin Books, 1982), 9.17, 238.

believed to be most effectively organized and recalled *visually*. Cicero asserts in *De Oratore*: "It has been sagaciously discerned by Simonides or else discovered by some other person, that the most complete pictures are formed in our minds of the things that have been conveyed to them and imprinted on them by the senses, but that the keenest of all our senses is the sense of sight, and that consequently perceptions received by the ears or by reflexion can be most easily retained if they are also conveyed to our minds by the mediation of the eyes."[69] Cicero is invoking here the classical technique of memory (mnemotechnics), according to which there are two kinds of memory—natural and artificial. The natural memory is that which is engraved in one's mind simultaneously with thought. Artificial memory is a memory strengthened or confirmed by training. Mnemotechnics, the cultivation of artificial memory, consisted of Cicero's well-known process of assigning places or images to that which is to be remembered.[70]

Answering Cicero's call for a Roman history equal in presentation and eloquence to that of the Greeks, Livy adopts the techniques of a Ciceronian orator. Cicero had asserted that Roman histories could not be compared with Greek histories because the former lacked *ornatus*, or attractive presentation.[71] Apparently in an attempt to answer Cicero's summons and to distinguish himself from the historians before him, Livy crafted a history congruent with the elements of Cicero's "art of memory." Impressed that memory is most effective when organized visually, Livy crafts history as a visual narrative. He forges from history "episodes" punctuated by speeches that act as visual testimony to moral and political truths. To convey, for example, the importance of diversity and of the need for the patricians and the plebeians to reconcile their differences and to create unity, Livy stages the story of the Fabii clan, an aristocratic family of three hundred that volunteers to single-handedly protect Rome from invasion. Although they initially fight valiantly, they are easily lured by the enemy into a trap and are eventually slaughtered.[72] Livy's dramatic rendition is a visual testimony to an important political idea—the necessity of diversity in the preservation of Roman liberty.

Livy's condensation of scenes also parallels the technique of mnemotechnics. By locating the human figures and the action in one place, as

69. Marcus Tullius Cicero, *De Oratore*, trans. J. S. Watson (London: Henry G. Bohn, 1855), 2.87, 327.

70. Frances A. Yates, *The Art of Memory* (Chicago: University of Chicago Press, 1966), chap. 2.

71. Livy, *The Early History of Rome*, 2.48–51.

72. Serres, *Rome: The Book of Foundations*, 183.

recommended by Cicero, not only is dramatic tension increased, but the likelihood of recollection is also improved. Thus in Livy's version of the rape of Lucretia, unlike Ovid's and Dionysus of Halicarnassus's, all action occurs in Lucretia's *domus*. Lucretia does not travel to her father's house to apprise him of her violation (as she does in DH's version) nor is her husband met on the road by a messenger telling him of his wife's fate (as he is in both other versions). Rather, all of the figures of the drama are gathered in one space and hear from Lucretia herself of the rape, just as they are each witnesses to Lucretia's suicide (in Ovid's version, Brutus arrives after Lucretia is dead).

Livy's visual staging of history serves to make the founding of Rome itself theatrical, a spectacle for emulation. The staging also blurs the distinction between the real origin and the representation of the origin. Livy has given power both to the real, that founding moment to which it is impossible to return, and to the representation, the memory that can be endlessly recalled and repeated. Rome never ceases to be founded; the memory of her founding is endlessly recalled and thus potentially reenacted. As Michael Serres argues: "The essential is not to learn to distinguish between the real and the representation, but rather the essential is to see these differentiated spaces forming, to see that there is not one space that is either real or represented . . . but that there are numbers of them, finely and inextricably imbricated in still others."[73] In other words, at the founding the real and the representation are intertwined; the founding is itself both real and representational. Consider, for example, how the rape of the Sabine women, one of the founding stories of the first pentad, braids together both discursive spaces, the representational and the real: the Sabine men are at the theatre indulging in the representational, while the Romans are in the real, stealing their sisters and daughters.[74] For Livy, this is not a cautionary tale about the dangers of representation, but rather an illustration of how the two are embroiled. The process of founding requires both spaces. Livy's history is itself the representation, the theatre, the spectacle of the once-real founding of Rome, inviting representation, repetition and refounding in the real, now-present age of Augustus.

73. Ibid., 182.

74. Christina S. Kraus makes the argument in her essay, "Initium Turbandi Omnia a Femina Ortum Est: Fabia Minor and the Election of 367 B.C.," in *Phoenix: The Journal of the Classical Association of Canada* 45 (1991): 314–25, that the story of Fabia Minor can be understood as a doubling of the Lucretia story.

IV. OVERVIEW

Livy's rendition of the story of the rape of Lucretia defines and in some ways anchors the themes that the following chapters pursue and develop. The double narrative of Brutus's fantasized parthenogenesis and Lucretia's sexual violation articulates a recurring and pivotal theme in this genealogy—the desire for male autonomy, which inevitably requires the supplement of female power. Although femininity takes substantively different forms in each thinker's work, the dilemma of male power, revealed as in some way inadequate or insufficient, preoccupies both Machiavelli and Rousseau.

Livy's history structurally personifies founding as a process rather than as a one-time inauguration. Although Livy's tale is significantly more violent than either Machiavelli's or Rousseau's, his history still maintains the possibility for political renewal and greatness. Lucretia's story is told in such a way as to ignite rather than forestall political action. Indeed, Lucretia-like stories are repeated several times within his history—for example, in the rape of Verginia and in the comic seduction of Fabia Minor.[75] These repetitions suggest that both decline and renewal are cyclical and repeatable events.

In addition, Livy's story of the rape of Lucretia reconceives the role of the founder. Here the founder is seen as renewing the bonds of the community as well as delivering Rome from the vulture of tyrannical power. Republican founding becomes more than simply giving one's form to matter in the way that Romulus did initially, but rather a process of both rescue and renovation. Thus, the *virtù* necessary to found a republic becomes the ability to rejuvenate the principles embodied in the original act of foundation. Renewing the spirit of the foundation is, in interesting ways, more of the focus than the founding itself. And again, this reconceptualization invites an examination of the role of women and of female power as the demands of *virtù* become deeply entwined with formulations of femininity. As the following chapters will explore, femininity becomes particularly salient when it is crafted, as it is in both Machiavelli and Rousseau, as specularity, performance and contingency.

75. Interestingly, by the time Livy was writing this history, praise for Romulus as a model founder was muted; although Romulus was still applauded for the initiative of his founding, he was also simultaneously chided for his tyrannical impulses. Thus, Livy's reformulation of the founder was designed, in part, to offer a more noble hero.

3

La Mandragola AND THE SEDUCTION OF LUCREZIA

I. THE COMEDY OF POLITICAL THEORY

Although some readers of Machiavelli dismiss his plays as insignificant to his political thinking[1] or as marking his utopian turn away from reality and political education,[2] Machiavelli's plays are not simply entertainment or a manifestation of his alienation and frustration with political life. Rather, they are a continuation of both his political thinking and his civic education in another form.

Once in political exile, Machiavelli adjusted both the form and content of his civic education to his new audience. This was a mark not of despair but of the Machiavellian strategist. Just as in *The Discourses* Machiavelli celebrated Brutus for his mantle of idiocy that allowed him to move about unnoticed as he set out to destroy the tyrants and liberate his country, so there is reason to believe that Machiavelli was also assuming a "mantle of idiocy" in writing comedies.

Machiavelli begins bemoaning his reduction to playwriting in the prologue to *La Mandragola*:

The author, with pastimes debonair,
Has sought to mask his impotence,
Since he's reduced to indolence
And has no other way to turn,
Condemned to an enforced sojourn,
All worthwhile occupations barred
Or, at least, denied reward.

1. See, for example, Quentin Skinner's *Machiavelli* (New York: Hill and Wang, 1981).

2. See, for example, "Introduction," in *Machiavelli and the Discourse of Literature,* ed. Albert Russell Ascoli and Victoria Kahn (Ithaca: Cornell University Press, 1993).

Ostensibly, Machiavelli is referring to his political exile from Florence. He has been banished from active political life and thereby reduced to playwriting. He implies that writing plays is not a worthwhile activity; he would not have stooped so low if he had been able to pursue his political career as planned. But there is reason to suspect his humility. For what could *seem* greater folly than for a political theorist to write comedy? And what could emerge as greater wisdom than for an exiled political actor to act politically through theatre? Unlike the fools of Machiavelli's comedies, who remain blindly anchored to their misconceptions, who cannot imagine changing themselves and who refuse to see the reverse side of things,[3] Machiavelli alters the form of his politics with the shifting of circumstances. And as he notes in a letter to Vettori, these changes parallel Nature herself.[4] His movement to comedy is Machiavelli's adaptation to the whims of Fortuna.

Machiavelli's turn to theatre also highlights his conception of the impossibility of literal duplication of the past. Unlike Plato's conception of recollection, Machiavelli's formulation is not one simply of retrieval but of creation as well.In a different historical period the recreation of the past takes a different form—from Livy's tragic rendition of the founding in the rape of Lucretia to Machiavelli's comedic repetition of the seduction of Lucrezia in *LaMandragola*. This conception of recollection is also manifest (as this chapter will detail) in Machiavelli's mockery of both Coluccio Salutati's humanist and Saint Augustine's Christian interpretations of the story of Lucretia. From Machiavelli's perspective, each of these renditions misunderstands its relation to the past.

This adaptation to a new form, theatre, resonated in important ways with Machiavelli's own conception of the space of politics. That is, the early 1500s marked a distinct change in the form of theatre itself. Previously, medieval theatre had created an explicit dialogue between the members of the audience and the actors on stage by continually referring to the spectators and conceiving of the stage as simultaneously part of, and distinct from, the audience's world. With the adaptation of Roman theatre to the Renaissance stage, however, the stage was understood as a completely

3. See Guilio Ferroni, "Transformation and Adaptation in Machiavelli's *Mandragola*," in *Machiavelli and the Discourse of Literature*, ed. Albert Russell Ascoli and Victoria Kahn (Ithaca: Cornell University Press, 1993), 95–97.

4. Letter to Vettori, January 1514, no. 159, in *Machiavelli: The Chief Works and Others*, trans. Allan Gilbert (Durham: Duke University Press, 1989), 2:960.

autonomous fictive space. The audience had no place in the world of the characters on stage and was no longer acknowledged by them: "Instead of alluding verbally and symbolically to a world which existed off stage, Roman drama was attempting to drag that world on stage in recognizable form, and to become a convincing slice of reality in its own right."[5] The stage was thus conceived as an enclosed space with its own internal logic. Also, at this time, illusionistic perspective sets, using the techniques established in sculpture and painting, were used to create visually the separateness of the stage from the audience.

In his political writings too, Machiavelli was trying to establish politics as an autonomous, if not fictive realm. He was seeking to establish political space as a place governed by its own logic and necessities, a space where the ethics of Christianity and of humanist decorum did not direct political decisions. Again, this is apparent in Machiavelli's critique of Salutati's and Augustine's versions of the Lucretia story. For example, Machiavelli mocks Augustine's chastisement of Lucretia for her pagan values, an ethics that Machiavelli reinterprets as political savvy.

Because theatre was beginning to enjoy this autonomy, that is, to become less dependent on the feedback of the audience during its performance, the stage begins theoretically to parallel Machiavelli's expectations for political space. For example, the audience in Renaissance theatre was not directly addressed but was allowed to eavesdrop on a world that resembled their own. Members of the audience were fashioned as spectators. Theatre was a visual spectacle, full of seeming and appearance, with the power to inspire imitation while simultaneously inviting the judgment of the spectator. Similarly, Machiavelli's address to Florentine political actors allows them to witness a world, ancient Rome, which closely resembles theirs and from which they can learn how to act. Machiavelli crafts his political actors as spectators, not to ensure their passivity, but rather because he believes that spectacle incites people to action. What is pivotal in theatre, as in Machiavelli's politics, is the staging of the action, not necessarily the action itself. Consider Machiavelli's reincarnation of the founding story in *La Mandragola*. What invites republican politics is not reenacting the rape of Lucretia, but simply being *witness* to it.

Finally, the repetition of Roman theatre on the Renaissance stage,

5. Richard Andrews, *Scripts and Scenarios: The Performance of Comedy in Renaissance Italy* (Cambridge: Cambridge University Press, 1993), 26–27.

like Machiavelli's mimetic subversion of the mirror of princes genre as well as his repetition of Livy's *Discorsi*, serves to expose what Luce Irigaray calls "the scenography that makes representation feasible."[6] In other words, Machiavelli's theatre, like his political treatises, makes visible, by the effect of playful repetition, what was supposed to remain invisible. He exposes the complicated relation one has to the past, the inadequacy of *virtù* and the consequent necessity of a certain dependence upon Fortuna. By claiming to repeat the past but actually inventing it, Machiavelli demonstrates that part of what makes a good mimic is not being completely absorbed by the function. By juxtaposing Machiavelli's version of the Lucretia myth with Salutati's, we see that Machiavelli is, in part, satirizing Salutati's rather slavish devotion to the past and his naive (from Machiavelli's perspective) humanist belief that the past can be duplicated in the present.

* * *

The best-known definition of comedy during the Italian Renaissance was from Cicero: "Comedy is an imitation of life, a mirror of manners and an image of truth." Crystallized in this definition were quintessential features, not only of the Renaissance, but of Machiavelli's political thinking: imitation, mirrors and perspective. It is not surprising, then, that it is comedy rather than tragedy that Machiavelli writes. Indeed, sixteenth-century formulations of comedy make it the genre par excellence for the articulation of Machiavelli's political theory.

Imitation was conceived by Renaissance commentators as a device particularly appropriate to comedy not only because comedy offered an imitation of everyday life but also because laughter was derived both from the aping of character by other characters in the play and from the mimetic mockery of previous models of comedy.[7] Nonetheless, as Cicero notes, comedy was also assigned a didactic purpose as an "image of truth." It was a favorite Renaissance argument that comedy was among the best sources of instruction for youth. Comedies provided important lessons in moral conduct, for they exhibited lively mirrors of human action for the edification of the spectator. A Renaissance commentator on the value of Terence's comedies said: "And there is this beauty in comedies; they contain much in few words that other writings are wont to unfold in long-winded

6. Luce Irigaray, *The Sex Which Is Not One*, trans. Catherine Porter (Ithaca: Cornell University Press, 1985), 75.

7. Marvin T. Herrick, *Comic Theory in the Sixteenth Century* (Urbana: University of Illinois Press, 1950), 20–21.

disputation."[8] Comedy thus had the advantage of being able to present multiple aspects of an issue without the weariness of a learned polemic.

Particular also to comedies was the learning achieved by confrontation with the unexpected. Interestingly, Renaissance commentators attributed both the laughter and the edification of comedies as coming from this encounter with the unforeseen. Pleasure was derived from both the unexpected turn and from one's learning something new: "For it becomes evident to him that he has learnt something, when the conclusion turns out contrary to his expectation and the mind seems to say, 'How true it is! but I missed it.'"[9] Thus there is a contagion between the delight provided by comedy and the learning one derives.

Working within these Renaissance conceptions of comedy, Machiavelli chooses comic theatre as an appropriate political medium. For what could be more apropos than a genre whose primary tool is imitation, specifically imitation of everyday people and events; a genre that multiplies perspectives as it mirrors reality; and, finally, a genre whose "image of truth" is achieved through examples and spectacle rather than through disputation and principled argument? Indeed, in his "Discourse on Language," Machiavelli echoes Cicero's definition of the purpose of comedy: "to hold up a mirror to private life, nevertheless, its way of doing it is with a certain urbanity and with terms which incite laughter, so that the men who run to that great delight, taste afterwards the useful example that is underneath."[10]

For Machiavelli, comedy is *not* frivolous. Laughter is a pretext that creates the opportunity for people to consider later the "deeper" meaning of the performance. As *commedia erudita,* the plays were considered sophisticated narratives that could be interpreted on several levels. They were satisfying to the multitude, while also communicating "subtle truths" to political leaders and scholars.[11] Moreover, the image of the mirror held up to private life was understood from several perspectives. First, there was the rather obvious didactic function of the mirror. The audience looks into the mirror and sees itself reflected on the stage. Through this representation of

8. Ambrosius Berndt Iuterbocensis, quoted in Herrick, *Comic Theory,* 76.

9. Renaissance commentator Madius, quoting Aristotle's *Rhetoric,* in Herrick, *Comic Theory,* 45.

10. Machiavelli's "Discourse about Our Language," quoted in Mera J. Flaumenhaft, "The Comic Remedy: Machiavelli's *Mandragola,*" in *Interpretation: A Journal of Political Philosophy* 7 (May 1978): 36.

11. Douglas Radcliff-Umstead, *The Birth of Modern Comedy in Renaissance Italy* (Chicago: University of Chicago Press, 1969), 11–15.

themselves, they understand better who they are and how to improve their follies. Yet, from another perspective, the mirror held to private life was an opportunity for the prince to see how the subjects look. The prince as spectator at the theatre sees himself reflected on the stage and has the opportunity to observe how his subjects perceive themselves and others.

Machiavelli chooses comedy rather than tragedy in part because *consilium* (counsel) was considered an important part of Renaissance comedy: "Comedy is nothing unless it is the image of human counsels and events."[12] And, these counsels concerned contingent matters, involving consultations about what is right and wrong, what is expedient and so forth, and thus naturally belonged to a deliberative discourse. Tragedy, on the other hand, was understood as the manifestation of a universal principle or aspect of mankind. There was little contingency in tragedy, and the denouement was foreordained in the opening of the play. Tragedies, according to Renaissance theories of the genre, expressed the abandonment of life, while comedies celebrated its commencement.[13] Thus for Machiavelli, comedy was more political—offering the possibility of a world that could be otherwise and was dependent on the interventions and machinations of mankind.

Although Aristotle's conception of the proper function of tragedy (i.e., the arousal of pity and fear) was not widely known early in the sixteenth century when Machiavelli was writing his plays, Donatus's commentary on Terence offered a detailed explanation of the emotions aroused by tragedy and comedy. Relying on Quintilian, Donatus asserted that tragedy aroused more violent emotions, "pathos," while comedy incited gentler and more calm emotions, "ethos." Pathos was understood "to command and disturb," whereas ethos "persuaded and induced a feeling of goodwill."[14] Ethos was connected with ethics and thus with Renaissance conceptions of judgment.

For Machiavelli's political purposes, then, comedy was a more appropriate didactic tool. Comedy modeled the process of judgment and created the conditions for judgment with its arousal of ethos. Tragedy, on the other hand, invited persuasion or dissuasion on the basis of strong emotion; there was little opportunity for reflection. In comedy there was the possibility for both reflection and invention. Comedy was credited as the genre that put people's emotions in order: "The end of comedy is cheerful, and employs

12. Renaissance commentator Melanchthon, quoted in Herrick, *Comic Theory*, 14.

13. Herrick, *Comic Theory*, 59.

14. Ibid., 69.

a quieting of the emotions which do not increase to a tragic perturbation. . . . Comedy sets human desires in order, so they may beget heroic strength."[15] Thus, comedy was perceived as the golden mean that contained and directed human emotions rather than enflaming them. Comedy, like Machiavelli's political writings, sought to educate human desires rather than simply to ignite them.

Another reason why Machiavelli preferred comedy to tragedy was that comedy was understood as the genre of blaming, while tragedy was the genre of praise.[16] Comedy detailed bad actions and characters who were worse than average but not wicked: "The Ridiculous may be defined as a mistake or deformity not productive of pain or harm to others; the mask, for instance, that excites laughter, is something ugly and distorted without causing pain."[17] Tragedy, on the other hand, praised great actions and heroic men, often from history, who had suffered dreaded outcomes. Tragedies began with order and ended with downfall, whereas comedies began with turbulence and concluded with peace and reconciliation. Given that Machiavelli wanted Renaissance Florence to recognize the possibility for her rebirth and renewal, comedy offered the more optimistic venue. Since Machiavelli believed that Florentine men were not so corrupt as to be beyond redemption, comedy afforded him the opportunity to chide and mock them for their flaws and failures without representing those defects as irreversible and determinant.

Finally, during the early sixteenth century there was little analysis of what is perhaps the most complex feature of comedy: what makes people laugh. References were often made to Caesar's assertion in Cicero's *De Oratore* that although he (Caesar) had examined various treatises to explain the phenomenon, what he found was that all who tried to formulate a theory of laughter merely made themselves objects of laughter. Caesar asserts that although laughter is a great advantage in speaking, "it cannot be taught by any rule or art."[18] Renaissance theorists acknowledged, like the Greeks and Romans before them, that what makes people laugh is contingent and contextual. This is an important aspect of comedy for Machiavelli, because here is a recognized virtue that cannot be taught by rules or learned through imitation. Rather, this virtue, knowing how to

15. Renaissance commentator Petrus Marsus, quoted in Herrick, *Comic Theory,* 71.
16. Herrick, *Comic Theory,* 17.
17. Aristotle, *The Poetics,* trans. S. H. Butcher (New York: Dover Publications, 1951), 74.
18. Cicero, *De Oratore* 2.56.

make others laugh, necessitates sensitivity to context, demands judgment and, of course, requires impeccable timing; it resembles nothing if not the *virtù* that Machiavelli celebrates for his political actors. In other words, the *virtù* required to produce comedy is much like the *virtù* demanded of successful Machiavellian actors: it is contingent, contextual and changing.

While Machiavelli is often read as a "realist," he is one for whom the real is elusive, changing and full of appearances. To be a realist in Machiavelli's terms is to be concerned constantly with distortion, inversion and opacity *because* power itself deceives and dissimulates. For Machiavelli the "real" is not stable, apparent and singular. It is changing, dependent on circumstances and perspective as well as on the whims of Fortuna. Politics, for Machiavelli, does not have its roots in human nature; he does not formulate a conception of human nature that then finds its articulation in politics. Or perhaps more succinctly, politics is not a manifestation of human nature but rather a realm in which human nature is, in some ways, irrelevant.

Although contemporary theorists of realism often argue that Machiavellian politics is interest politics par excellence,[19] this book argues that producing and articulating "interest"—political, rather than natural—is itself the project of Machiavellian politics. Politics is not, then, the arena for the articulation and contestation of an a priori interest.

Although Machiavelli does occasionally seem preoccupied with force and with the "armed citizen," close examination of his discussions of force expose his focus on the "reputation of force," the "display of power" and "appearing to trust one's citizens,"[20] rather than on the mere deployment of force. What preoccupies Machiavelli in his discussions of force, specifically in *The Discourses,* is how that force is narrated—what is said about one's ability, how that force appears and how it is later remembered. Consider,

19. Hans Morganthau, *Politics Among Nations: The Struggle for Power and Peace* (New York: McGraw-Hill, 1993).

20. See for example, *The Discourses* 1.19 and 2.14, where Machiavelli gives numerous examples of the necessity of kings often to wage war in order not "to appear effeminate . . . and be esteemed little" and "because the zeal of the prince's friends will be chilled on seeing him *appear* feeble and cowardly" (my emphasis). In fact, Machiavelli goes so far as to say that "I do not mean to say by this, however, that arms and force are never to be employed, but that they should be reserved as *the last resort* when other means fail" (2.31; my emphasis). Consider further that Machiavelli also asserts that "the surest guaranty of victory" is "to inspire the soldiers on the eve of battle with confidence." Of course, this confidence is the result of Machiavelli's willingness to manipulate the auguries when required (*Discourses,* 1.14, "The Romans Interpreted the Auspices According to Necessity, and Very Wisely Made Show of Observing Religion, Even When They Were Obliged in Reality to Disregard It; and If Any One Recklessly Disparaged It, He Was Punished").

for example, Machiavelli's assertion in *The Discourses* that "artifices [of force] may safely and with advantage be employed when they have more the appearance of reality than of fiction."[21]

My argument is simply an acknowledgment that for Machiavelli, politics is the manipulation of what counts as the real in a particular context rather than an enduring search for the real itself; politics is the creation of meaning rather than the search for truth. Politics is a matter, also, of being able to judge whether an artifice will have sufficient "reality" for a particular situation and/or audience.[22] Politics involves judgment, the evaluation of what is necessary in a particular situation. And comic theatre seems to provide an ideal vehicle for the edification of this judgment.

In *La Mandragola,* Machiavelli's comic theatre is shown to be neither mere entertainment nor the utopian politics of a desperate exile. Rather, *La Mandragola* is the comic staging of the republican founding story of Lucretia, integral not only to Machiavelli's conception of political foundings but also to his formulation of political action, *virtù* and spectacle. *La Mandragola* is not only a rewriting of Livy's story of the rape of Lucretia, but it is also a rewriting and commentary on other Lucretia stories in circulation during the Italian Renaissance, specifically, Saint Augustine's in *City of God* and Coluccio Salutati's in *Declamatio Lucretia*. Machiavelli's rendition is thus testament to his understanding of his relationship to the Roman past as well as to his Christian and humanist present. In this chapter attention will be focused on Machiavelli's response to Augustine's and Salutati's version; in the next, analysis will center on Machiavelli's reinterpretation of Livy's version.

II. *La Mandragola*: LUCRETIA MACHIAVELLI STYLE

The comedy *La Mandragola* is ostensibly the story of how Callimaco, with the cunning assistance of Ligurio, plots to sleep with Lucrezia,[23] the

21. *Discourses* 3.14, 459.

22. For example: "Here it is well to observe that such artifices may safely and with advantage be employed when they have more the appearance of reality than fiction; for then their seeming strength will prevent the prompt discovery of their weakness. But when they are manifestly rather fictitious than real, they should either not be employed or they should be kept at such a distance that their real character cannot be so quickly discovered" (*Discourses* 3.14, 459–60).

23. N.B.: The different spellings of Lucretia: "Lucrezia" is the Italian form of the Roman name. Machiavelli's character in *La Mandragola* is Lucrezia, as is Lucrezia Borgia, Cesare's sister. Only in Livy's story is her name Lucretia.

beautiful and famously virtuous wife of Messer Nicia. The plot is driven by the various machinations each of the conspirators pursues in order to fulfill his desires. The story begins, as does the story told by Livy in his *Early History of Rome,* with one of Lucrezia's relatives bragging about her beauty and grace to a Florentine, Callimaco, then living in Paris. In order to see the celebrated beauty, Callimaco returns to Florence and becomes "inflamed with such burning desire to be with her, that [he] can not bear it."[24]

Lucrezia, however, is reportedly as chaste as she is beautiful. Nonetheless, Callimaco perceives several weaknesses in Lucrezia's defenses: the stupidity of her husband, Nicia; the couple's desire to have a child; and finally, the compromising nature of Lucrezia's mother, Sostrata. In order to fulfill his desires, Callimaco enlists Ligurio, a clever charlatan, to devise a plan that will ensure Callimaco's success at becoming Lucrezia's lover.

In Ligurio's scheme, Callimaco poses as a learned physician who concocts a draught of mandragola guaranteed to make any woman conceive: "If it were not for that, the Queen of France and countless other Princesses of that realm would be barren" (2.6, 195). The only hitch is that the first man to have sex with a woman who has drunk the potion will die within a week. Therefore it is necessary, the pseudo-physician asserts, to kidnap some unsuspecting youth to draw off the poison. This "unsuspecting victim," of course, will be the desirous Callimaco.

The remainder of the play chronicles the frauds and deceptions required to get Callimaco into Lucrezia's bed without Nicia's knowledge but somehow with something resembling Lucrezia's consent. Lucrezia finally agrees to drink the mandrake potion, which is, of course, a ruse, and to sleep with the captured youth in order to draw off the poison so that she can eventually be impregnated by her husband. Enlisted in this process are a friar, Lucrezia's mother, and her own husband, Nicia.

The play concludes, as comedies do, with several happy resolutions. Callimaco reveals himself and his love to Lucrezia, who remarkably reciprocates his love and takes him as "my lord, my master and my guide" (5.4, 269). Nicia is promised the much longed-for heir, and the greedy, hypocritical friar has been paid 300 ducats for his duplicitous role in the outcome.

Quite simply, the play can be read as Machiavelli's commentary on how corrupt and fallen Renaissance Florence is when compared with

24. *La Mandragola* 1.i, in *The Comedies of Machiavelli,* ed. and trans. David Sices and James B. Atkinson (Hanover: University Press of New England, 1985), 167. Citations in the text hereafter are from this edition.

ancient, republican Rome. In fact, Machiavelli notes in his prologue to *La Mandragola*:

> *Today the ancient virtues flicker*
> *And high endeavors disappear;*
> *For who would dare to preserve*
> *In undertakings long or short,*
> *Which nagging censure will abort,*
> *And works on which fond hopes are pinned*
> *Are cloaked in fog, or gone with the wind.*

Apparently, Florence is so infirm that it can neither maintain the ancient virtues nor even be cured if anyone sought to remedy her malady. The most obvious sign of the fallen state of Renaissance Florence, where the play is set, is the status of Lucrezia's rape. In *La Mandragola,* she is not raped but seduced, allegedly enjoying "the chance to appreciate the difference between [Callimaco's] technique and Nicia's, between the kisses of a young lover and those of an old husband" (5.4, 267). In fact, Lucrezia seems rather easily "converted" to adultery.

In addition, the only person who considers suicide in Machiavelli's version is Callimaco, and then, while worrying whether something will spoil his plans to seduce Lucrezia: "If that should happen, this will be the last night of my life, because I'll throw myself into the Arno, or hang myself, or jump out of that window up there, or plunge a dagger into my breast right on her doorstep" (4.4, 243). His last suggestion of plunging a dagger into his breast is the only echo of the Roman Lucretia's suicide.

Yet rather than a commentary on how far Renaissance Florence is from the Roman ideal, the comedy actually illuminates Machiavelli's conception of the process of foundings more generally. Even the Roman republic, Machiavelli acknowledges, was not ideal at its founding. First, there was the initial fratricide: Romulus kills Remus, which Machiavelli suggests would be suspect, except that it resulted in a common good. Second, Rome did not have a great legislator such as the Spartan Lycurgus at her foundations. Having been founded by Romulus as a monarchy, Rome "lacked many of the institutions essential to liberty."[25] Consequently,

25. *The Discourses,* trans. Leslie J. Walker, S.J. (London: Penguin Books, 1970), 1.2. Citations in the text hereafter are from this edition.

she had to wait years before she was able to achieve these "perfections." Furthermore, "although the founder of Rome was Romulus, to whom like a daughter she owed her birth and education," his laws were insufficient for "so great an empire" and it was subsequently necessary for Numa to establish religion as the foundation for Roman civil society (*Discourses* 1.11). Finally, popular power was waning until the people rebelled and the Tribunes were created. Nonetheless, as Machiavelli details, Fortuna favored the Roman Republic, and she was eventually able to achieve a combination of the three powers that finally rendered her constitution perfect (*Discourses* 1.2).[26]

This conception of the founding as a process explains why Machiavelli remains optimistic about the possibility of founding/renewing the Florentine republic. His use of examples from the past is not designed to suggest how far fallen contemporary Florence is from the ideal of classical Rome, but it is rather to remind Renaissance Italians that the founding of the Roman Republic was itself a process of beginning, that it took years before Rome achieved her perfection. Moreover, Machiavelli believes that what is worse than beginning awry is beginning in perfection and then going astray. Better it is, he asserts, to start in corruption and work toward perfection (*Discourses* 1.10).

Thus, Machiavelli is a political thinker for whom the present is *not* beyond repair. Rather, so strongly does he believe in the power of renovation that he insists that "those are the best constituted bodies, and have the longest existence, which possess the intrinsic means of frequently renewing themselves, or such as obtain this renovation in consequence of some extrinsic accident" (*Discourses* 3.1). This is why he retells the founding story of the rape of Lucretia—confident that the memory of a former liberty will stir the people's return to their first principles. For the story of Lucretia takes place, as Machiavelli himself notes in *The Discourses,* at a time before Rome was completely corrupt: "The Romans being not yet corrupted when they recovered their liberty, were able to maintain it after the death of the sons of Brutus and the expulsion of the Tarquins, by means of such laws and institutions as we have treated above. But if the people had been corrupt, then there would have been no sufficient remedies found in Rome or

26. Consider further that Machiavelli tells his republican founding story in theatrical form—itself an unstable medium open to interpretation, a medium that blurs the boundaries between the real and the imitation, between appearance and being, between the original and the copy.

elsewhere to maintain their liberty" (1.16). Rome at the time of the republic, just like Florence in 1519 (the performance date of *La Mandragola*) is still not so corrupt as to be beyond redemption. The memory of Soderini's republic lies in the not-too-distant past.

Interestingly, Janus, the Roman god of beginnings, was represented in Roman art with two faces. These faces were shown looking in opposite directions, symbolizing the god's knowledge of both the past and the future. In fact, the name *Janus* was also frequently used as a common noun (a *janus*), which Cicero defined (*De Natura Decorum* 2.67) as "a crossing place with a roadway."[27] Implicit, clearly, in the Roman conception of beginnings was duality. Beginnings were understood as neither singular nor complete. As the two-faced god signifies, beginnings were themselves complicated interventions between the past and the future, a crossroad at which several directions were possible. And this is the conception of beginnings, of foundings, to which Machiavelli, like Livy, subscribes. It is partially because of this complicated sense of beginnings that Machiavelli believes that one must depend on the *virtù* of only one person, the founder, to inaugurate, although not complete, the process of beginnings.

Thus, *La Mandragola* has also been understood by political theorists as a political allegory for *The Prince*. Callimaco represents Duke Lorenzo de'Medici; Lucrezia is Florence; and Nicia stands for the ill-fated Piero Soderini, Machiavelli's patron in the Florentine chancery. Ligurio is the political theorist, Machiavelli.[28] Even when historical figures are not attached to the characters, the play tends to be reduced to a translation of *The Prince* in which Callimaco is the "redeemer . . . who cures her [Italy] of those sores that have been festering for so long"[29] and under whose "banner this country may be ennobled"; in other words, he is the founder of a unified Italy.

While this is an apt reading of the play in some respects, it neglects the significance of the role of Lucrezia. The momentum of the play is not simply toward the installation of a new prince but rather toward the founding conditions of a republic and a republican citizenry. The play articulates

27. Mark Morford and Robert Lenardon, *Classical Mythology* (New York: Longman, 1985), 467.

28. Editor's Note to "The Mandrake Root," in *The Portable Machiavelli*, ed. and trans. Peter Bondanella and Mark Musa (New York: Penguin Books, 1979), 430–32.

29. *The Prince*, trans. Peter Bondanella and Mark Musa (Oxford: Oxford University Press, 1984), chap. 24, 112.

Machiavelli's conception of the republican founding as well as the qualities of *virtù* required for a successful republic. Despite the corrupting incongruities between other "serious" versions and Machiavelli's comedic rendition,[30] there is still a way in which the comedy is Machiavelli's rather optimistic rendition of the possibility, rather than impossibility, for a republican founding. *La Mandragola* is crafted specifically as a memory to ignite political imitation and action; the play is a spectacle fashioned to seduce a Renaissance audience to their not-quite-forgotten liberty.

Importantly for Machiavelli, the founding story of the rape of Lucretia is not based on verifiable historical fact. Indeed, as commentators have noted, the story occurs in Livy's narrative at the limit between legend and historical fact.[31] The founding is a myth, as Hanna Pitkin notes, "and thus, cannot be a genuine solution to any problem in the real world."[32]

Machiavelli turns to a mythic story at this most crucial moment because of what the founding is meant to achieve. The fable, the myth, the story is a nonfoundational politics that is still legitimate and authoritative. Although Machiavelli's rendition claims to be a recovery of origins, it erases the violence and ambiguity that marked the original act of founding. Machiavelli's comedy prohibits further inquiry into the origins and protects the republic's center of illegitimacy from scrutiny. Machiavelli wants to recall the founding for its power to incite political action but to forestall close examination of its violent foundations.

The founding story is simultaneously meant to generate piety in the sons/citizens toward the initiative of their father/founder *and* to thwart their desire to follow his example completely. For example, Brutus founds the republic but kills his sons, according to Machiavelli, in part, because they were trying to be fully autonomous. Brutus's sons behave as fathers rather than as sons of the republic; they act as aristocrats rather than as members of the populace. Machiavelli justifies Brutus's killing of his sons, as well as six other "memorable executions," "because they were extreme and noteworthy . . . [they] made men draw back to their proper stations"

30. See the introduction of Chapter 4 for a discussion of the role of the comedic and serious in Machiavelli.

31. Robert M. Ogilvie, Introduction, *A Commentary on Livy: Books 1–5* (Oxford: Clarendon Press, 1965).

32. Hanna Pitkin, *Fortune Is a Woman: Gender and Politics in the Thought of Niccolo Machiavelli* (Berkeley: University of California Press, 1984), 294.

(*Discourses* 3.1). And this proper station (*segno*) or mark recalls the people to the beginnings of the republic but does not reenact it.

Machiavelli continues his use of the example of Brutus's killing of his sons by noting that as these "memorable executions" became rarer, "they also gave men more room for growing wicked. . . . For this reason, from one such enforcement of the law to the next, there should be a lapse of not more than ten years . . . and if something does not happen to bring the penalty back to their memories and renew fear in their minds, so many offenders quickly join together that they cannot be punished without danger." Importantly, what must be brought back to the people's memories is the punishment they suffered before they became republicans.[33] In other words, the people must remember not only the valor of the founders but also the fear and insecurity they felt before the founding of the republic. Machiavelli wants his contemporary Florentines to recall both the initial calculations of Brutus (i.e., his feigned idiocy in order to secure his opportunity for the founding) and his severity in maintaining the republic after its founding (i.e., the killing of his sons). Both aspects of Brutus' strategy are important: Brutus's coy deceptions are an important lesson to the virtuous man Machiavelli hopes will restore the republic; Brutus's killing of his own sons is a lesson to the multitude. While the founder will imitate other great men, the multitude must not. And the punishment of Brutus's sons is an object lesson for them. The multitude must recall the injuries of tyranny and strive to be noble sons of the republic. Machiavelli's use of the image suggests that the desired imitation for the multitude is of the son, not the father; what needs renewal is the reverence of the son, not the resurrection of the father; the son must recall the father, not replace or be the father.

Furthermore, the exemplar of Brutus's killing of his sons suggests why Machiavelli tries to instill both a sense of autonomy—"only those defenses are good, certain and durable, which depend on yourself alone and your own ability"[34]—and of dependence in republican citizens. On the one hand, the sons feel overshadowed by the father, so Machiavelli is trying to restore their sense of autonomy and independence, to encourage them

33. See *Discourses* 3.1: "By revising the government they meant inspiring such terror and such fear in the people as they had inspired on first taking charge, for at that time they punished those who, according to that kind of government, had done wrong."

34. *The Prince*, chap. 24.

with a sense of their own possibilities for political action. On the other hand, he needs to forestall their desires to *be* the father by maintaining a reverential memory of the father/founder as a source for imitation.[35] Thus here, as elsewhere, one of the primary ways Machiavelli details for the people to recognize their place is through spectacle[36]—the memorable and noteworthy spectacles of the executions of the law.

III. SATIRE OF AUGUSTINE'S PAGAN LUCRETIA: MAKING THE PRIVATE POLITICAL

In Livy's account, the rape of Lucretia highlights how a private transgression has public, political reverberations. Lucretia's private violation and suicidal confession reveals, in part, a cultural secret. In Machiavelli's account, however, there is no such distinction between the public and private, nor any such seeming revelation. All there is for Machiavelli's Lucrezia is politics and the realm of appearances. What concerns Machiavelli is not the distinction between, or violation of, the public and private spheres, but rather the politicization of virtue. In his domestic comedy, Machiavelli tries to demonstrate the necessity of making private morality answer to public necessity rather than vice versa. He is eager to demonstrate, not simply that everything is political, but rather that everything, including, specifically, moral decisions, has the potential to be politicized. Nothing is ontologically or naturally *not* political.

Lucrezia's conversion to adultery becomes for Machiavelli not a sign of her moral failing but of her political savvy. Lucrezia becomes a "bad woman" in order to be a "good citizen";[37] she forfeits her chastity in order to ensure her status as citizen. Through her seduction, the possibility for the republican founding is conceived; her participation is integral to the founding's success. Her private immorality serves a public good. Being a good citizen necessitates her willingness to act against the principles of private, and in this case Christian, morality. Lucrezia is willing to do this and thus personifies an ideal Machiavellian political actor.

In fact, her readiness to forfeit the ideal of chastity is, in part, Machiavelli's satire of Saint Augustine's critique of Lucretia's rape and suicide. In

35. It also may begin to explain why the founder takes the form of a woman, Lucrezia, in *La Mandragola*. I will discuss this further in Chapter 4.

36. The other ways are war and acts of God such as natural disasters, which often also bring men back to their "first principles."

37. Jean Bethke Elshtain, *Public Man/Private Woman: Women in Social and Political Thought* (Princeton: Princeton University Press, 1981), 94.

The City of God Saint Augustine is concerned with *why* Lucretia killed herself.[38] He asserts that "while the will remains firm and unshaken, nothing that another person does with the body, or upon the body, is any fault of the person who suffers it, so long as he cannot escape it without sin."[39]

Augustine, consequently, offers two explanations for why Lucretia decided to kill herself: first, perhaps Lucretia knew she was guilty because she had secretly enjoyed the rape and therefore decided she deserved the punishment for adultery—death; or second, and more likely, since she was a pagan and not a Christian, she was more concerned with her reputation than with the state of her conscience. A Christian, Augustine insists, would have been content that: "in the sight of God, [she was] esteemed pure . . . [she would] ask no more: it suffices [Christians] to have opportunity of doing good and they decline to evade the distress of human suspicion, lest they thereby deviate from the divine law."[40] Lucretia, as a pagan, is prompted instead by the burden of shame and the fear that others will suppose that she did not resent the wrong done against her, even if she knew in her heart that she was innocent. She has a sense of heroic virtue rather than of private morality. Lucretia, according to Augustine, is more attentive to her reputation, to appearances, than to her conscience or representation before God.

And this, of course, is Machiavelli's Lucrezia. Machiavelli is insisting that *reputation* is the most important aspect of the violation, that what matters is not the morality or immorality of the deed but the context and purpose for which it is performed. Lucrezia's willingness to be deceived, to be seduced to adultery, is emblematic of a citizen able to judge when to seize opportunity, when to lie and when to tell the truth. In fact, Machiavelli rewrites the story so that Lucrezia's consent or nonconsent is not at issue. He mocks Augustine's argument regarding intention in the words of

38. Augustine makes four arguments condemning suicide: first, that no private individual may take it upon himself to kill a guilty person, even if that person is oneself; thus Judas is not forgiven for his suicide nor is his suicide proof of his repentance. Second, the suicide who takes his own life has killed a man and thus breaks the sixth commandment, thou shalt not kill; this later became the justification for suicide as a felony in civil law. Third, the truly noble soul will bear all suffering; the pains we suffer are not our own but are undergone in the service of Christ. Fourth, since many Christians in the early centuries killed themselves for fear of falling before temptation, Augustine argued that suicide was a sin greater than any they could avoid by its commission, and thus the suicide dies the worst of sinners. See Henry Romilly Fedden, *Suicide: A Social and Historical Study* (New York: Benjamin Bloom, 1938), 116–17.

39. Saint Augustine, *The City of God,* trans. Marcus Dods (New York: Modern Library, 1950), book 1, chaps. 16–20.

40. *City of God,* 25.

the hypocritical Friar Timoteo: "As for the act itself, it is only an old wives' tale that it is a real sin, for the will is what commits sin, not the body. The real sin is going against a husband's wishes, and here you are following his wishes; or taking pleasure in it, and here you are filled with displeasure."[41] Here Machiavelli remakes Augustine's argument: while Augustine asserts that the violation is not a sin because it was done to the body without the will of the mind, Machiavelli's friar is asking Lucrezia *to agree* to the violation because only her body will be stained.

Interestingly, just before the passage cited above, the Friar also alerts Lucrezia to the importance of perspective: "There are many things that, seen from afar, seem awful, strange, unbearable; and then when you get up close to them, they turn out to be ordinary, familiar, bearable. That is why it is often said that their bark is worse than their bite. This is one of those things." Again, this is Machiavelli's suggestion that private morality needs to be examined and its consequences considered from a political perspective. There is also an echo here of Machiavelli's assertion that virtues can become vices, and seeming vices, virtues when understood properly.[42] The importance of perspective also recalls Machiavelli's own conception of the role of the theorist: "for, just as those who paint landscapes place themselves in a low position on the plain in order to consider the nature of the mountains and the high places, and place themselves high atop mountains in order to study the plains, in like manner, to know well the nature of the people one must be a prince, and to know well the nature of the princes one must be of the people."[43] Political acumen, as well as political theory itself, requires adjusting the position from which one looks and judges.

Although it is evident that Machiavellian politics is little concerned with fulfilling the necessities of the body and at this level seems to reproduce Aristotle's distinction between the realm of the *oekios* and the *polis,* Machiavelli's conception of politics itself makes it difficult for him to maintain the naturalness or the "given-ness" of the distinction between the public and private. Instead, his plays indicate that this distinction between

41. *La Mandragola* 3.11, 225.

42. "And yet he must not mind incurring the scandal of those vices, without which it would be difficult to save the state, for if one considers well, it will be found that some things which seem virtues would, if followed, lead to one's ruin, and some others which appear vices result in one's greater security and well being" (*The Prince,* chap. 15).

43. *The Prince,* Preface.

the public and the private is itself open to contestation and negotiation. For example, consider the ways in which women and servants figure so prominently in his plays—Lucrezia in *La Mandragola*, Sofronia in *Clizia*, and Davo, the servant, in *The Woman from Andros*. Each is a private person who becomes a political actor.[44] Often it is these characters who are the plot's catalysts, instrumental in orchestrating the play's outcome. For instance, in *Clizia* it is Sofronia's machinations that bring her husband, the patriarch Nicomaco, back to himself and his responsibilities.

In addition, the domestic conflict of Machiavelli's comedies highlights the importance he attributes to conflict for the maintenance of the republic.[45] The liberty of the republic depends on the conflict and opposition between the people and the nobles. In fact, Machiavelli argues that a more vital and dedicated form of civic cooperation will emerge from conflict and opposition than from a situation in which harmony and cooperation are stressed: "I maintain that those who blame the quarrels of the Senate and the people of Rome that which was the very origin of liberty . . . they do not consider that in every republic there are two parties, that of the nobles and that of the people; and all the laws that are favorable to liberty result from the opposition of these parties to each other."[46]

From this perspective, *La Mandragola*'s domestic strife is emblematic, not necessarily of corruption, but of the dissension Machiavelli expects and encourages between the nobles and the people. From the beginning of the play, Nicia and Lucrezia's marriage is shown to be one of struggle and negotiation. Indeed, in the first act Ligurio notes that Lucrezia governs Nicia, and Nicia complains that he must struggle always to gain her compliance. There is also the obvious conflict between Nicia and Callimaco, with Nicia playing the noble fool who refuses to adjust to changing circumstance, while Callimaco, like the populace, knows how to enlist the help of a superior man, Ligurio.

Nonetheless, because Machiavelli, unlike Aristotle, does not privilege a model of harmony, the resolution of these conflicts is always open. What the outcome will be is not predetermined. And since Machiavelli's

44. I am indebted to J. Peter Euben for calling to my attention that Machiavelli uses the term "political actor" rather than subjects or citizens to describe members of republics.

45. Neal Wood, "The Value of Asocial Sociability: Contributions of Machiavelli, Sidney and Montesquieu," in *Machiavelli and the Nature of Political Thought*, ed. Martin Fleisher (New York: Atheneum, 1972).

46. *Discourses* 1.4, in *The Prince and the Discourses*, trans. Luigi Ricci (New York: Modern Library, 1950), 119.

political model is neither static nor wedded to the fulfillment of natural or universal principles, a space is exposed for the consideration that the relation between men and women, or more specifically between masculinity and femininity, is also neither static nor predetermined, and that the struggle between them might not necessarily result in the subordination of femininity and the triumph of masculinity. In other words, in his domestic comedies, Machiavelli's victor is not always, or even usually, the patriarch. In the resolution of *La Mandragola,* although Lucrezia has seemingly been seduced, she has not been completely dominated or eclipsed. Instead, she holds with her conspiratorial knowledge a pivotal power for the success of the founding of the republic.

It is also interesting that unlike other Renaissance comedies, *La Mandragola* does not make everything known to everyone in the end. Rather, at the play's end Lucrezia's husband, Nicia, still remains duped, perhaps indicating Machiavelli's belief that the retention of "the semblance of old forms" (*Discourses* 1.25) is imperative for reforming the government. For Nicia, the image of truth is sufficient veracity. Like the majority of humankind, Nicia is "satisfied with appearances, as though they were realities, and often even more influenced by the things that seem than those that are" (*Discourses* 1.25).

Thus in Machiavelli's willingness to contest political hierarchy, he simultaneously, although perhaps not deliberately, opens up the possibility for the subversion of other "given" hierarchies. His politicization of virtue as well as his domestic conflicts not only radicalize the public space of politics but make manifest the possibility of doing so elsewhere. When politics becomes less about the fulfillment of universal principles and more about the creation of meaning through the negotiation of and with circumstances, the possibility develops for other principles (i.e., natural gender hierarchy) also to be contested. As Maurice Merleau-Ponty has noted, Machiavelli tells a story in which "history is a struggle and politics a relationship to men rather than principles."[47] It is partially because Machiavelli conceives of politics as a *relationship* that women as well as forces identified as feminine, specifically in the form of Fortuna, are not completely banished from his conceptions of political life.

47. Maurice Merleau-Ponty, "A Note on Machiavelli," in *Signs,* trans. Richard C. McCleary (Evanston: Northwestern University Press, 1964), 219.

Consider, in this regard, Machiavelli's discussion of the role of women in the ruin of the state.[48] It is because of the *relation* men have to women and, even more important, that men have to each other, that women become the catalyst for the state's ruin. Although it remains a profoundly misogynist formulation, it is not because of women's nature or essence, or indeed because of anything that they do, but rather it is because of what women *mean* in their signifying relations with men, that "some injury in a matter of women, either by whoring them or raping them or by breaking off marriages" becomes destructive of the state's stability. This is an important distinction, because Machiavelli docs not conceive of women as naturally inferior or destructive but rather understands their role to be one derived in large part through their relations with men. Although this is not a particularly liberating conception of women's role, it is also not one that assigns their place because of their essential nature or difference from men. Rather, because women's role is derived from their relation to men, there remains the possibility that this relation can be changed.

Indeed, Machiavelli gives several examples in which women, in a changed world and/or relationship to men, do act politically and are quite savvy about it. Recall, for example, Machiavelli's account of Madonna Caterina, who after the slaughter of her husband and the capture of herself and her children, convinces her captors to allow her to return to her fortress, leaving her children as collateral. Once she returns inside her city's wall, she threatens the conspirators with revenge and demonstrates that she does not care about her children by showing them her genitals and saying she still has means for producing more children (*Discourses* 3.6). This story is intended, Machiavelli asserts, as a warning to conspirators of the primary danger after an assassination: anyone left to avenge the prince. The story of Caterina, however, seems to demonstrate something else as well: that women, like savvy male political actors, can accommodate changing circumstances, even by forfeiting something as seeming "natural" as the claims of motherhood. With her husband's death, Caterina becomes a Machiavellian political actor for whom political necessities override all other concerns. The mistake of her conspirators was to misjudge her "nature" and thus to neglect her potential to avenge the slaughtered prince.

48. See *Discourses* 3.26.

IV. SALUTATI'S HUMANIST LUCRETIA: MACHIAVELLI'S CRITIQUE OF HUMANIST AUTHORITY

A comparison of Machiavelli's Lucretia's story and humanist Coluccio Salutati's version reveals one of the significant differences between Machiavelli and his humanist contemporaries: their different conceptions of how to fashion a relation to the past. As Chancellor of Florence from 1375 to 1406, Salutati sought to rewrite Florence's origin story by weakening the association between Florence and the tyrant Caesar and strengthening, instead, the link between Florence and republican Rome.[49] Rewriting Livy's story of the rape of Lucretia served such a purpose. Since the revision was to serve this rather didactic political purpose, Salutati tried to re-present the text in as unmediated a fashion as possible. As Stephanie Jed argues in *Chaste Thinking*, "The restoration of a pure or chaste text becomes a part of the rhetorical defense against tyranny."[50] Salutati is interested in Livy's story of the rape of Lucretia as part of a project of genealogical inheritance. The story must be rendered without calling attention to the differences between ancient Rome and fifteenth-century Florence. Any variation in the Renaissance rendition would be interpreted as a contamination and corruption of the text and thus as a symbol of Florence's inadequacy as an inheritor of Roman greatness.

Salutati's treatise, *De Clamatio Lucretia,* reproduces the argument among Lucretia; her father, Lucretius Spurius; and her husband, Collantinus Tarquinius, when she announces her intention of killing herself. Her father and husband urge her to live so that she may see Tarquin punished and to "let him see you exalting in his punishment."[51] They also echo Augustine's argument that only Tarquin was the adulterer since Lucretia's will was resistant. Besides, her husband and father remind her, "A woman will not be thought to be innocent who afflicts herself with punishment as a criminal" (150). Lucretia's retort is that no one will believe her unless she proves her strength and courage by dying. She is also worried that unless they avenge her death, Tarquin's lust will spread and violate other women. She asks, "For indeed, what woman will be safe if Lucretia has been raped?" (151).

49. Hans Baron, *The Crisis in the Early Italian Renaissance* (Princeton: Princeton University Press, 1956), 63.

50. Stephanie Jed, *Chaste Thinking: The Rape of Lucretia and the Birth of Humanism* (Bloomington: Indiana University Press, 1989), 45.

51. "Translation of *Declamatio Lucretiae,*" in Jed, *Chaste Thinking,* Appendix, p. 150. References in the text are to this translation.

Lucretia is further dismayed by the possibility that she may be pregnant as a result of the rape. She also laments that it was her chastity, not her beauty, that did her this injury. Oddly, Lucretia is also concerned that having once been violated she may eventually begin to enjoy shameful acts. She dies begging, "Let not Lucretia be given as an example to Roman women, so that, on account of my life, they may convince themselves that life is lawful for the unchaste" (152).

In this version, Lucretia kills herself because she is convinced that she is a contaminant to society. Although her husband and father urge her not to abandon her roles as wife, daughter and mother, Lucretia argues that each of these has been irreparably defiled. How can her husband enjoy her embraces when he thinks he is holding the whore of Tarquin? How can her father be proud of her when it is the very chastity he taught her that has brought her shame? And her children—how can they respect their mother when her womb may shelter the seed of the tyrant? Rape is a crime that has violated all the roles she plays as a woman; it is a private violation with public consequences. Here, Lucretia's rape trespasses the boundaries meant to preserve the private from public view. Salutati's Lucretia feels that the rape exposes her to public scrutiny; that which should have remained private and hidden has become public and visible.

Furthermore, Salutati's Lucretia (like Livy's and Machiavelli's) reminds her male kin of their failure to protect her from transgression: "Consider that you promised to keep our marriage bed inviolable to insult." In fact, her husband and father both unwittingly condemn themselves when they remind Lucretia that they inaugurated her disgrace: "Will you not recall, my Lucretia, how a few days ago we came here along with that vile adulterer, who saw you then for the first time?" (151).

Through her suicide, Lucretia hopes to liberate herself from contamination by another's lust and thus to restore her body to its former integrity. Similarly, as Jed notes, humanist rhetoricians sought to liberate ancient texts from textual errors and contamination and thus to restore them to their former integrity—an integrity that, in Salutati's case, he hoped would serve as a secure foundation for republican Florence: "As a result of Lucretia's refusal to live with the contradiction of chastity within a corrupt body, a new freedom is born which reproduces in Florence and in the Roman texts supporting Florentine identity, this same contradiction—the claim to restore a pure or integral descent from Republican Rome as proof of a political mission."[52]

52. Jed, *Chaste Thinking*, 45.

In contrast, Machiavelli's revision of the Lucretia story is a satire on this humanist ambition for an unexpurgated rendition of antiquity. Indeed, Machiavelli wants to expose rhetorically the seductions and desires that create "errors" in texts. For Machiavelli the uninterrupted descent of Florence from republican Rome cannot be achieved through unexpurgated texts. Indeed, for Machiavelli both aspects of this rhetorical ambition are fictitious. First, there is *no* uninterrupted descent from republican Rome, because Rome herself was corrupt and contaminated at the origin. And second, unexpurgated texts cannot account for what is pivotal in political life—accommodations to change. Texts must alter and be altered as circumstances vary. Thus, rather than conceiving of these changes as "corruption" and "contamination," Machiavelli marks them as the signs of the seduction, desires and interests that govern political life. Indeed, there is a way in which *La Mandragola* can be read as an anatomy of the modes of desire[53] and of the ways various political actors respond to those desires.

Machiavelli begins *The Discourses* with the claim that he is trying to correct the perception that the times have changed and to disabuse the majority of their mistaken belief that "heaven, the sun, the elements, and men had changed the order of their motions and power, and were different from what they were in ancient times. Wishing therefore, so far as in me lies, to draw mankind from this error, I have thought it proper to write upon those books of Titus Livius that have come to us entire despite the malice of time."[54] Nonetheless, Machiavelli well knows that all ten books of Livy's *Discourses* are *not* extant. The malice of time has corrupted Livy's work; there is no uncontaminated text to which to return. This is as much as to say that Machiavelli's rendition of Livy is just that—*his*. Machiavelli's readings of the past are part of his writing of the present. How and why he reads the past is a reflection and reinterpretation of his conception of his political present.

The traditional Renaissance humanist was torn between a methodological desire to instruct (i.e., to help Renaissance men become more like the Roman ideal) and a theoretical recognition that part of what the imitation of the past requires is the teaching of judgment and interpretation. For Machiavelli, his humanist contemporaries erred too far on the side of merely mimicking the ideal. In contradistinction to many humanists,

53. Wayne Rebhorn, *Foxes and Lions: Machiavelli's Confidence Men* (Ithaca: Cornell University Press, 1988), 47.

54. *Discourses*, Introduction to book 1.

Machiavelli has no specific method or procedure. Method, like the Greek *techne*, implies mere application of a standard procedure. For traditional humanists, the role of antiquity in contemporary Renaissance politics cannot be theorized because Rome is always already understood as the method, as the rule par excellence. If there is only one method, there can be no choice, no practical deliberation.[55] Machiavelli's approach, on the other hand, theorizes a relation to antiquity and is available only to those who understand it, those who employ judgment and interpretation. This explains why there is no systematic Machiavellian philosophy but rather, primarily, examples requiring interpretation. To read Machiavelli's texts is, somehow, to use them.

Salutati's version of Lucretia's story is pedagogically motivated; he wants to teach the history of Florentine identity. Hence, unlike Machiavelli, he is resistant to any version of the story that might suggest its undecidability. As an early humanist, Salutati uses examples such as the story of Lucretia's life to illustrate a particular point, in this case the republican origins of Florentine identity; however, he resists a more theoretical approach to the story. Although his use of the example of Lucretia's rape requires some interpretation by his readers (i.e., they must recognize the story of Lucretia's dilemma as analogous to their own quest for political identity), it suggests that there is one and only one answer to the question of Florentine identity.

For Machiavelli, on the other hand, theory is itself "a metapractice or practice about practice, one that is necessarily bound up with desires, interests, and intentions to persuade."[56] His writing both imitates the classical Roman tradition and is meant itself to stimulate imitation; as a theorist, he is himself both spectator and spectacle. He claims to be following in the paths of great men and history *and* to be creating texts, both as treatises and as theatre, as sources for imitation. In the Introduction to *The Discourses*, Machiavelli asserts that he is "open[ing] a new route ... show[ing] the way to others." He positions himself here as a spectacle for imitation. Although he claims that he is merely transcribing Livy, offering a literal and transparent imitation of the past, what he actually constructs is a spectacle of the past, an artificial re-presentation, something not simply to be imitated but rather to be fulfilled and completed.

55. See Victoria Kahn, "Humanism and the Resistance to Theory," in *Rhetoric, Prudence and Skepticism in the Renaissance* (Ithaca: Cornell University Press, 1985).

56. Ibid., 389.

Thus, Machiavelli conceives of his project, in part, as educating the reader's judgment. Acknowledging the unreliability of his contemporary readers, he seeks to train their judgment, not so much by teaching them what to think, as how to think. And that is why Machiavelli's work is full of examples rather than principles. Examples involve the reader in a practice of interpretation, which is essential for the exercise of political judgment. Examples are not merely illustrations of a theory or a principle but are themselves calls for judgment.[57] Machiavelli is inviting *phronesis,* practical wisdom, not teaching *techne,* technical skill. His examples do not invite the reader merely to imitate or avoid single instances of virtue or vice, success or failure, but rather to emulate Machiavelli's deliberation as embodied in the rhetorical practice of his work as a whole. He invites the reader to witness how he makes a judgment. Often at the beginning of a chapter he poses a quandary: "whether it is better to be loved or feared," "which of the two is more ungrateful, the people or a prince," and "whether it is better, when fearing an attack, to wait at home or to carry the war into an enemy's country." He then usually details the arguments for both sides until he finally concludes with his position, arrived at often in a way that highlights judgment, not principle: "And if one should follow out the reasons, there is something to be said on either side; but if one should examine their outcome, one would take the side of the nobles" (*Discourses* 1.5). Thus, even when Machiavelli concludes, he is still attentive to the possibility that the "right conclusion" depends on how one judges. This is particularly true in his comedy *La Mandragola* when the interpretation of the "happy ending" varies from one character to the next.

Machiavelli's version of the Lucretia story, unlike Salutati's, suggests the undecidability of meaning through the seduction rather than the rape of Lucretia. Moreover, as theatre, Machiavelli's rendition stages the instability of imitation. And this is why, as the next chapter will detail, comedy is an ideal vehicle for the theorist who wants to educate judgment without the didacticism of strict adherence to a short list of principles. Because Machiavelli is creating a "practice about practice," comedy, with its focus on the variability of human life, is a particularly edifying medium.

57. Ibid., 377.

4

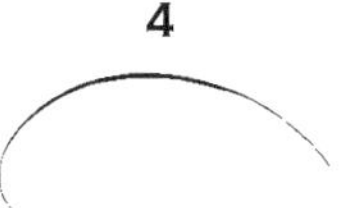

The Seriously Comedic, or Why Machiavelli's Lucrezia Is Not Livy's Virtuous Roman

I. The Seriously Comedic

In a letter to Vettori, Machiavelli describes the relationship between the comedic and the serious in their correspondence:

> Anyone who saw our letters, honored friend, and saw their diversity, would wonder greatly, because he would suppose now that we were grave men, wholly concerned with important matters, and that in our breasts no thought could fall that did not have in itself honor and greatness. But then, turning the page, he would judge that we, the very same persons, were light-minded, inconstant, lascivious, concerned with empty things. And this way of proceeding, if to some it may appear censurable, to me it seems praiseworthy, because we are imitating Nature, who is variable; and he who imitates her cannot be rebuked.[1]

While ostensibly commenting on the variability in his correspondence, Machiavelli is also implicitly offering a justification for writing comedy as well as political treatises: he is simply imitating Nature. Yet it is a rather peculiar, indeed, "Machiavellian" conception of Nature that he has in mind. Machiavellian Nature is not ordered, determined and stable; it is variable, contingent, an inevitable process of change. Indeed, part of Machiavelli's sense of humor derives from mocking those fools who mistakenly believe Nature is staid and who fail to accommodate her whimsy.

1. Letter to Vettori, no. 159 in *Machiavelli: The Chief Works and Others,* trans. Allan Gilbert (Durham: Duke University, 1989), 2:961.

Thus, Machiavelli's comedies, particularly *La Mandragola,* are themselves articulations of this interplay between the serious and the comedic. *La Mandragola,* obviously, represents the comedic element of his political writings. But the play also enacts a relationship between the serious and the comedic: it is a comedy with a serious political element as well as a serious political argument presented in a comedic medium.

La Mandragola is both engaged with the New Plautine comedy of the period and implicitly a critique of it. The principal elements of the New Comedy formula are present: the lover(s) blocked by interested elders or others, escape or hiding within or without the city enclosing an ordered society, and an eventual harmonious reconciliation.[2] In Machiavelli's play, however, there are two significant divergences. First, unlike most Plautine comedies, there is no deus ex machina or marvelous discovery to create a happy resolution. The only forces propelling the plot are those of human ingenuity and opportunism. Characters achieve their goal because of their own wit or scheming.

Second, unlike the traditional Plautine plot line, the seemingly happy resolution of Machiavelli's comedy conceals narrative duplicity. In the end, the course of events as perceived by some of the dramatic characters is not the real course of events as understood by the audience of *La Mandragola.* As noted in the previous chapter, the audience and several of the stage characters share the knowledge of a secret kept from other members of the play's society: all has not been revealed at the end. There is a discrepancy between the two simultaneous stories unfolding and supposedly settled in the fifth act. One ending is the harmonious closure of New Comedy, the happy resolution of the play: Nicia can anticipate the arrival of his much-sought-after heir, and Callimaco has made Lucrezia his lover. The other ending is an unfinished contingent plot: Nicia has unwittingly authorized his own continued cuckolding by offering a key to his home to both Ligurio and Callimaco; he remains unaware of their role in the plot. And Lucrezia, by paying the Friar a purseful of money, seems implicitly to be asking for the continued sanction of her adultery. Her conversion has been complete but unrevealed. She and Ligurio remain the only dramatic characters who are aware of all of the machinations of the others. Thus, this second ending is unstable, requiring assiduous attention to the mutability

2. Jackson Cope, *Secret Sharers in Italian Comedy: From Machiavelli to Goldoni* (Durham: Duke University Press, 1996), 5.

of fortune. The comedy thus has an unresolved ending with the potential for the resolution not to remain happy.

With this incomplete ending, however, Machiavelli creates an ideal vehicle for the edification of the audience's political judgment. The humor of the play invites the audience to laugh with the conspirators, to identify with the wits (Ligurio and Lucrezia) rather than with the buffoon (Nicia). As a result, at the conclusion the audience is placed in a position of complicity: "What we, the viewers, agree to silence is our awareness that events at the 'end' are not closed back in a great circle that creates a renewed social harmony but one that opens onto vistas of disruption and deception . . . the play is more cynical than carnivalesque."[3] The audience's identification and collusion is not simply an object lesson in Machiavellian politics; it is a participatory event. The comedy makes the audience actors in its world. From the prologue—"May you be tricked as she was"—to the ending—"Who wouldn't be tickled?"—the audience is invited in. And for Machiavelli, the audience's identification with the machinations of the protagonists is the necessary catalyst for political action.

Consider, in this regard, several letters Machiavelli wrote to Vettori in 1513 in which he asserts that the reason the Swiss have become a force to be feared is because they have begun to imagine themselves as Romans.[4] Machiavelli perceives a contagion here between imagination and reality: "I believe that as Nature has given each man an individual face, so she has given him an individual disposition and an individual imagination. From this it results that each man conducts himself according to his disposition and his imagination."[5] Unable to change their dispositions, Machiavelli thus strives for influence over men's imaginations. And comedy presents a powerful medium. The laughter of comedy, with its destabilization of traditional forms and its sense of transgression, creates in the audience a sense of being unbalanced and thus open to possibilities. And it is then that Machiavelli's lesson begins.

The most difficult moment in leading people to political action, according to Machiavelli, is getting them to conceive of themselves as political actors. He is confident, however, that once they imagine themselves as republicans, the republican process itself will actually make them

3. Ibid., 5.

4. See, for example, Letters No. 131, August 10, 1513, and No. 134, August 26, 1513, in *Machiavelli: The Chief Works and Others*, 2:915–21 and 922–26.

5. No. 116. "Letter to Soderini, January 1512 (1513)," 2:895–97.

so; what they lack in nature, artifice, in the form of the law and institutions, will augment.[6] It is as if Machiavelli knows that men are not republican by disposition but hopes that the process of imagining themselves as such will make them so.[7] Machiavelli needs only to spur the people's desire, not change their nature. Words, not steel, he believes, will suffice to recall them to their imagined republican selves.

And so *La Mandragola* becomes a source of political edification. Its invitation to the audience, its seduction of their laughter, induces identification with those characters who behave as Machiavelli deems necessary for political action. The instability of the ending necessitates judgment; the play does not end with a packaged didactic lesson. There is no satisfied catharsis that the world is ordered and stable; rather the audience's nervous laughter at the unfinished ending is an implicit acknowledgment of a Machiavellian worldview. Constant vigilance and agility is required to maintain one's place on the wheel of fortune.

So while the content of the comedy is ostensibly a reinterpretation of Livy's tragic rendition of the story of the rape of Lucretia (as the remainder of this chapter will detail), Machiavelli's sense of humor—laughter generated by human ingenuity rather than the marvelous, his enjoyment of narrative duplicity rather than happy endings—illuminates as much about his serious political argument as his reconfiguration of the story itself.

II. Why Lucrezia Is Not Livy's Noble Roman Matron

The most significant textual justification for a parallel reading of *La Mandragola* and Livy's *Early History of Rome* lies in how the mandrake works. Tellingly, the mandrake functions in Machiavelli's play in much the same

6. See, for example, *Discourses* 1.58: "And if princes show themselves superior in the making of laws, and in the forming of civil institutions and new statutes and ordinances, *the people are superior in maintaining those institutions, laws, and ordinances,* which certainly places them on a par with those who established them" (italics mine).

7. It is for this reason that Machiavelli disagrees with Livy and other ancient writers regarding the nature of the people. While Livy asserts that the multitude are inconstant, Machiavelli insists that the defect is not in the nature of the people themselves, but is a function of each person's response to the law: "The difference in their [the prince's and the people's] conduct is not due to any difference in their nature (for that is the same, and if there be any difference for good, it is on the side of the people); but to the greater or less respect they have for the laws under which they respectively live" (*Discourses* 1.58). In addition, "a licentious and mutinous people" can be brought back to good conduct by the persuasion of a good man. An evil-minded prince, on the other hand, can only be overcome with violence.

way as Lucretia's rape and suicide function in Livy's version. The mandrake, like the rape, is both a poison and a cure.[8] Just as Lucretia's body enacted the founding through her contamination by Tarquin (tyranny) and her expunging of this pollution through her suicide (the founding), so the mandrake both poisons Lucrezia, requiring "someone to sleep with her right away . . . to draw off all the poison of the mandrake after one night"[9] *and* cures her, thus enabling her to conceive, "there is nothing more certain to make a woman conceive than to give her a potion made with the mandrake root" (2.6, 195).

As a result, Lucrezia is positioned both to purge the society, having inhaled its contaminants, and to restore it to health. Machiavelli echoes this process in *The Discourses*: "For in nature as in simple bodies, when there is an accumulation of superfluous matter, a spontaneous purgation takes place, which preserves the health of the body" (2.5). Interestingly, like her predecessor's, Lucrezia's downfall and contamination results from the carelessness of her kinsfolk. In both versions, it is the bragging of a relative that ignites the plot: in Livy's, Lucretia's husband brags about her virtue; and in Machiavelli's, a cousin traveling abroad does so. In *La Mandragola* Lucrezia is further polluted by the corruption of those around her: her husband, Callimaco; her mother, Sostrato; and her confessor, Frate Timoteo.

Machiavelli also reflects on and satirizes the motif of paternity that Livy suggests with Brutus's kiss of Mother Earth. *La Mandragola*, too, is preoccupied with images of conception, birth and motherhood. The primary impetus for Nicia's cuckolding is his own desire to have an heir. Here Machiavelli, like Livy, highlights male anxiety about feminine power and the difficulty of guaranteeing the birth of a republic. Just as a man can never guarantee the paternity of his children, so a political founder cannot guarantee the success of his republic. While Livy suggests solo male procreation and implicit renunciation of the feminine as a resolution, Machiavelli advises seduction of the feminine. Obviously, there is no certainty of paternity in *La Mandragola* when Nicia is cuckolded by Callimaco. Certainty of paternity, like final domination of Fortuna, is impossible. It is interesting

8. For an extended discussion of Lucretia as *pharmakons* see Ronald L. Martinez's "The Pharmacy of Machiavelli: Roman Lucretia in *Mandragola*," in *Renaissance Drama as Cultural History: Essays from Renaissance Drama 1977–1987*, ed. Mary Beth Rose (Evanston: Northwestern University Press, 1990), 31–73.

9. *La Mandragola* 2.6, in *The Comedies of Machiavelli*, ed. and trans. David Sices and James B. Atkinson (Hanover: University Press of New England, 1985), 197. Citations in the text hereafter are from this edition.

to note, too, that the paternity of feminine power is itself ambiguous for Machiavelli. In his poem, "Fortune" written to Soderini, Machiavelli writes:

Whose daughter she might be, or from what seed Nobody knows,
Only one thing is sure:
Her might can make Jove, too, watch out in dread.[10]

Lucrezia's own paternity is unspecified in *La Mandragola*. Her father is neither present nor mentioned, and her mother is presumed to have been promiscuous in her youth.[11] This absence of paternal authority grants a surprising autonomy to femininity in the play.

Nonetheless, while paralleling Livy's version in several interesting ways, Machiavelli's story is more engaging in its differences. In Livy's account the rape of Lucretia highlights how a private transgression has public, political reverberations. Lucretia's private violation and suicidal confession reveals, in part, a cultural secret. In Machiavelli's account, however, there is no such distinction between the public and private or any such seeming revelation. All there is for Machiavelli's Lucrezia is politics and the realm of appearances. What concerns Machiavelli is not the distinction between, or violation of, the public and private spheres, but rather the politicization of virtue. In his domestic comedy, Machiavelli tries to demonstrate the necessity of making private morality answer to public necessity, rather than vice versa.

Lucretia forfeits her chastity in order to ensure her status as citizen. Through her seduction the possibility for the republican founding is conceived; her participation is integral to the founding's success. Her private immorality serves a public good. Being a good citizen necessitates her willingness to act against the principles of private, and in this case Christian, morality. Lucrezia is willing to do this and thus personifies an ideal Machiavellian political actor.

Another important distinction between the two versions is announced in the very frontispiece of *La Mandragola*. The frontispiece is the image of the classical centaur except that instead of holding the usual arrow, he is serenading with a violin (Fig. 1), suggesting that persuasion, "sweet nothings," not force, will determine the outcome of the play. The stage is set

10. "The Capitoli," in *Lust and Liberty: The Poetry of Machiavelli*, trans. Joseph Tusiani (New York: Obolensky Press, 1963), 113.

11. Theodore Sumberg, "*La Mandragola*: An Interpretation," *Journal of Politics* 23 (1961): 327.

FIG. 1

for Machiavelli's belief that often cunning and fraud, even seduction, are more effective than force (*Discourses* 2.13).

In contrast, the dagger is the pivotal symbol in the Roman version. Tarquin menaces Lucretia with a knife, Lucretia kills herself with a dagger, and Brutus swears upon the same knife to drive the Tarquins from Rome. The only dagger in *La Mandragola* is the pathetic stick Nicia arms himself with just as he arranges for his own cuckolding: "He's wearing a little cloak that does not cover his ass. What the hell does he have on his head? He looks like a cross between an owl and a monk, and down below he has a little blade sticking out."[12]

Also suggestively, Nicia's "little blade" is Machiavelli's not-so-subtle illusion to the diminishing masculinity of his compatriots, resulting, in part, from the enervating influence of the Catholic Church: "Though it may appear that the world has grown effeminate, and Heaven has laid aside her arms, this without doubt comes chiefly from the worthlessness of men who have interpreted our religion according to sloth and not according to vigor" (*Discourses* 2.2). Pagan religion, in contrast, was full of pomp and

12. *La Mandragola* 4.8. This image also clearly mocks Nicia's sexual impotence in the same way that the dagger invokes Tarquin's potency.

magnificence. The pagans cultivated worldly glory rather than the humility and contemplative life of Christianity. Nonetheless, Machiavelli defends Christianity as the victim of "false interpretation." Christianity does not create effeminate men, rather it is the result of "worthless men" who have misunderstood what Christianity intends: "For if they consider that it [Christianity] allows us the betterment and the defense of our country, they would see that it intends that we love and honor her and prepare ourselves to be such that we can defend her" (*Discourses* 2.2). Thus, Machiavelli does not discount the importance of religion to the political,[13] only interpretations of religion that render men unfit political actors. The contrast evoked between the spectacle of Nicia's "little blade" and that of Brutus's heroic retrieval of the dagger from Lucretia's breast demonstrates just how unfit Machiavelli imagines this misinterpretation of Christianity has rendered Renaissance men.

Nonetheless, while in some respects highlighting Florence's deficiencies in comparison with her Roman ancestor, Machiavelli's rewriting of Lucretia's rape is simultaneously a reconfiguration and contestation of Roman authority. Machiavelli's rewriting allows for the possibility of political action without the tyranny of Roman authority. Machiavelli wants to maintain in some form both Roman authority and its innovation. As Hanna Pitkin notes, it is unclear when one strives to imitate the Romans whether one imitates *them* or their capacity for innovation.[14] Machiavelli's compromise is echoed by Hannah Arendt when she asserts about the American founding that its authority was the "authority of reconstitution itself; an authority inherent in its own performances."[15] That is, republican authority must be exercised in a way that further politicizes the people rather than in a way that renders them quiescent. And that is exactly what Machiavelli's rendition of the founding in *La Mandragola* does. His revision demonstrates the capacity for the founding to be amended and augmented. Set in contemporary Renaissance Italy rather than in ancient Rome, the play sets the beginning, the possibility for founding, in the present. Foundation is, as it were, continuous foundation. This maintenance of Roman antiquity

13. See, for example, *The Discourses* 1.11: "And whoever reads Roman history attentively will see in how great a degree religion served in the command of the armies, in inspiring the people and keeping men good, in making the wicked ashamed."

14. Hanna Pitkin, *Fortune Is a Woman: Gender and Politics in the Thought of Niccolo Machiavelli* (Berkeley: University of California Press, 1984), 88.

15. Hannah Arendt, *On Revolution* (New York: Viking Press, 1963), 202.

is achieved through an augmentation that takes place by way of translation.[16] Machiavelli maintains the authority of Rome through a rendition, a translation of a traditional story, Livy's story of the rape of Lucretia. And this translation is manifest, in part, in the way in which in Machiavelli's account, Lucretia's rape becomes not only bloodless but consensual.

In contrast to the comedy, however, the founding stories that Machiavelli recounts in *The Discourses* and *The Prince* each involve violence—Romulus kills Remus; Verginia is slain by her own father; and Tarquin rapes Lucretia. Nonetheless, oddly, Machiavelli remains confident that the Italian republic he is seeking to renew can be renovated without violence. Apparently, Machiavelli believes that words will be sufficient to renew the republic since the Florentine people are not entirely corrupt: "For a licentious and mutinous people may easily be brought back to good conduct by the influence and persuasion of a good man . . . words suffice to correct those [defects] of the people whilst those of the prince can only be remedied by violence" (*Discourses* 1.58). When trying to dislodge a corrupt prince, violence is necessary; but when attempting to reform a wayward people, words (and spectacle) are sufficient. Persuasion, not force, founds the republic. For it is easy to persuade the people initially, but more difficult to "keep them in persuasion. And so it is necessary to order things so that when they no longer believe, they can be made to believe by force."[17] Machiavelli's advice to innovators is not only to begin with persuasion and to use force only when necessary, but also "to order things so that when they no longer believe, they can be made to believe" (*Prince* 7). In other words, for Machiavelli, even force works rhetorically as persuasion. It too must be staged.

Although Machiavelli does occasionally seem preoccupied with force and the "armed citizen," close examination of his discussions of force often expose his focus on the "reputation of force,"[18] the "display of power,"

16. Jacques Derrida, "Deconstruction in America: An Interview with Jacques Derrida," *Critical Exchange* 17 (1985): 24–25.

17. *The Prince* in *Machiavelli: The Chief Works and Others,* trans. Allan Gilbert (Durham: Duke University Press, 1989), 26.

18. See, for example, *The Discourses* 1.19 and 2.14, where Machiavelli gives numerous examples of the necessity for kings often to wage war in order not "to appear effeminate . . . and be esteemed little" and "because the zeal of the prince's friends will be chilled on seeing him *appear* feeble and cowardly" (my emphasis). In fact, Machiavelli goes so far as to say in 2.31: "I do not mean to say by this, however, that arms and force are never to be employed, but that they should be reserved as *the last resort* when other means fail" (my emphasis).

and "appearing to trust one's citizens."[19] His reliance is rather on how force is narrated—what is said about one's ability, how that force appears and is later remembered. It is interesting to note in this regard that Machiavelli is credited with being the first to organize a military parade.[20] Apparently, after establishing the citizen militia in Florence in 1506, Machiavelli arranged a parade through the streets of Florence. For Machiavelli, spectacle and narrative are the materiality of power and of the real.

It is possible to have a bloodless revolution, Machiavelli asserts, when the new government is established by the consent of a large group of people (*Discourses* 3.6). As an example, he cites the expulsion of the Tarquins as a transition from slavery to liberty in which "no one else suffered injury" except for the chiefs of state. On the other hand, if a government originates in violence, there is, of course, not only the violence of the revolution but also the threat of continued violence as a result of the desire for revenge by those injured by the establishment of the new government. Yet how can Machiavelli name the expulsion of the Tarquins "bloodless" when Lucretia is raped and commits suicide? What does he mean that "no one else suffered injury" when Lucretia dies as a result of her violation?

Elsewhere in *The Discourses* Machiavelli refers to "what happened to Lucretia" as both an "accident"[21] and an "excess."[22] While he acknowledges that her rape was a catalyst for the founding, he insists it was not a necessary one:

> Tarquin was driven from Rome, not because his son Sextus had violated Lucretia, but because he had disregarded the laws of the kingdom and governed it tyrannically.... If the accident of Lucretia had not occurred, some other would have produced the same effect; for had Tarquin conducted himself like the previous kings, when his son Sextus committed that crime, Brutus and Collantinus would have

19. This is ostensibly Machiavelli's argument when he discusses the injuries of relying upon fortresses. His critique centers not so much on their advantage or disadvantage in a specific battle plan as on how their use *appears* to others and what it *seems* to suggest about the prince's confidence in the valor of his own citizens. Here Machiavelli prefers to depend more on the goodwill of the citizens than on the strength of citadels.

20. Roberto Ridolfi, *The Life of Machiavelli,* trans. Cecil Grayson (Chicago: University of Chicago Press, 1963), 88.

21. "E se lo accidente di Lucrezia non fosse venuto, come prima ne fossenato un altro" (3.5).

22. "E come si è veduto in questra nostra istoria, l'eccesso fatto contro a Lucrezia tolse lo stato ai Tarquinnii" (3.26).

appealed to Tarquin for vengeance against Sextus, instead of stirring up the Roman people as they did. (*Discourses* 3.5)

Here, apparently, is the misogynist Machiavelli who seems to have earned every feminist invective against him. He expresses no moral outrage about the rape; and his silence, indeed, his interpretation of Lucretia's violation in terms of political expediency, is quintessential "evil Machiavel." What seems to matter to him is only how events correspond with the demands of political life. Yet is it sheer misogyny and opportunism that motivates Machiavelli's reading of Lucretia's rape? How does the "accident of Lucretia" figure politically in Machiavelli's conception of foundings?

First, Machiavelli's discussion of the expulsion of the Tarquins is found in a chapter entitled, "What Causes a Kingdom to Be Lost by a King Who Has Inherited It." Apparently, for Machiavelli, unlike Livy, the Tarquins are not usurpers but inheritors of the state. And thus to them he repeats advice that he gives in *The Prince*: "Princes should know, then, that they begin to lose their positions at the hour when they begin to break the laws and those old ways and customs under which for a long time men have lived" (*Discourses* 3.5).

The *political* principle at work in this chapter is that the ruler can maintain his power only with the concurrence of the people. Tarquin was driven out because he had "deprived Rome of all the liberty which under the other kings she had preserved." If Tarquin had lived like other kings, Brutus and Collantinus would have come to him for vengeance against Sextus rather than inciting rebellion against his father's rule. Instead, they incite revolution, for Tarquin has not demonstrated that he is a friend of the people who, like Brutus, would be willing to sacrifice his own sons for their preservation.[23] According to Machiavelli, Tarquin has incurred the people's wrath by reducing them to unsavory chores: "For he roused the populace as well against him, making them labor at lowly tasks, very different from those in which his predecessors had employed them" (*Discourses* 3.5).

In contrast, Livy notes that while Tarquin used the poorer classes to build the temple to Juno, the laborers thought it "an honorable burden with a solemn and religious significance and they were not, on the whole,

23. Harvey J. Mansfield, *Machiavelli's New Modes and Orders: A Study of the Discourses on Livy* (Ithaca: Cornell University Press, 1979), 314–16.

unwilling to bear it."[24] While Livy does note that the laborers were not as willing to be involved in some of Tarquin's more labor-intensive projects, he nowhere suggests that this "menial work" led to rebellion. For Livy, most of the injuries that Tarquin inflicts are against the Senate, not the people. In contrast, for Machiavelli it is because of Tarquin's violation of the people that he is driven from Rome in a bloodless revolution initiated with the consent of the people. And this, for Machiavelli, is the most important aspect of the rape of Lucretia and the expulsion of the Tarquins: the *consent* of the people for the founding. Here also is to be found a challenge (if not justification) for the overt misogyny of Machiavelli's formulation of "the excess against Lucretia."

The desire that ignites the expulsion, for Machiavelli, is not the excessive one of Sextus but rather the desire of the people to be well governed; as he notes in the same chapter, "For when men are well governed, they do not seek for nor wish any other liberty" (*Discourses* 3.6). It is the people's desire which spurs the founding and to which Machiavelli is most attentive. The foundation of the republic is the people, and this is his *political* reason for diminishing the significance of the rape of Lucretia. For Machiavelli, to highlight the link between the rape and the founding, as Livy does, is to locate the republican founding with the Senate/nobles rather than with the people.

It is noteworthy that one of Machiavelli's few overt disagreements with Livy concerns the nature of the people: "Titus Livius as well as all other historians affirm that nothing is more uncertain and inconstant than the multitude. . . . But as regards prudence and stability, I say that the people are more prudent and stable and have better judgment than a prince" (*Discourses* 1.58). For Machiavelli, there is nothing by nature that prevents the people from being both good judges and good governors of themselves. Although Machiavelli does not deny the importance of the founder, the consent of the people is pivotal to the founder's success.

At work also in this discussion of the people's nature is Machiavelli's reconfiguration of Roman authority. As Arendt notes, Roman authority (*auctoritas*) was constituted by a trinity of authority, religion and tradition: "Members of the Senate, the elders or *patres* (fathers) were endowed with authority which had been obtained by descent and by transmission (tradition) from those who had laid the foundations for all things to come, the

24. Livy, *The Early History of Rome* 1.57.

ancestors, whom the Romans called *maiores* (founders)."[25] Machiavelli's rendition of the expulsion of the Tarquins is an attempt to redraw the line of descent for this founding authority from the Senate to the people. For Machiavelli, both power and authority rest with the people; they are their own founders. Consequently, Machiavelli highlights consent, specifically the consent of the people, not the rape of Lucretia, in his account. Indeed, in Machiavelli's bloodless, consensual version of the founding story, *La Mandragola,* Lucrezia is neither raped nor does she commit suicide. Rather, she gives her reluctant assent to adultery: "Since your cleverness, my husband's stupidity, my mother's silliness, and my confessor's guile have led me to do what I would never have done by myself, I have to judge that this comes from a divine providence that willed it so. I am not capable of refusing what heaven itself wants me to accept" (5.5, 269).

The comedy's conspiracy to obtain Lucrezia's "consent" parallels the consent of the people necessary for the founding of the republic. In *La Mandragola* Lucrezia is the embodiment of the people, able to judge the common good and to adjust her actions accordingly. Her consent to Ligurio's scheme is what enables one dimension of the happy resolution of the comedy, the founding of a new domestic order.

III. SEDUCTION IN THE REALM OF APPEARANCES

The word *mandragola* in Italian refers to the phallic-like root of a plant presumed to have not only magical powers but also the quality of an aphrodisiac. *Mandragola* is also a cognate of *mostrar,* 'to deceive.' Tellingly, the mandrake potion in the play is a ruse; it is never administered. Ostensibly, Lucrezia will conceive, not because of a magic potion, but because of the heated passion of her young lover. In fact, there are several insinuations in the play that Lucrezia's husband is either impotent or a homosexual.[26] Moreover, the mandrake potion, if taken, is fatal to men (the first man to have sex with a woman treated with the potion dies), while the woman remains unaffected.[27] This is perhaps testament to the battle Machiavelli

25. Hannah Arendt, "What Is Authority?" in *Between Past and Future: Eight Exercises in Political Thought* (New York: Penguin Books, 1961).

26. Consider, for example, Nicia's early remarks that Lucrezia is always cold at night and is found on the floor praying on her knees, and his own rather keen interest in "checking" the anatomy of his "victim" in order to be certain that it is sufficient and functional.

27. Martinez, "The Pharmacy of Machiavelli," 67–68.

perceives between masculinity and femininity as well as between their respective counterparts, *virtù* and Fortuna. Nonetheless, it remains a battle without an obvious resolution in either *La Mandragola* or elsewhere in Machiavelli's writings.

Significantly, Machiavelli does not deny women's sexual and reproductive powers in *La Mandragola* (Lucrezia does live to give birth to a child[28]). Nonetheless, the mandrake could easily be read as a manifestation of Renaissance men's anxieties about feminine power; Machiavelli's characters overcome feminine power because the mandrake is only a ruse! However, although the mandrake may be a ruse, the play demonstrates that feminine power is not; rather, feminine power is potent in the world of appearances. The mandrake "works" because in Machiavelli's world, appearances have become the real.

* * *

Although Lucrezia is heralded in the prologue as "fit to govern a kingdom," she never appears alone onstage or leaves the interior of her home or the church. She, like the other Machiavellian actor, Ligurio, has no soliloquies, and we know of her primarily through the mouths of men.[29] Thus, Lucrezia's seduction is complicated by the fact that the audience only learns of her compliance from her would-be rapist, Callimaco. We are left to judge from appearances, by her willingness at the end of the comedy to play hostess to Callimaco in her home and to pay the friar a purse full of money for his blessing on her pregnancy. What is significant about Lucrezia is not her rape but the spectacle the dilemma her rape or seduction poses.

What *is* integral is appearances. For seduction is nothing if not a play on the appearance of things; seduction does not try to dispel appearance for the sake of a reality beyond.[30] Rather, seduction is a mastery of signs. As Jean Baudrillard develops, "To seduce is to die as reality and to reconstitute oneself as illusion."[31] Seduction is play, a challenge, a strategy

28. In *Clizia* there is a reference to the birth of child to Lucrezia and Callimaco through the miracle of the prayers of Friar Timoteo: "Don't you know that through his [Friar Timoteo's] prayers the wife of Messer Nicia, Madonna Lucrezia, who was sterile, became pregnant?" (Nicomaco to his wife, Sofronia, 2.3).

29. Of course, part of the reason that she is rarely on stage is that the part of Lucrezia would have been played by a young male actor. Apparently, the ability of a man to portray "the most beautiful woman in Italy" strained even Renaissance credulity.

30. Jean Baudrillard, *Seduction*, trans. Brian Singer (New York: St. Martin's Press, 1990).

31. Ibid., 69.

of appearances. And thus for Machiavelli, seduction, not rape, is the ideal metaphor for political action.[32]

An absolute, like rape, is illicit in Machiavellian politics because it is irresistible. This interpretation counters that of some who have argued that Machiavelli's *La Mandragola* makes a mockery of the reality of rape, that his revision of Livy's story argues against the very possibility of rape.[33] Yet, Machiavelli's Lucrezia is seduced, rather than raped, *because* Machiavelli recognizes the irreversibility of rape and wants to suggest a conception of political action less contingent, ironically, on violence and a literal determinism. "God, self-evident truths, natural law are all despotic because they are irresistible. And because they are irresistible, they do not persuade to agreement, they command to acquiescence."[34] Rape, too, is a command; seduction, however, is for Machiavelli quintessentially political. What Machiavelli reveals through his strategy of seduction is that politics, too, is about appearances, about the instability and disruption of the distinction between appearance and reality.

Seduction suggests also the contingency of political action, the uncertainty of outcome and the continual need to adjust to the vicissitudes of circumstances. Through his strategy of seduction, Machiavelli deploys not only a certain kind of femininity but also a form of mutuality necessary for political action. For Machiavelli politics is always agonistic. Yet he finds something other than violence and danger in struggle.[35] Rather than condemning tumult and conflict, he praises them for their ability to preserve the republic: "For whoever will carefully examine the result of these agitations will find that they have neither caused exiles nor any violence prejudicial to the general good, and will be convinced even that they have given rise to laws that were to the advantage of public liberty" (*Discourses* 1.4). Conflict is a sign of the vitality of politics. Political action is about

32. John Forrester notes, for example, that "seduction, unlike rape, has a positive and a negative face . . . rape is punctual, instantaneous, involving not only physical violence, but temporal violence. Seduction is interminable, and even the spiritual rapists may imitate this interminability through their endless repetition" ("Rape, Seduction and Psychoanalysis," in *Rape: An Historical and Social Enquiry,* ed. Sylvanna Tomaselli and Roy Porter [Oxford: Basil Blackwell, 1989], 82).

33. See Elshtain (1981) and Mary O'Brien, "The Root of the Mandrake: Machiavelli and Manliness," in *Reproducing the World: Essays in Feminist Theory* (San Francisco: Westview Press, 1989), 103–26.

34. Arendt, *On Revolution,* 202.

35. Maurice Merleau-Ponty, "A Note on Machiavelli," in *Signs,* trans. Richard C. McCleary (Evanston: Northwestern University Press, 1964), 211.

negotiation and accommodation, not about strict adherence to given principles. Without motion, without dissension, there would be no politics. Thus, a political actor inattentive to the changing whims of Fortuna would have little political power; one must recognize where one is on the wheel of fortune and leap accordingly.

It is this relationship of contest that Machiavelli urges between political actors and feminine power: political actors must engage with the feminine but still maintain their masculinity; they must be attentive to Fortuna's power but build the dikes to contain her dominion. Fortuna, like Lucrezia, must also be seduced, not raped. For she, as the feminine principle of political action, cannot be completely dominated or annihilated. As Machiavelli begrudgingly acknowledges, "She is the arbiter of one half of our actions but she still leaves the control of the other half, or almost that, to us."[36]

Although Machiavelli uses the language of conquest—"if you wish to master her, to conquer her by force"[37]—this is followed immediately by the reminder that "it can be seen that she *lets* herself be overcome by the bold rather than by those who proceed coldly."[38] Again, even the contrast with those who proceed *coldly,* intimates the alternative of passion and heat, the strategy of seduction. The relationship that political actors have with Fortuna is one of interminable seduction. They must constantly anticipate her desires, prepare for her arrival and adjust themselves to her whims.

Like Lucretia, who is seduced because of others' preparedness ("your cleverness, my husband's stupidity, my mother's silliness, and my confessor's guile"), so too Fortuna is seduced and domesticated by man's preparedness: "Where fortune is concerned: she shows her force where there is no organized strength to resist her; and she directs her impact where she knows that dikes and embankments are not constructed to hold her. . . . It does not follow that when the weather is calm we cannot take precautions with embankments and dikes, so that when they rise up again the waters will be channelled off or their impetus will not be either so unchecked or so damaging."[39] And this is part of the paradox of the feminine for Machiavelli. Although his images of women are riddled with sexual violence, in his political narrative it is the feminine that ultimately makes politics

36. *The Prince,* chap. 25.

37. Ibid.

38. "E si vede che la si lascia piú vincere da questi, che da quelli che freddamente procedono" (ibid.).

39. Ibid.

possible. Indeed, he suggests that it is the spectacle of the feminine that will bring the people back to themselves and thus enable the founding.

Nonetheless, although this strategy of seduction grants a certain recognition to the feminine other in the form of Fortuna, seduction is not without its own hierarchy of domination. That is, it is one thing for the feminine other to *yield* as Fortuna does, and quite another for her to demand what she wants. Yet there is still another complication. Fortuna yields because of the ability of the political actor to make a spectacle of himself; he considers how his power will be perceived and adjusts himself accordingly. For Machiavelli this capacity to see oneself as others do enables one to formulate an understanding of power. As Merleau-Ponty has noted, "Power bears a halo about it, and its curse is to fail to see the image of itself it shows to others."[40] In the case of the prince, he must learn to see himself from the perspective of the people and to alter his image accordingly.

Like Lucrezia's seduction, which suggests a process of founding rather than its one-time inauguration, so as theatre, *La Mandragola* is a ritual reenactment of the origin, repeated endlessly with each performance. This reenactment purifies contaminants from the society and solidifies communal bonds. And Machiavelli uses a medical lexicon to suggest the purification: "Every day some ill humors gather which must be cured."[41]

Spectacles, as Machiavelli reminds us throughout *The Prince* and *The Discourses,* help to bring the people back to themselves; because of memory lapses, the people may forget their founding principles and need to be reminded of them.[42] Ironically, for Machiavelli it is spectacle, not action, that brings the people back. Remembrance itself is a kind of seduction; recollection and temptation are twin impulses. The recollection of the past, manifested though spectacle, sparks a desire for imitation. Re-presentation of the past seduces political actors in the present. Thus, Machiavelli is careful about what he represents. Because there is a contagion effect about recollection, Machiavelli does not want to represent the most violent renditions of the past—the initial fratricide of Remus or the sexual violation of Lucretia.

For Machiavelli, the ability to make a spectacle of oneself is the mark of a successful prince. This capacity to see oneself as others do enables one to formulate an understanding of perspective. The prince can see himself

40. Merleau-Ponty, "A Note on Machiavelli," 216.

41. Ibid.

42. See Chapter 3 for a full development of this theme.

from the perspective of the people and alter his image accordingly. This formulation is Machiavelli's rather clever satire of the mirror of princes literature. Concurrently, Machiavelli subverts the conception of the object of the look as always already feminized and passive. Here he—or in the case of Lucrezia, she—who is most attentive to being looked at, has the most power. Lucrezia, like the prince, is a political actor, orchestrating her appearance, controlling how she is looked at.

In some respects, Lucrezia is the prototypical Machiavellian political actor. She adjusts when the circumstances demand,[43] seizes Fortuna and uses deception to achieve her ends. Upon her is Machiavelli's hope for the success of the play pinned: "How fortunate if you could be tricked in the way she was!"[44] Lucrezia is the embodiment of dissimulation *and* she reveals reality for what it is. Foremost, she is not what she seems—she proves through the course of the play that she is neither as chaste nor as naive as the other characters presume. She personifies dissimulation. Yet this dissimulation is reality; reality is not what it seems, and Machiavelli is continually urging political actors to be attentive to the duplicity of appearances and the fallacy of their judgments.

Quite interestingly, Lucrezia, and the Renaissance feminine in general, personify what Froma Zeitlin identifies as the paradox of theatre: "While theatre resorts continually to artifice, as it must, to techniques of make-believe that can only resemble the real, it can also better represent the larger world outside as it more nearly is, subject to the deceptions, the gaps in knowledge, the tangled necessities, and all the tensions and conflicts of a complex existence."[45] Lucrezia reveals to the male character that the world is other than he originally imagined it and that he cannot ultimately control it. For example, although the bragging of one of her relatives and the desires of Callimaco ignite the plot, they both ultimately lose control of the narrative. Although Callimaco achieves his desired end, he does not control the machinations that drive the plot; Ligurio, and, eventually, Lucrezia do.

Clearly, political actors do not exercise control over the unfolding of

43. Nonetheless, her transformation is probably not as rapid as Callimaco believes; Nicia revealed earlier that Lucrezia had already been deceived by a friar who tried to take advantage of her while she was saying her novenas. Indeed, Lucrezia was probably never as naive as the men believed.

44. *La Mandragola*, Prologue.

45. Froma Zeitlin, "Playing the Other: Theater, Theatricality and the Feminine in Greek Drama," *Representations* 11 (Summer 1985): 79.

events. What they *can* control, however, is how they respond to changing circumstances. At some level, *La Mandragola* is a story demonstrating that because men cannot control the effects of either their words (i.e., the brag) or their acts, they must learn how to change themselves according to how their words and acts are construed by others; they must change themselves as circumstances change. They must learn how to seduce the feminine Fortuna. Thus, Lucrezia is a "lesson" to men. She is Machiavelli's invitation to political actors to dissimulate. Moreover, Lucrezia shows men that the world is not as they imagined it to be. For example, she reveals to the characters of the play (and to the audience) that she is not as chaste as they presumed; in fact, she is relatively willing to be deceived herself and to conspire in adultery. But her conversion is not because she is corrupt, as some have suggested,[46] but because she is astute. She is adapting to circumstances, seizing opportunity before Fortuna passes by and only her bald head is visible.[47]

Lucrezia embodies the complexities appearance poses for Machiavellian politics—not only the indeterminability of seeming and being, but also the importance of being able to determine when to use force and when persuasion. Although Machiavelli's Lucrezia does not kill herself, she performs a similar narrative function to Livy's Lucretia. She controls how her story is told, how she is read. As spectacle, Lucrezia teaches the other male characters and spectators of the play how to be men, specifically, how to be successful, autonomous, political actors. She highlights the need for the other in order to know oneself, and she attests to the complexities and ambiguities implicit in achieving manhood. It is the spectacle of the female body, again, both literally and metaphorically, that constitutes the initial political "we." Lucrezia is testament to both Machiavelli's fascination with the power of Fortuna and the feminine, and his fear of her devastating power and influence.

For Machiavelli, men and women are sexual antagonists, just as are *virtù* and Fortuna. But this struggle with the enemy can aggrandize oneself and ensure one's own success. Throughout Book 2 of *The Discourses*, Machiavelli details "How Rome Became Great by Ruining Her Enemies." Rome

46. See Susan Behuniak-Long, "The Significance of Lucrezia in Machiavelli's *La Mandragola*," *Review of Politics* (Spring 1989): 264–80.

47. In one of Machiavelli's poems, he reiterates the popular image of Fortuna as bald from behind: "The back of my head is utterly shorn / In vain, therefore, men try to grab me, when / I pass them by, or if around I turn," in *Lust and Liberty: The Poetry of Machiavelli*, 128.

was able to become powerful through struggle, partially, as Machiavelli elaborates, because she fought *without* annihilating or completely impoverishing the conquered country. In a parallel vein, as demonstrated through *La Mandragola*, antagonism with Fortuna as well as with femininity enriches male *virtù*. Women serve as worthy enemies who augment men's *virtù*; contestation and struggle with women both teaches men and empowers them. And, as a "worthy enemy," Machiavelli grants women, as personified by Fortuna, autonomous power. She does, after all, still control half of men's actions.

For Machiavelli, stability is ephemeral, and politics itself is about the contestation of meaning. Politics means manipulating appearances in order to achieve a desired end. Machiavelli embraces the dilemma of the instability of each to the other and articulates a politics that assumes the mediation of appearances and adjusts itself according. This antagonism and reconciliation is personified in Machiavelli's articulation of the relationship between *virtù* and Fortuna. Machiavelli is the realist who recognizes the "real" as the realm of appearances.

Focusing on Machiavelli's theatrical texts foregrounds what risks neglect in traditional formulations of realism. For Machiavelli, power is not simply about domination, empire and glory; rather, Machiavelli's Renaissance relationship to the Roman republican tradition (primarily through Livy) articulates his celebration of contestation rather than domination, of the people rather than empire, and of the common good as well as of glory. These themes are most fully developed in Machiavelli's theater, where he both imitates and innovates the Romans, where he repeats and rewrites history and where he re-presents reality in the realm of appearances.

Finally, the story of the rape of Lucretia raises the theme of violence in Machiavelli in a register other than that of competing state and self-interests. The story of the rape suggests, first, the violence of any beginning, the problem of asserting command before the principles of that authority are secured. Yet Machiavelli's rendition of the story, in which Lucrezia is not raped but seduced, suggests that neither politics nor political foundings rests solely on force. Secondly, this pivotal story of the founding implies that politics does not enjoy the autonomy on which political realism would like to insist. In fact, the play details the ways in which political power is inscribed in the body; in other words, Machiavelli's plays take quite seriously the metaphor of the "body politic." Notions of masculinity, of femininity and of sexuality are revealed as integral to the founding as well as to the maintenance of politics. The domestic comedy of *La Mandragola* is, in part, a recognition that political power does not exist solely in the relations between states or in the relation between the state and the citizen, but rather that power also asserts itself through imposing interpretative grids on the human body, particularly in constructions of masculinity and femininity.

5

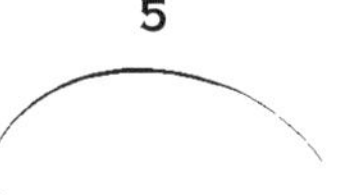

The Paradox of Rousseau's Politics and the Return to the Founding

Like Machiavelli, Jean-Jacques Rousseau is a theorist in a prolonged contest with his own time. Just as Machiavelli was simultaneously of his time in his veneration for Roman antiquity and against it in his renunciation of humanist formulations, so Rousseau is both a student of the Enlightenment and one of its most provocative critics. Like other philosophes, Rousseau looked to both Sparta and Rome as models rather than to the golden age of Christianity. Yet rather than celebrate the martial and heroic aspects of classical republican *virtù,* Rousseau recommends a rather sentimental and domestic *virtù,* best exemplified, interestingly, by Rousseau's women, such as Lucrèce of "La Mort de Lucrèce" and Julie of *Nouvelle Héloïse.*

Rousseau also rests uncomfortably between republicanism and liberalism. As an unpersuaded reader of Hobbes and Locke, Rousseau nonetheless takes seriously the dilemmas posed by their work. For example, although Rousseau has a republican conception of the common good, he maintains a rather liberal formulation of the individual; that is, Rousseau's individual acts politically without public deliberation but in accord with a general will. The general will is in service to the common good but is achieved through self-consultation. Thus, Rousseau shares Hobbes's critique of language but is reluctant to forfeit the possibility of a public good that transcends majority self-interest.

Nonetheless, Rousseau is not simply a theorist of contradictions. Rather, he is, as he acknowledges, a subtle thinker of paradox: "Pardon me my paradoxes; it is necessary to make them when one thinks."[1] Thus, to understand Rousseau's complications, one must resist the temptation to

1. *Emile, or On Education,* trans. Allan Bloom (New York: Basic Books, 1979).

reconcile and/or dismiss all these tensions. Indeed, as Tracy Strong has recently argued, to attempt to define and limit Rousseau is to read him against his own conception of what it means to be human.[2] Instead, to read Rousseau fruitfully two centuries after his death is to ask how and why particular paradoxes develop as a result of his thinking. In other words, a genealogical method similar to the one Rousseau narrates in his *Second Discourse on the Origins of Inequality* offers the contemporary reader the possibility of understanding how the paradoxes came into being, what problems Rousseau sought to highlight through them, and how his solutions themselves created new dilemmas. Toward that end, these two chapters on Rousseau, in addition to recounting his version of the story of the rape of Lucretia, initiate such a genealogy.

* * *

Among the paradoxes resulting when Rousseau thinks, perhaps the most difficult to comprehend is Rousseau's conflicting responses to the theatre. Although he is a successful playwright, he writes one of the most well-known renunciations of theatre, *Letter to D'Alembert on the Theatre*. Even his birth city, Geneva, embodies the paradox: it is a city that forbids theatre but that supports for many years a successful playhouse just outside its city gates at Carouge.

Theoretically, as well, there is paradox. Rousseau accords to human nature a theatrical capacity, pity, which is simultaneously the fount of human goodness and the inevitable source for human misery. When pity is good, *"amour de soi,"* it becomes more intense as the one who observes identifies with the one who suffers; Rousseau's notions of justice are linked with observation and the development of empathy. Nonetheless, it is also this capacity for self-conscious identification with the other which, when it becomes distorted in society, *"amour-propre,"* leads men into reckless comparisons, jealousies and the loss of self-esteem.[3]

2. Tracy Strong, *Jean-Jacques Rousseau: The Politics of the Ordinary* (Thousand Oaks, Calif.: Sage Publications, 1994).

3. Importantly, one only pities those who are less fortunate than oneself and those with whose suffering one can identify; however, after the onset of *amour-propre,* one compares oneself to those whom one envies and who enjoy talents, luxuries, and merits one does not possess. Thus in the latter instance, identification (and comparison) with the other is preoccupied with the inadequacy of the self. In the former case, on the other hand, pity is derived from a sense of commonality, a kind of "there but for the grace of God go I." This explains why in *Emile,* Rousseau can assert that the boy who is among riches is unhappy, while the boy who is among the suffering is happy:

Virtue, for Rousseau, then, depends on pity being located literally "in the eyes of the beholder"; the beholder must be unaware of the reciprocal gaze of the beheld. Once men recognize that they are both the beholder and the beheld, spectator and spectacle, the natural connection of pity is weakened, if not destroyed. Consequently, theatre is for Rousseau a manifestation of humanity's corruption. As David Marshall has persuasively argued: "Theatre, then, in Rousseau's descriptions, represents the fall from the state of nature. . . . The rise of a theatrical perspective turns people into actors and encourages them to make spectacles of themselves: it also weakens the natural bonds between people by making them into spectators."[4] Theatre replaces genuine sympathy with the imitation of sympathy and releases people from responsibility or action: "In giving out tears to these fictions, we have satisfied all the rights of humanity without having to give anything more of ourselves."[5] Theatre replaces the pity of *amour de soi* with the self-aggrandizement of *amour-propre.*

Nonetheless, as many readers have noted, Rousseau continues to depend on "theatrical formulations" for the success of his various projects.[6] For example, in *Considerations on the Government of Poland,* Rousseau urges the ruler "not to neglect the need for a certain amount of public display; let it be noble, imposing, with a magnificence which resides rather in men than in things. It is hard to believe to what an extent the heart of the people follows its eyes, and how much it is impressed by majestic ceremonial."[7]

Like Machiavelli, Rousseau remains attentive to the power and seduction inherent in spectacle. Indeed, even in the *Letter to D'Alembert,* Rousseau recommends the cultivation of festivals as appropriate substitutes for theatre going. Because Rousseau draws an important distinction between

---

"The boy among riches feels jealous and inadequate in comparison to he who has riches, while the boy among the suffering feels pity and gratitude that he does not suffer" (*Emile,* 230).

4. David Marshall, "Rousseau and the State of Theatre," *Representations* 13 (Winter 1986): 86.

5. *Letter to D'Alembert on the Theatre,* trans. Allan Bloom (Ithaca: Cornell University Press, 1960), 25. Citations in the text are to this edition.

6. See, for example, Marshall Berman, *The Politics of Authenticity: Radical Individualism and the Emergence of Modern Society* (New York: Atheneum, 1970); Michael Brint, *Tragedy and Denial: The Politics of Difference in Western Political Thought* (Boulder: Westview Press, 1991); and Jean Starobinski, *Jean Jacques Rousseau: Transparency and Obstruction,* trans. Arthur Goldhammer (Chicago: University of Chicago Press, 1988).

7. *Considerations on the Government of Poland,* trans. Frederick Watkins (Madison: University of Wisconsin Press, 1986), 173.

theatre and festival, his renunciation of theatre does not include all spectacles. That is, Rousseau distinguishes festivals from theatre by insisting that in festivals "the spectators become an entertainment to themselves ... each sees and loves himself in the other so that all will be better united" (*D'Alembert*, 126). Festivals are akin to *amour de soi*; at a festival each individual is both spectator and spectacle but without the consciousness of performing for the gaze of the other. As Rousseau details, the object of these entertainments will be "nothing, if you please" (*D'Alembert*, 126). Thus, what Rousseau dislikes about spectacle is the resultant self-alienation—performing for the gaze of the other and addressing a viewer outside oneself. Yet what he wants to maintain in spectacles (through festivals) is their power for civic education.

Repeatedly, Rousseau argues that men will not be sufficiently virtuous if their only motive is duty or interest. Rather, what is required is the motivation of passion; as Rousseau notes, "Our passions are the principal instruments of our preservation."[8] And passion, as Rousseau both worries and applauds, is aroused by imagination. Imagination determines the course of one's passions (*Emile*, 219).

Imagination arouses men not only sexually (witness Rousseau's repeated assertions that what is not seen and must thereby be imagined is more seductive than what is manifest), but also socially and politically. Consider, in this regard, Rousseau's praise for the Romans for whom the august display of royal power impressed the subjects: "The object that is exhibited to the eye shakes the imagination, arouses the curiosity, and keeps the mind attentive to what is going to be said" (*Emile*, 322). Recognizing this potent link between spectacle and imagination, Rousseau wants to maintain some aspects of theatre for communal edification.

Consequently, although Rousseau writes several plays, it is to the epistolary novel and to dialogues that he ultimately turns in order to preserve the elements of spectacle most compelling to his project of civic education but without the destructive proclivities of theatre. And this transition in Rousseau from playwright to epistolary novelist is most clearly demonstrated in his early (and incomplete) rendition of Lucretia's story in his tragedy, "La Mort de Lucrèce" and his eventual refashioning of the tale in his epistolary novel, *Nouvelle Héloïse*.

The epistolary novel, popular in the eighteenth century, preserves

8. *Emile or On Education*, 212.

the reciprocity and exchange of pity, but unlike the theatre (and salon), it limits the possibilities of performing and addressing the judgment of others. In Rousseau's formulation, the exchange of letters, like the festival, is one in which the participants become an "entertainment to themselves." Unlike the actors of the stage, the letter writers do not pretend to be someone else, and the readers are not seduced by the imitation of feelings. Rather, through letter writing and exchange, Rousseau believes, as did other early members of the republic of letters, that men more fully manifest themselves.[9]

Furthermore, in ways the next chapter will detail, the epistolary novel, like the general will of Rousseau's *The Social Contract,* is a rhetorical form of "asocial collectivity." Rousseau's epistolary novel maintains a republican conception of politics based on the reciprocal exchange of conversation among equals yet avoids the pitfalls Rousseau attributes to theatre (and salons), such as dependence on the gaze of the other, the deception of the actors and the feminization of men.[10]

This chapter and the next offer detailed readings of Rousseau's "La Mort de Lucrèce" and his epistolary novel *Nouvelle Héloïse* not only in order to examine this transition in form from theatre to the epistolary novel, but also to consider what Rousseau's reformulation of the story of Lucretia reveals about his conception of political life and citizenship. This chapter is a detailed exegesis of "La Mort de Lucrèce," specifically as it reflects on Rousseau's conception of the republican tradition and his own relationship to the past. Rousseau's reinterpretation of the story of Lucretia reveals a theorist still optimistic about the possibility of innovation under conditions of corruption.

The following chapter, "*Nouvelle Héloïse* and the Supplement of Sexual Difference," addresses how several of Rousseau's various political analytics (i.e., the legislator, the general will) are illuminated through an understanding of Rousseau's conceptualization of sexual difference. For Rousseau, sexual difference is a haven *for* politics. Rousseau's world of domesticity is a place where men can be political without the dangers Rousseau attributes

9. See Dena Goodman, *The Republic of Letters: A Cultural History of the French Enlightenment* (Ithaca: Cornell University Press, 1994), chap. 3.

10. In addition, because the epistolary novel does not offer an omniscient narrator but only the perspectives of the various letter writers, readers are compelled to make their own judgments. Formally, the epistolary novel is Rousseau's challenge to the scientism of Enlightenment approaches to politics; that is, it is partially his attempt to restore state*craft* to statesmanship.

to politics in the public sphere. The domain of women is not one without politics; rather it is a world that enables and preserves Rousseau's asocial formulation of politics. Indeed, it is a world constructed largely to solve the problem(s) of politics.

I. "La Mort de Lucrèce"

In Rousseau's unfinished tragedy "La Mort de Lucrèce,"[11] Lucrèce was initially betrothed to her would-be rapist, Sextus, son of the tyrant Tarquin. The play opens with Lucrèce's maid Pauline lamenting that Lucrèce's father, Lucretius, broke off the engagement that had fulfilled the desires not only of the king, Tarquin, but of the Roman people as well. Pauline further suggests that perhaps Sextus, as heir to the crown, would have been a more worthy husband for the virtuous Lucrèce than the commoner Collatin. Lucrèce chides her for this indiscretion, insisting that she prefers "the constant and peaceful love of Collatin to the fiery passions of Sextus" (1.1).

The play continues with the arrival of a letter from Collatin telling Lucrèce that he is returning home with the son of the king, Sextus and urging her to prepare suitable accommodations since "it is upon him [Sextus] that the lot and fortune of your spouse depends" (1.2). Lucrèce sends a message back to her husband that she is too ill to receive any guests other than her husband and that he will have to entertain Sextus alone.

Pauline, however, suspects that Lucrèce is feigning illness in order not to have to see her former lover. She confides this to her own lover, Sulpitius, who is himself an adviser to Sextus. Apparently Sextus is conspiring with the two servants by promising to arrange their marriage if they can successfully arrange a secret meeting for him with Lucrèce. Pauline, nonetheless, remains ambivalent about her role in "tempting" Lucrèce. After working in Lucrèce's service for six months, she is beginning to believe that Lucrèce is "not capable of feeling anything but for her spouse and her duty." Sulpitius, on the other hand, insists that Lucrèce only wants others to believe she is virtuous and that no one ever puts their virtue before their own happiness.

In this rendition of Lucretia's story, Brutus also knows of Lucrèce's love for Sextus, although he tells her father, Lucretius, that Lucrèce herself is ignorant of her own sentiments. Besides, he asserts, "conquered passions

11. Text in *Jean-Jacques Rousseau Oeuvres Complètes*, ed. Bernard Gagnebin and Marcel Raymond (Paris: Bibliothèque de La Plèiade, 1964), 2:1024–46. All translations of the play are my own, although I am indebted to Charles Butterworth for his assistance.

are a more powerful spur for heroic souls than lessons of cold wisdom" (1.5). He even goes so far as to assert that Lucrèce is "more than a man," while her husband, Brutus worries, is "only a woman."[12]

Thus, while Sextus is planning his secret liaison with Lucrèce, Brutus is already preparing to drive the tyrants from Rome. He needs only to enlist the help of Collatin, Lucrèce's husband. To do so, he tells Collatin of Sextus's love for his wife; he urges Collatin to avenge this insult to both his wife and himself. Yet Collatin cares little that Sextus loves Lucrèce, saying only, "I know the virtue of Lucrèce's heart" (2.4). Brutus persists, but Collatin is reluctant to make war. He worries about the possibility of anarchy, slavery and civil strife after the monarchs are driven out. Lucretius accuses him of puerile ambitions for which it is easier to serve the tyrants and thus satisfy his own desires than to fight for liberty and equality. Finally, Lucretius persuades Collatin with the assurance that when Rome is free, he, Collatin, will reign over the people of Rome. Nonetheless, in an aside, Brutus and Lucretius agree that Collatin is "ambitious, weak and of little skill" (2.4).

This is the last complete scene of Rousseau's tragedy; the remainder of the play can only be conjectured from four pages of fragments. Among these fragments is a scene between Sextus and Lucrèce in which he tells her of his love and asks for her help in overcoming his passion: "It is because of your virtue that I will obey the laws" (fragment 1). Yet, apparently he does not contain his passions, because in an additional fragment he laments that the "virtue deserving of adoration by the gods" has been soiled by him, "the vilest of mortals" (fragment 11). He, then, apparently kills himself. Whether Lucrèce is raped or consents remains ambiguous; however, in one of the last fragments, she too commits suicide, insisting that she is still virtuous, although she paradoxically adds that she can punish herself only after "having shared in the crime" (fragment 18).

* * *

In *The Confessions*, Rousseau describes his most immediate reason for writing "La Mort de Lucrèce": "I planned a prose tragedy on no less a subject than Lucrèce, with which I had some hope of overcoming derision, even though I ventured to bring that unfortunate woman back to the stage when she had become an impossible subject for the French theatre."[13] In part, Rousseau was lamenting the contemporary comedic representations of Lucretia's plight. Jean François Regnard and Charles Dufresny, two

12. Fragment 2. Fragments are quoted from *Oeuvres Complètes*, where they are numbered at the end of the unfinished play.

13. *The Confessions*, trans. J. M. Cohen (New York: Penguin Books, 1953), 8:368.

contemporary playwrights, had produced a comedy of Lucretia's rape similar to Machiavelli's *La Mandragola*. Also a scorned and inept tragedy, *Lucrèce*, written by Pierre Duryer in 1638, had been briefly revived. Rousseau's initial goal in writing "La Mort de Lucrèce" was to restore Lucretia's status as a tragic heroine and to give to contemporary Parisian audiences a "useful heroine": one with whom they could identify.

For Rousseau, the story of the rape of Lucretia is, in part, an apt encapsulation of deterioration and renewal: an allegory for the loss and potential rebirth of the republic. And for Rousseau, women are the perfect emblem of both corruption and the possibility of renewal. Who else in eighteenth-century French society has fallen further than women, specifically the bourgeois women of the salons? Yet upon whom else can the possibility for renewal be placed? If even the wretched can be redeemed, made into the virtuous nursemaids of the republic, surely there is still reason to believe in the possibility of a republican rebirth.

Rousseau's conception of deterioration and renewal, however, departed sharply from both the Christian idea of time as a gathering dimension guided by Providence toward a culminating fulfillment (i.e., salvation) and from the Enlightenment formulation of progress associated with the "new science." Like Machiavelli before him, Rousseau argued instead that there was a cyclical dimension to history, that there was an inevitability to both the foundation of societies and states, and an equal inevitability to their destruction: "If Sparta and Rome have perished, what State can expect to last forever? . . . The body politic, as well as the human body, begins to die from its birth, and bears within itself the causes of this destruction."[14] Nonetheless, this story of deterioration and renewal raises several predicaments for Rousseau. If the republic is the ideal form of government, why did it initially deteriorate? Similarly, if human nature is inherently good, as Rousseau seems to insist, what is the origin of the current debauchery? Moreover, if unlike Machiavelli, Rousseau is unwilling to accept *seeming* virtuous rather than *being* virtuous, how will he develop a moral politics?

* * *

In Rousseau's version of the rape of Lucretia, the story begins not in innocence but in corruption. Lucrèce's is a world in which fathers forfeit their daughters' happiness for political gain, in which servants conspire secretly

14. *The Social Contract: An Eighteenth-Century Translation Completely Revised* (New York: Hafner Press, 1947), 79.

against their mistresses and in which tranquil appearances mask inner turmoil. The heroine is herself a compromised figure. Lucrèce has been consigned to a rather loveless marriage with Collatin, a man so consumed with ambition that he is oblivious to his wife's desires. Even Collatin's own father-in-law chastises him: "With a more sensitive heart and a less blind ambition, you would not have been ignorant for so long" (2.4). In addition, Sextus, although he claims to love Lucrèce, resorts to stealthy artifice, employing his servant Sulpitius, as well as Lucrèce's own servant, to achieve what his simple devotion to her could not—her consent.

Thus like Lucrezia in *La Mandragola,* Lucrèce is a solitary figure struggling to maintain her virtue. In Machiavelli's version, Lucrezia's isolation prompts her to political *virtù*—seizing opportunity, responding to the whim of fortune and expediting her own interests. In Rousseau's tragedy, Lucrèce is the paragon of virtue struggling in a corrupt time. She, like Julie of *Nouvelle Héloïse,* is determined to maintain her virtue despite temptation. Of course, keeping Julie's story in mind, one wonders whether Rousseau's Lucrèce kills herself, finally, not from shame but because the conflict between desire and duty is too great.

Although Rousseau's Lucrèce is married to Collatin, she is believed by both the people of Rome and by family servants to still be in love with Sextus, the man to whom she was originally betrothed. Like Julie of *Nouvelle Héloïse,* her virtue is jeopardized because of the shortsightedness of patriarchal authority. Lucrèce's father, Lucretius, revoked her engagement in order to forge a more politically expedient union with Collatin. It is this predicament thrust upon her that precipitates her dissolution. Although like the Lucrezia of *La Mandragola,* she is tainted by the corruption of those around her, Lucrèce's denouement is calculated to demonstrate how societal corruption coerces the virtuous and compels them toward vice. Unlike Lucrezia, who is willingly seduced by knavery, Lucrèce is the tragic victim of a bankrupt society colluding against her. Lucrèce's plight is tragic because she struggles valiantly. When Collatin writes to ask her to entertain Sextus, Lucrèce, uncertain of her own fortitude, seeks God's intercession: "Oh, God, who sees my heart, clarify my judgment. Guarantee that I do not cease to be virtuous; you know that although I want to be, I will always be if you want it as well!" (fragments for 1.2). Here Lucrèce casts the shadow on her own chastity; she marks the flaw in herself—her love for Sextus—that will be her undoing.

Rousseau has several motives for beginning his founding story in corruption. First, by beginning in decline he asserts that there is no need for an innocent origin, no need for a return in order for there to be rebirth or simply reform. In other words, contemporary society does not need to be purified before the republic can be reborn. Unlike other Enlightenment thinkers, Rousseau does not postulate conditions of innocence. For example, Rousseau does not begin, as Mariux does in his play *La Dispute,* with man in the state of nature. For Rousseau, even in *Le Narcisse,* which parallels many of the themes of *La Dispute,* man is always already in society.

Importantly, Rousseau's "ideal" is not the state of nature. His ideal is that liminal state (the second state of nature) that has both the best qualities of human nature and the worst, with their consequent potential for destruction. Rousseau's project is invention and renovation, not return to a pristine origin. The conditions for the founding need not be those of foundational innocence; rather, Rousseau argues, the republic can be reborn from the ashes of horror and death; or again, less dramatically, simply reformed from corruption.

Rousseau recounts Lucretia's story as tragedy in part because he believes that humanity responds to horror; we learn about ourselves and the past when confronted with the horrible, the tragic; "it arouses our natural pity" (*D'Alembert,* 31–34). Rousseau crafts the story so as to highlight the horror of contemporary society—a society so corrupted that the love between Lucrèce and Sextus (and later, between Julie and Saint Preux) cannot endure because of society's perverse artifices. Rousseau does not tell a story of sweet innocence with the hope that audiences will recoil with the recognition of how far they have fallen. Rather, he paints the vivid consequences of their fall. The story is both to remind audiences of what they have become *and* to offer the possibility of redemption from Lucrèce's ashes.

Like Machiavelli, Rousseau recognizes the difficulty of innovation once "customs are established and prejudices have taken root." His motivation for choosing tragedy is partially articulated in the *Social Contract:* "This does not mean that . . . there may not sometimes be violent epochs in the lifetime of states, during which revolutions do for people what certain crises do for individuals; when horror of the past takes the place of oblivion, and when the state, consumed by civil wars, is reborn, so to speak, from its ashes, and recovers the vigor of youth as it leaves the arms of death. Such was Sparta in the time of Lycurgus; such was Rome after the Tarquins."[15]

15. "Of the People," *Social Contract,* 40.

It was Rousseau's hope that this re-presentation of a past horror would jolt oblivious French audiences into recognition and spur the birth of a new republic.

Secondly, by beginning "La Mort de Lucrèce" in decline, Rousseau has the opportunity to make his specific criticisms of contemporary society. The play challenges not only paternal authority but also social conventionality and the realm of appearances. Moreover, the play is full of conspiracy and of characters who are not what they seem and are neither faithful nor loyal. And this characterization of what ancient Rome allegedly embodies features, of course, the very qualities and criticisms that Rousseau makes of his own time.[16]

Thirdly, by beginning in corruption, Rousseau can also show how some of nature's good qualities resist defilement. The power of Lucrèce's virtue is manifest in her maid Pauline's reluctance to conspire against her: "Away from her eyes I want all that pleases you, but in front of her, I no longer want anything but honesty" (fragment 8). Even Sextus is contrite after the rape, praising Lucrèce for "a virtue deserving of adoration by the gods" and cursing himself as the "vilest of mortals!" (fragment 11).

And finally, the corruption in "La Mort de Lucrèce" manifests Rousseau's early renunciation of Christian salvation. The founding of the republic is not dependent on God's grace. Even in a state of disgrace, republican redemption is possible. The cycles of deterioration and renewal are testaments to the possibility of a republican birth, even in conditions of disgrace. Instead of one original Fall, Rousseau postulates many falls, each with the promise of redemption. Rousseau, like Machiavelli, unlinked the secular and the theological in order to remove political renovation from the salvation schedule.

It is this cyclical conception of time that Rousseau is also partially trying to justify in *The Second Discourse*. Here Rousseau postulates two rather contradictory characteristics of nature. On the one hand, he wants to insist that nature is good; and yet on the other, that there is a certain "natural" inevitability to the crisis that necessitates the foundation of society and humanity's eventual misery. The paradox is the result of Rousseau's twin impulses—first, to assert a natural order that is good and thus offers the possibility for renewal without divine intervention; and second, to explain

16. It is interesting to note that while Machiavelli sets his play in his own time, Rousseau sets the story of Lucrèce in ancient Rome, suggesting that there is no pristine place to which to return, that man is always already corrupt or corruptible, even in ancient Rome.

how we arrived at the point of again (and even continuously) needing renovation.

Rather than reading this complexity as a contradiction that negates itself, it is possible to conceive of these two impulses as fundamental to Rousseau's rereading of the republican tradition. Although "La Mort de Lucrèce" begins in corruption, the play is not a talisman of Rousseau's despair. Like Machiavelli, who also set *La Mandragola* in corrupt times, Rousseau's representation of corruption is part of a genealogy meant to evoke the possibility of reconstitution. Although one can read Rousseau as nostalgic, the overwhelming impetus of his thought is toward renewal and reinterpretation.[17] For Rousseau there is no possibility of retrieving the past; the past he "remembers," as he acknowledges in *The Second Discourse,* never was; he has set the facts aside. His purpose instead is to offer a genealogy of Parisian society in order to suggest the potential for intervention.

Rousseau is trying both to explain why eighteenth-century society is in decline and to develop a more utopic vision of a retrievable past. Interestingly, the past that Rousseau heralds is not the origin but a secondary stage of development. Rousseau lauds this secondary moment in humanity's evolution because he is *not* a primitivist, or even the romantic he is often perceived to be. And this ideal, this secondary stage of nature, is itself the beginning of convention, a less than perfectly transparent association:

> Thus although men had come to have less endurance and although natural pity had already undergone some alteration, this period of the development of human faculties, maintaining a golden mean between the indolence of the primitive state and the petulant activity of our vanity, must have been the happiest and most durable epoch . . . and he must have come out of it *only by some fatal accident,* which for the common good ought never to have happened.[18]

Thus, the story of Lucrèce seems to begin after "the fatal accident"—that is, after Lucrèce's broken engagement to Sextus, when she is married to Collatin and Rome is living under Tarquin tyranny. This is a Rome in decline, long past the secondary golden era. Although this is not an ideal moment, it is the period from which Rousseau imagines rebirth is possible.

17. See, for example, Arthur Lovejoy's "The Supposed Primitivism of Rousseau's *Discourse on Inequality,*" *Modern Philology* 21 (1923): 165–86.

18. *The Second Discourse,* in *The First and Second Discourses,* trans. Roger D. and Judith R. Masters (New York: St. Martin's Press, 1964), 151; italics mine.

Indeed, his ambition is to return humanity to this golden stage but with the knowledge they will have gained after the "fatal accident." For Rousseau, men and women return to their "natures" as a consequence of their fall, rather than despite it.

As in both Livy's and Machiavelli's renditions, Lucretia's violation and her subsequent demonstration of *virtù* redeemed teaches men how to be republican citizens. For Livy, Lucretia is a moral exemplar because she is always chaste and because she forfeits her life for a reputation of virtue; she recalls Augustan Romans to their former greatness. For Machiavelli, Lucrezia is a model of *virtù* because she recognizes that *virtù* demands the accommodation of circumstances; she seduces Renaissance men to the requirements of historical contingency. And for Rousseau, Lucrèce is a model for men's civic education because she has been tempted, has fallen and has then been redeemed. She mimics Enlightenment corruption and models the possibilities for rebirth. In fact, temptation and redemption are integrally linked for Rousseau.

Lucretia's redemption is most fully manifest in the second part of *Nouvelle Héloïse*. In the second preface to *Nouvelle Héloïse*, Rousseau insists that it is only because Julie has been debauched that she can be such a good model of virtue: "Bring your models a little lower, if you want people to try to imitate them. To whom do you vaunt purity which has not been sullied? Well! Tell us about purity which can be recovered; perhaps at least someone will be able to get your meaning."[19] Indeed, Rousseau even holds out the possibility that the tyrant Sextus could have been reformed. In "La Mort de Lucrèce" Sextus not only kills himself in despair after his vile deed, but he anticipates that his violation of Lucrèce will not achieve what he desires: "Alas, in possessing her I will still be quite far from the supreme happiness I formed a ravishing idea of for myself. Ah, Sulpitius, when you have given me Lucrèce, tell me, what will you do to make me happy?" (2.1). Here, *virtù* is shown to be a sentiment rather than a martial value, even for a tyrant. Sextus is revealed as caught between the demands of an ancient formulation of *virtù* that requires that he bend the world to his will to ensure his immortal glory, and a Rousseauist conception of *virtù* that entails self-examination and the reconciliation of collective justice and personal happiness.

19. "Julie, or the New Héloïse: Letters of Two Lovers in a Small Town at the Foot of the Alps," unpublished translation by Philip Stewart and Jean Vaché, iv.

For Rousseau, the possibility for renovation relies predominately on those who have struggled with their own passions: "Learn that passions to be conquered are a more powerful spur to heroic souls than cold lessons of wisdom which, finding no obstacle, acquire no strength through resistance."[20] It is perhaps this aspect of Rousseau's thinking that Judith Shklar had in mind when she called Rousseau "the Homer for the losers."[21] That is, if by "losers" one means those who begin by being defeated by "fatal accidents" and other contingencies beyond their control, yet who struggle nobly to compensate and overcome them once they have been defeated. These "losers" accommodate what is done to them as well as their own flawed natures, rather than engrave the world with their form. Thus, Lucrèce's *virtù* is shown in how she responds to what is done to her; consequently, upon her the rebirth of the republic can depend.

Interestingly, Sextus is, in Rousseau's account, considered to be among those who has also faced obstacles (i.e., patriarchal conventions that took his beloved from him); however, he did not acquire the strength sufficient to resist vice. Oddly, in Rousseau's version Sextus is portrayed in many respects as a more sympathetic character than Lucretia's husband. Collatin is depicted as a rather stupid man, obsessed with his own ambitions and reputation, who must be cajoled into fighting for the republic. He is Rousseau's despised *nouveau bourgeois*; he is apparently beyond redemption in the new republic. Both Lucretia's father, Lucretius, and Brutus secretly agree that he will be of little value.

Apparently, what makes Collatin incapable of rebirth is his failure to recognize his own shortcomings as well as his reluctance to give up the privileges and security he has enjoyed under Tarquin rule. He is, like members of the Parisian bourgeois, unable to understand what the "fatal accident" has cost, so indentured is he to his own *amour-propre*. Rousseau thus leaves the possibility for the renovation and renewal of the republic in the hands of those who have suffered most from what has been lost[22]—whether tyrants[23] or virtuous women. In other words, for Rousseau it is

20. Brutus to Lucretia's father, Lucritius; 1.5.

21. Judith Shklar, "Jean Jacques Rousseau and Equality," *Daedalus* 107 (Summer 1978): 24.

22. It is noteworthy that Karl Marx was a great reader and admirer of Rousseau. Interestingly, this Rousseauist formulation of renovation bears some uncanny resemblances to Marx's theory of revolution. And for bringing early to my attention the Rousseau in Marx, I am indebted to my undergraduate teacher, Kurt Tauber.

23. It is significant that Rousseau never hated the aristocracy as much as he hated the rich. Maurice Cranston makes a compelling argument for why: "For Rousseau believed himself to be a

the consciousness of loss and the subsequent response to that loss which spurs *virtù*.

Importantly, however, even though Rousseau suggests that Sextus might be redeemed, his redemption rests on the spectacle of Lucrèce's virtue. As Sextus himself notes: "Vice is in my heart; I feel it and admit it with trembling. But you [Lucrèce] make me love innocence and purity; in you, I adore their celestial image; and if, far from your eyes, my imagination wanders away in recollecting your charms, their presence calms my furious passions while doubling my rapture and your touching and modest glances bring me back to virtue" (fragment 1). Lucrèce, as a virtuous woman, possesses the capacity of recalling a man to virtue. She, like both Julie of *Nouvelle Héloïse* and Sophie of *Emile*, becomes a spectacle that redirects a man's imagination. And she does this by offering resistance, "an obstacle" (i.e., her virtue), which Rousseau argues is what spurs heroic souls: "strength through resistance" (1.5). In other words, just as the world does not always give men what they want, so Rousseau's women, by simultaneously inflaming and containing men's passions, teach them how to accommodate a world of undecidability.[24]

Indeed, Rousseau's republican attentiveness to contingency and mortality is marked, in part, by his conception of the role of accidents in history. Rousseau tries to account for that which cannot be controlled, for the unexpected and the unforeseen, but without defining exactly what those forces are. His reference to a "fatal accident" that must have caused man to lose his happiness is a warning, in part, of the instability of man's flawed nature, as well as of the insecurity of bonds among men. There are two other references to the role of "accidents" in *The Second Discourse*: (1) "the chance combinations" and "different accidents that were able to perfect human reason while deteriorating the species" (140); and (2) the "happy accident" that introduced man to fire (143).

---

man of superior merit, yearning for a society ruled by an aristocracy of virtue, and he found a certain affinity with the kind of French nobleman who looked back sadly to the feudal world which the absolutist monarchy had destroyed, the world of chivalry and chateaux forts and shining honour, where the noblese d'epee et de race was answerable to no one but God. Between their obscure memory of a lost world and Rousseau's dream of a world unborn there was much in common, a shared capacity to imagine something better than the prevailing alliance of despotic government with materialist culture" (*The Noble Savage: Jean Jacques Rousseau 1754–1762* [Chicago: University of Chicago Press, 1991], 160).

24. This point is explored later in Chapter 6 in an analysis of Rousseau's formulation of rape and consent.

These unnamed accidents are methodologically akin to Michel Foucault's conception of the undecidability and productivity of power;[25] the conception that power does not always follow a calculable linear trajectory. These accidents parallel for Rousseau what *fatum* was for Livy and *fortuna* for Machiavelli. While Livy believed that the greatness of Rome was inevitable, he still insisted that the cultivation of individual *virtù* was pivotal to the success of the republic (see Chapter 2). Similarly, for Machiavelli, although the Florentine republican founding was not fated, the inevitability of Fortuna's vicissitudes was integral to the potency of men's *virtù*. Rousseau's "fatal accident" is his synthesis of both views. What is inevitable for Rousseau, indeed almost fated, is man's self-destruction—what Nietzsche calls "the iron hand of necessity shaking the dice-box of chance."[26] For Rousseau the "dice-box of chance" is how man responds to the inevitability of his own flaws.

Interestingly, there is something rather Greek about Rousseau's formulation. Like Sophocles' *Oedipus Rex*, the tragedy for Rousseau is how men choose to respond to their fate—a fate, ironically, which they have created for themselves. Like Oedipus, Rousseau's man paradoxically creates his own fate and then manifests his *virtù* by choosing how he responds to it.[27] Thus, despite the "fatal accident," humanity's freedom, and hence the possibility for republican renovation and rebirth, depends on how each reacts to this tragic flaw. This is perhaps most clearly articulated by Rousseau's modern-day Lucrèce, Julie of *Nouvelle Héloïse*. What makes Julie the paragon of *virtù* for Rousseau is how she responds to her inevitable fall. Despite her youthful seduction, Rousseau defends Julie as a moral exemplar because her *virtù* rests not in her having always been virtuous but in her ability to cultivate *virtù* despite the temptations of profligacy.

* * *

Rousseau's genealogy of the founding of the republic is not meant to be an exposure of meaning hidden at the origin. He is not searching for an exact essence; in fact, he does not assume that such forms even exist. Rather,

25. See, for example, Michel Foucault's *The History of Sexuality: An Introduction*, trans. Robert Hurley (New York: Vintage Books, 1978).

26. Frederick Nietzsche, *Daybreak: Thoughts on the Prejudices of Morality*, trans. R. J. Hollingdale (Cambridge: Cambridge University Press, 1982) no. 130, p. 81.

27. For a persuasive and insightful account of this aspect of Sophocles' *Oedipus*, see J. Peter Euben's "Identity and Oedipus Tyrannos," chapter 4 in *The Tragedy of Political Theory: The Road Not Taken* (Princeton: Princeton University Press, 1990).

Rousseau's genealogical method is an interpretation of the founding for a particular end. Because he is more concerned with the fulfillment of his aim (the renewal of the republic) than with the search for the Truth of the founding, Rousseau writes and rewrites the origin story in the *First and Second Discourses,* in "La Mort de Lucrèce" and in *Nouvelle Héloïse* in ways that respond to the needs of the present rather than that correspond to the past. His founding stories are themselves spectacles for imitation. Rousseau's histories of the founding become, then, in Nietzsche's terms, "effective history." They are histories not of rediscovery but of discontinuity. Unlike traditional histories, which read the past as a patient and continuous development seeking completion, effective history insists on the singularity and randomness of events. Effective history addresses "moments when there is a reversal of a relationship of forces, the usurpation of power, the appropriation of a vocabulary, turned against those who had once used it . . . the entry of a masked other."[28]

Rousseau's retellings of the story of the rape of Lucretia mark just such an "event." The story of Lucrèce is not an origin story but a narrative of "a reversal of a relationship of forces" between masculinity and femininity; of "the usurpation of power" in the movement from tyranny to republicanism; of "the appropriation of a vocabulary" in the reformulation of *virtù* from a martial to a domestic virtue; and finally, of "the entry of the masked other": woman.

Rousseau's effective history of the origin is the affirmation of knowledge as perspective. For Rousseau, there is nothing that is sufficiently stable to serve as the basis either for self-recognition or for understanding other men. For Rousseau the story of the rape of Lucretia is, in part, about the constitution of the subject within a historical framework. His political philosophy is concerned with the constitution of the citizen through education, including the most minute details of diet, child rearing and sexuality. His retellings of the story of Lucretia, his repetitions of the origin story, are not about tracing the impact of external events on a transcendental subject, but rather about the constitution and reconstitution of the subject in a particular historical and social milieu. Thus, when his early rendition of the origin story, "La Mort de Lucrèce" is unsuccessful, Rousseau changes both genre and story line and rewrites the origin tale in *Nouvelle Héloïse.*

28. Michel Foucault, "Nietzsche, Genealogy and History," in *The Foucault Reader,* ed. Paul Rabinow (New York: Pantheon Books, 1984), 89.

6

Nouvelle Héloïse AND THE SUPPLEMENT OF SEXUAL DIFFERENCE

I. *Nouvelle Héloïse* AS A FOUNDING NARRATIVE

Rousseau began working on *Nouvelle Héloïse* shortly after putting aside "La Mort de Lucrèce" (circa 1754–56); indeed, he refers to *Nouvelle Héloïse* in both his correspondence and *Confessions* as his attempt to render a more useful heroine than Samuel Richardson's popular *Clarissa*, itself a British rewriting of the rape and suicide of Lucretia: "The character of Julie provide[s] a far more useful history ... of an ordinary woman who was tempted, as women are, and fell as women do and will, but who was redeemed, as any woman can be and so few are."[1]

Paralleling the story of Lucrèce, Julie is prohibited by her father from marrying her lover, Saint Preux. Indeed, due to a physical assault from her father, Julie miscarries the child she has conceived illegitimately with Saint Preux. Nonetheless, at her father's insistence she marries Wolmar, a cold, passionless man: "Bound by an indissoluble tie to the fate of a husband, or rather to the will of a father, I [Julie] am entering a new way of life which is to end only with my death."[2] Her life then becomes an internal struggle between the demands of virtue and honor inside the constraints of patriarchal marriage and the feelings of love and passion that she feels outside its confines.

1. William Mead, "*La Nouvelle Héloïse* and the Public of 1761," *Yale French Studies* 28 (Fall–Winter 1961–62): 18.

2. *Eloisa, or a Series of Original Letters,* trans. William Kenrick (1803; Oxford: Woodstock Books, 1989), 2:277. Kenrick's translation has served as the primary source for the translations in this chapter, although I have also consulted a yet-unpublished translation by Philip Stewart and Jean Vaché, "Julie, or the New Héloïse: Letters of Two Lovers in a Small Town at the Foot of the Alps."

After her marriage to Wolmar, however, Julie becomes the paragon of virtue, having seemingly extinguished her feelings for Saint Preux. Her husband arranges repeated "tests" for the former lovers, much as Rousseau does for Emile, in order to measure how completely Julie has overcome her feelings. Indeed, the second half of *Nouvelle Héloïse* is a rather utopian tract of long letters detailing this ideal community and the philosophy that governs it.

The novel's denouement, however, offers a challenge to the stability of this ideal. Julie wills her own death after she rescues her child from a near-fatal drowning. She dies, apparently, in order to end her struggle with temptation and thus to ensure that she dies virtuous: "I glory in my past life: but who could have answered for my future years? Perhaps, were I to live another day, I should be culpable." She dies voicing the hope that she and Saint Preux will someday be united in death. Her death, like Lucrèce's, is both a testament and an attempt to guarantee her innocence.[3]

3. Like Livy, but unlike Machiavelli, Rousseau's founders, Lucrèce and Julie, both kill themselves. Yet suicide is one of those practices about which Rousseau has complicated things to say. On the one hand, all of his primary female characters kill themselves; in fact, Rousseau is often charged with inspiring a romantic change toward the theme of suicide in love. Yet on the other hand, *Nouvelle Héloïse* also presents what is perhaps one of the eighteenth century's most persuasive arguments against suicide.

In *The Persian Letters,* Montesquieu justifies suicide as the preeminent right of the individual. He asserts that suicide is forbidden because "we imagine that the annihilation of a being as perfect as ourselves would degrade the whole of Nature." Voltaire too finds this reasoning false and defends the individual's right to commit suicide. Rousseau, typically, offers arguments both for and against suicide, although *Nouvelle Héloïse* as a whole implicitly argues that suicide is justifiable *only* if a man has become useless to his fellow citizens.

In Part 3 of *Nouvelle Héloïse,* Saint Preux writes to Lord Edward Bomston, asserting that "when our life becomes a misery to ourselves and is of advantage to no one, we are at liberty to put an end to our being." Saint Preux pointedly argues against those who would assert that life is a gift from God that therefore needs to be preserved. Instead, he insists that suicide does not violate God's power because God's power extends far beyond the mere confines of a man's body; arguments against suicide thus place too much emphasis on the body. Besides, Saint Preux argues, those who appeal to the gospel for prohibitions against suicide will not find them there, because such proscriptions are pagan; they were appropriated by Lactantius and Augustine from Plato's *Phaedo.*

Against those who assert that suicide is the way of cowards, Saint Preux retorts, "O Rome, the victor of the world, what a race of cowards did your empire produce! Let Arria, Eponina, Lucretia be of the number; they were women. But Brutus, Cassisus and the great and divine Cato, who did share with the gods the adoration of an astonished world . . . thy proud admirers never thought that one day in the dusty corner of a college, vile Rhetors would prove thou a mere coward for having preferred suicide to imprisonment." Nonetheless, Saint Preux does acknowledge that some men have duties to others that prohibit their committing suicide; yet he maintains that for those without such responsibilities, suicide is not culpable.

Demonstrating both her role as legislator and her capacity for female autonomy, Julie orchestrates her final days, instructing each member of her family and community, including her minister, on her views and expectations of them after her death. She even writes the equivalent of a suicide note to Saint Preux, explaining what her death means to her and how she wants him to interpret it.

Like all of the Lucretias before her, Julie's death also testifies to the failure of her male kin—first, her father was unable to be with her on her deathbed because he had stumbled down a flight of stairs when he mistakenly believed Julie had already drowned in rescuing her child. And secondly, she dies, not in the arms of her husband or her lover, but in the "sweet embrace" of her best friend, Claire; her only request of her husband Wolmar is that he deliver the letter testifying to her love of Saint Preux to him.

A: Founding and the Law: The Role of Woman as Legislator

For Rousseau the act of founding the republic is not simply one of social compact but of law. In contrast to Hobbes, for Rousseau the social contract

---

Lord Bomston replies to Saint Preux that each man's life has some design, some end, some moral object. "Were you placed on earth to do nothing in this world? Did not Heaven when it gave you existence give you some task or employment?" he asks. "Point out to me the just man who can boast that he has lived long enough." Insisting that the evil Saint Preux sees in the world is actually in "the disposition of your own mind," Lord Bomston urges him to correct his "irregular appetites," and not to "set your house on fire to avoid the trouble of putting it in order."

Afflictions of the mind, the kind that motivate suicide, Bomston asserts, are in direct opposition to the evils of the body. The latter become worse the longer they continue, while those of the mind are effaced over time: "Grief, disquietude, regret, and despair are evils of short duration, which never take root in the mind; and experience always falsifies that bitter reflection which makes us imagine our misery will have no end." Thus, only the acute pain of the body can justify suicide.

Bomston also reminds Saint Preux of his obligations to Julie, who would suffer inconsolably if he were to kill himself. And finally he chides Saint Preux for invoking the examples of Roman suicides, "Did Brutus die a lover in despair, and did Cato plunge the dagger in his breast for his mistress?" No, he contends, the Romans committed suicide in service to their country, as part of the fulfillment of their duty rather than its evasion.

As a result of this exchange, Saint Preux does not kill himself; instead, he agrees to Lord Bomston's suggestion that he travel the world as part of a sailing expedition. Yet what is one to make of this exchange between Saint Preux and Bomston when one considers the suicides of Lucrèce and Julie, as well as of Sophie? Why do these women kill themselves, and what do their suicides signify in Rousseau's political economy?

Although each woman seems to kill herself for love in defiance of Bomston's insistence that each life has a God-given purpose and design that must not be violated, each woman's suicide actually fulfills rather than defies her purpose in life. Rousseau's women die, not as silly mistresses to love, but as Roman heroines in service to their husbands and kin, as well as to their country.

is nothing in itself: "It is absurd and unreasonable if, instead of uniting inwardly the individual wills, it compels them to unite by the use of external physical coercive measures."[4] That is, Rousseau does not want individuals to unite out of fear, but rather because each one's particular will, as such, has ceased to be. The will must no longer demand and desire for itself but must exist and will only from within the framework of the general will.

The priority Rousseau gives to the legislator and to the law rather than to justice is an important distinction to the formulation of several of his Enlightenment contemporaries. Although Rousseau begins his discussion of law with the assertion that "all justice flows from God . . . and is undoubtedly universal and emanates from reason alone,"[5] he concludes with the observation that "laws of justice are vain among men." Because of man's inability to receive accurately the "laws from on high," conventions and civil laws are a necessity.

In contrast, both Diderot and Voltaire have an a priori theory of justice. For example, Diderot: "If we understand by just and unjust the moral qualities of action which are the foundation [of those terms], the propriety of things, natural laws, without contradiction all these ideas are quite antecedent to law, since law builds on them and may not contradict them."[6] Rousseau, on the other hand, supposes that the laws themselves give people the idea of justice, not vice versa.

Furthermore, the laws need to be crafted to a particular people as well as the people crafted to the law. Rousseau imagines different laws, different conceptions of justice, for different people: "For as a regimen proper for persons in health will not agree with invalids, so a corrupted people cannot be governed by the same laws that will suit a good people."[7] Although Rousseau begins his discussion of the legislator with the observation that "to discover those happy rules of government which would agree with every nation could only be the work of some superior intelligence . . . gods would be required to give laws to mankind," his project is *not* to "give laws to all mankind" but rather to give laws to a specific people. The project of the legislator is not to develop the ideal law but to craft the

4. Ernst Cassirer, *The Philosophy of the Enlightenment,* trans. Fritz C. Koelln and James Pettegrove (Princeton: Princeton University Press, 1951), 260.

5. "Of the Law," in *The Social Contract: An Eighteenth-Century Translation Completely Revised* (New York: Hafner Press, 1947), 33.

6. From Diderot's "Juste," quoted in Lester Crocker, "The Priority of Justice or Law," *Yale French Studies* 28 (Fall–Winter 1961–62): 35.

7. "Of the Roman Comitia," *Social Contract,* 107.

law ideal to particular citizens: "*and* to craft the citizens to those laws: The laws themselves will cultivate the people necessary to appreciate them."[8]

This priority of law instead of justice means politically that whatever is willed, is considered just.[9] Rousseau is oddly less concerned with the content of the laws than that they are appropriate for the people they will govern. Moreover, *how* the law is created is more significant than its content; if laws are crafted in accordance with the general will, then they are "just." That is, although the outcome of the general will may not always be right, the legitimacy of its constitutional foundations ordains the general will as "just."

Crafting the general will, then, becomes the primary task for the legislator. For Rousseau, it is the legislator who inaugurates the republic, "I call a republic any state that is ruled by laws."[10] While the social compact gives "life and existence" to the body politic, the law gives it "motion and will." And, Rousseau adds, "For the original act by which the body is formed and united determines none of the measures that ought to be taken for its preservation" (*Social Contract*, 32). In other words, the methods of the social contract are distinct from those required for the renewal and subsequent preservation of the republic. Thus, "La Mort de Lucrèce" is concerned primarily with the second step of this process, renewal of the republic, while *Nouvelle Héloïse* addresses both steps. In "La Mort de Lucrèce" when Collatin is reluctant to join Brutus in the liberation of Rome, Brutus reminds him that the laws of Rome are stronger than its tyrants and that Rome has been free since its birth; it is only necessary "to subtract some of what it has too much," that is, tyrants.[11] All that is required is to recall Rome to herself.

In *Nouvelle Héloïse,* on the other hand, Rousseau details how to fashion individuals into "a people" (i.e., the initial social contract) through the organization of Clarens, Julie's ideal community. *Nouvelle Héloïse* is the story of both the initial social compact and the formation of the republic. Clarens is a community that begins with a "people who are already united

8. "Of the Legislator," *Social Contract,* 38.

9. Rousseau's formulation of the priority of law is also in part the origin of the critiques (mistaken in my opinion) made of Rousseau's political philosophy as potentially authoritarian. That is, because laws are crafted by the general will by and for a specific people, each state is allowed to create its own values without being required to recognize any transcendental or universal categories of morality, justice or truth.

10. "Of the Law," *Social Contract,* 34.

11. "La Mort de Lucrèce," 2.4.

by some original bond of origin, interest, or convention, but who have not yet had any established system of law ... and are thus in the best state to receive laws."[12]

In *The Social Contract* the impetus for social association highlights the failure of man's first nature. The catalyst for association, Rousseau asserts, is a crisis that arose "when the strength of each individual [was] insufficient to overcome the resistance of the obstacles to his preservation." Consequently, they "form by aggregation an assemblage of forces that may be able to overcome the resistance."[13] Rousseau does not detail what these obstacles are or what constitutes resistance, but he does say that the fundamental problem his work strives to address is how "every person, uniting himself with all, can obey only himself and remain as free as before" (*Social Contract,* 15). The irony, of course, is that this "freedom before" is exactly the crisis that necessitated the contract in the first place.

As a result, the general will seeks to restore man to his nature while forestalling what caused him to need the general will initially—that is, the failure of his nature itself (!). To resolve this quandary, Rousseau fashions a legislator who is engaged in "an enterprise exceeding human power and executed by an authority which is not an authority."[14]

Nonetheless, Rousseau wants to be careful not to give the legislator too much power, so he frames these responsibilities, not as foundational, but as a form of clarification. Rousseau insists that the general will that precedes the legislator is always right, but that the judgment that guides it is not always enlightened: "It is therefore necessary to make the people see things as they are, and sometimes as they ought to appear, to point out to them the right path which they are seeking, to guard them from the seducing voice of the private wills, and helping them to see how times and places are connected, to induce them to balance the attraction of immediate and sensible advantages against the apprehension of unknown and distant evil.... From thence is born the necessity of a legislator."[15] Rousseau's expects that this "increase in public knowledge" will result in the "union of judgment and will in the public body." The people will desire what is their duty. There will be no contest between individual happiness and the public good such as Hobbes postulated. Rather, through the civic education of the legislator, men will be cultivated as citizens.

12. "Of the People," *Social Contract,* 45.
13. "Of the Social Compact," *Social Contract,* 14.
14. "Of the Legislator," *Social Contract,* 37.
15. "Of the Law," *Social Contract,* 35.

The contrivances necessary for the success of the legislator remind us that the resulting general will is itself a convention. In order to create a "people," one must transform each individual, "remove from man his own proper energies to bestow upon him those which are strange to him, and which he cannot employ without the assistance of others." One of the paradoxes here is that in order to be free, one must be in a state of dependence; the most "solid and perfect institution" is one in which "each citizen is nothing but when combined with all the other citizens."[16]

Tellingly, Rousseau's ideal woman embodies the qualities he attributes to the legislator in *The Social Contract*: someone who "understands man's passions without being liable to them," someone who has "no affinity to our own nature but who understands it perfectly," and finally, someone who "condescends to make us the object of his care."[17] And, who better understands and enflames men's passions without being liable to them than a virtuous woman? In *Emile,* Rousseau details extensively how a virtuous woman masks her own desires and thus regulates her suitor's passions. Who, again, but a woman has no affinity to men's nature but understands it perfectly? In *Nouvelle Héloïse* Julie criticizes Saint Preux for his failure to recognize the inherent differences between men and women, and in *Letter to D'Alembert,* Rousseau suggests that "if you want to understand men, look to women." And, finally, who condescends to make men the object of care but she for whom "it is the fate of [her] sex always to govern ours"? Rousseau repeatedly observes (worries?) that women rule but that they must disguise this power and create the illusion of their dependence upon men: "The empire belongs to women and cannot be taken from them, even if they abuse it."[18]

Although the laws themselves will eventually cultivate the people necessary to appreciate them, *initially* the legislator has no other recourse but illusions. Remarkably, Rousseau chides those who presume to think otherwise: "And while the pride of philosophy and the blindness of party prejudice will see in these men only fortunate impostures, the true political thinker admires in their institutions that great and comprehensive genius which presides over durable establishments."[19] Like Machiavelli, Rousseau is in some way saying that dissimulation is not dissimulation, lying is not lying, if it is to some good purpose, if the intention is honorable. Like

16. Ibid.

17. "Of the Legislator," *Social Contract,* 36.

18. *Emile, or On Education,* trans. Allan Bloom (New York: Basic Books, 1979), 361.

19. "Of the People," *Social Contract,* 39.

Machiavelli's *The Prince* and against advocates of natural law, Rousseau's is a notion that the wielder of the highest political power is subject to no legal conditions and limitations.

Perhaps because the legislator's task is so awesome, Rousseau proposes the use of techniques that will later be anathema in the maintenance of the republic. The legislator, like woman, is permitted recourse to artifice and calculation. Women require these artifices, Rousseau insists, because they are regulating man's desires as well as maintaining the appearance, if not the reality, of female virtue. Women's use of these artifices suggests, in part, the failure of male desire; that is, "natural" male desire is insufficient and thus requires the supplement of feminine seduction. In a parallel vein, the "nature" of the citizen is inadequate to guarantee the founding of the republic. Thus, like Plato's reliance on "noble lies," despite the supposed transparency of Reason, Rousseau too drafts his own noble lies—civil religion, women—despite the alleged natural goodness of man.

Because Rousseau gives the legislator these extraordinary powers—the sanction of dissimulation, the invocation of Heaven for justification of some laws, and so forth—he asserts that the proof of the legitimacy of the legislator is to be found in "the magnanimous spirit of the legislator [which] is the sole miracle which must prove his mission."[20] Thus, it is noteworthy that all of Rousseau's ideal women (i.e., Lucrèce, Julie and Sophie) are paragons of virtue. Indeed, the legitimacy of that virtue is demonstrated, in part, by a kind of contagion effect. The manifestation of a woman's virtue urges others also to goodness. For example, the maid, Pauline, who is conspiring against Lucrèce in "La Mort de Lucrèce," is so affected by Lucrèce's virtue that she begins "to lose the courage and the will to soil a soul so pure" (1.3). In fact, even Brutus admits his dependence on Lucrèce for the success of the liberation of Rome: "I do not know what voice shouts to me from the bottom of my heart that it is she [Lucrèce] who has to break our chains. Without doubt it is under the auspices of virtue that the birth of liberty is invited" (fragment 2).

In addition, Brutus's appeal to Lucrèce is a mark of Rousseau's reformulation of *virtù* as a domestic rather than a martial virtue.[21] Unlike Machiavelli, who when confronted with chance in the personification of Fortuna,

20. "Of the Legislator," *Social Contract,* 39.

21. There are, of course, also numerous examples of Julie's domestic virtue as she tries "to make people see things as they are or as they ought to appear." In her letters to Saint Preux she is continually advising and correcting his interpretations. For example, she chides him for his failure

employed the martial virtues as well as seduction, Rousseau employs only the domestic virtues as the salvation to the demands of contingency. For Rousseau, the form-giving, the very action of *virtù* has been abandoned in favor of a *virtù* of sentiment, of emotion and of spectacle. In fact, so domesticated is Rousseau's formulation of *virtù* that only women still seem to manifest its more traditional elements.

B: Narcissism and the Empire of Public Opinion: The Necessary Death of the Legislator

Rousseau is acutely afraid, in ways that Machiavelli is not, of the potential loss of individuality in political communities. As a result, Rousseau is caught between his republican impulse for a community organized around a "common good" and his desire for a guarantee of individual autonomy, not necessarily as a liberal conception of individual rights, but as differences that resist collapse into either narcissism or the empire of public opinion. Consequently, Rousseau becomes obsessed with the process by which citizens are created, with the crafting of differences that will both resist authoritarianism (of the kind that he castigates in the form of public opinion) and preserve the unity of the political community (as it is threatened by the aggrandizement of *amour-propre*).

These anxieties about narcissism and the empire of public opinion are encapsulated in the long prelude to Julie's death in *Nouvelle Héloïse*. Although Julie spends her life creating Clarens, her ideal community, her death raises the specter of what Rousseau fears could destroy his newly founded republic—narcissism and public opinion.

First, Julie's death ensures that in her role as founding legislator she will not violate the prohibition against uniting in one individual "both legislative authority and the sovereign power."[22] She dies, in part, for the preservation of the community. As a true legislator, she has worked to inscribe the laws of this new state that she hopes will thrive after her death

---

to understand the moral distinctions between the sexes, for his hysteria when her letters take too long to arrive, and for his seduction by the amusements of Parisian society. Interestingly, it is most often from Julie's pen that Rousseau expresses his own views. What this suggests is not only the significance of Julie, and perhaps of women, for the articulation of Rousseau's political philosophy, but also his own identification with the role of the legislator.

22. "Of the Legislator," *Social Contract*, 37. Rousseau notes that when Lycurgus gave laws to his country, he began by abdicating royal power. Rome, he asserts, revived tyranny by failing to follow this prohibition against unifying power of legislation and governing. This also seems to be the most powerful textual evidence against those who would argue for Wolmar (who is very much alive at the end of *Nouvelle Héloïse*) in the role as founder.

in the hearts of her citizens. She has been attentive to manners and morals, customs and opinions: "These are means unknown to our political thinkers, but on which the success of everything else depends. To them [manner and morals] the great legislator directs his secret care, though he appears to confine his attention to particular laws, which are only the curve of the arch, while manners and morals, slower to form, will become at last the immovable key-stone."[23]

Rousseau's formulation assumes not only that the laws are an expression of the people but also that the laws actually help to constitute "the people." In a moment reminiscent of Machiavelli's own formulation of the law, Rousseau recognizes that good laws help to create good citizens. The legislator must unify individual interests with those of the collectivity. For Rousseau, the way to achieve this is to fashion men whose individual interests are identical to the interests of the common good. This is not about denying men's natures or repressing their desires but rather about transforming their nature, about giving them an alternative nature: "Those who dare to undertake the institution of a people must feel themselves capable, as it were, *of changing human nature, of transforming each individual,* who by himself is a perfect and solitary whole, into a part of a much greater whole, from which he in some measure receives his being and his life."[24]

Of course, it is rather paradoxical to suggest that men's natures can be changed, "nature" being one of those categories that is traditionally recognized as stable and essential. Nonetheless, what Rousseau's genealogy reveals is that "nature" is itself unstable, accidental and thus available for reformulation. The legislator will construct an alternative nature for her citizens. Rousseau's political philosophy, much like Plato's in *The Republic,* is attentive to the entire education of the citizen; everything from diet to parenting to sexuality is important in the constitution of the citizen. Rousseau's recognition of the mutability of nature, that one can "substitute a moral and partial existence" for a "physical and independent one," is a radical articulation of a thesis of social construction. Rousseau wants to socialize a "nature" that will contribute to the maintenance of his ideal republic.

Thus, Julie strives to transform each individual into part of a much greater whole. During the last days before her death, she continues to etch

23. "Of the Division of the Laws," *Social Contract,* 49.

24. "Of the Legislator," *Social Contract,* 36.

in the hearts of her kin, her future citizens, her hopes for the community. She has separate conversations with each family member about how she hopes each will continue her work into the future: "I will remain with you: in leaving you thus united, my heart, my soul, will still reside among you; you will see me continually among you; you will perceive me perpetually near you" (*Eloisa*, 4:252). Moreover, her death serves as the authority for her community; it justifies her "authority which is not an authority."[25] She borrows legitimacy from death.[26] Her staging of her own death helps to guarantee the community she has established. She spends her last days dining and drinking with her friends, giving instructions for the education of her children and debating with her pastor. She is trying to forge the sentimental bonds that will keep the members of her family/community together. She is articulating female *virtù*—that is, creating in others through her own performance the feelings that will secure the community.

Nonetheless, what is most revealing of Rousseau's trepidation about the possibility of securing this ideal community is his account of Julie's "second death." When Julie's father's servant arrives after her death, he believes her corpse looks at him and makes a signal to him with her head. He then tells everyone that Julie is not dead and "everyone easily believed what he wished might be true, and sought to give others pleasure, by countenancing the general credulity" (*Eloisa*, 4:269). Indeed, what could be a more dramatic and potent demonstration of Rousseau's fear of the power of public opinion than the immediate conversion of an entire household to a single man's testament to a dead woman's resurrection? Indeed, Wolmar, Julie's husband, asserts, "The moment of false hope, so soon and so cruelly extinguished was the most afflicting of my whole life" (*Eloisa*, 267). Somehow the imaginary "second death" was more affecting than the real death; even Wolmar was initially imbued with hope, despite the fact that he had witnessed Julie's death with his own eyes.

Wolmar, consequently, has a difficult time persuading the people of the house that Julie is *really* dead, and he thus decides to display her body for thirty-six hours so that he will not be accused as "a parricide of a husband, who had buried his wife alive." This is a typically Rousseauist response to the problem of public opinion; rather than cultivate the people's reason through dialogue, he appeals to their imagination through spectacle.

25. Ibid, 37.

26. Elisabeth Bronfen, *Over Her Dead Body: Death, Femininity and the Aesthetic* (New York: Routledge, 1992), 80.

Because Rousseau recognizes the enormous power of imagination, he seeks to regulate it through the contrivance of an orchestrated spectacle. Rather than build a fortress against imagination, Rousseau tries to conceive of a spectacle that will capture the imagination for the goals of reason. Imagination is not itself contaminated by unreasonableness for Rousseau; rather, one must learn how to use imagination for reasonable ends. In this instance, it is the display of a dead woman's body that is the ideal spectacle. Like Lucretia before her, Julie manifests her *virtù* by her ability, even in death, to make a spectacle of herself.

Wolmar finally buries Julie when the heat has begun to disfigure the corpse. Claire then covers Julie's face with a veil, which had been a gift from Saint Preux, warning: "Accursed be that sacrilegious hand which shall presume to lift up this veil! Accursed be that impious eye which shall dare to look on this disfigured face!" This action had such a profound effect on the spectators, Wolmar claims, that Julie was put into the coffin dressed as she was and immediately buried.[27]

Representations of female death, as Elisabeth Bronfen argues, refer to the absence of full meaning by signaling the presence of meaning elsewhere.[28] In this scene, the display of Julie's corpse marks again the failure of her male kin—her father, her husband, and perhaps even Saint Preux, who is alternately presented in the novel as inside and outside the patriarchal circle.[29] Julie's corpse, as spectacle, points to what is absent—male sufficiency.

Moreover, Rousseau's graphic mention that the body begins to decay and must then be buried is also a talisman of Rousseau's anxiety about the stability/reliability of spectacle in general. In her second death, "Julie" is an unstable representation; she is a spectacle designed to secure unity among

27. Earlier in the novel, Saint Preux had a dream foreshadowing Julie's death in which she is covered with his veil. Rousseau then suggests in a footnote that even this spectacle was staged by Julie herself: "Events are not always predicted because they are to happen; but they happen because they were predicted" (Part 6, Letter 11, p. 738).

28. Bronfen, *Over Her Dead Body,* 85.

29. The fact that Saint Preux is not there with Julie at her deathbed can be interpreted as an indication that Rousseau considers him one of the architects of the community who must therefore be banished. Or, his absence can be read as a sign of Rousseau's own identification with Saint Preux and his ambivalence about the role of the tutor/theorist in the new community. In the sequel to *Emile,* for example, Emile laments that his tutor deserted him and nearly charges him with the disgrace into which he and Sophie have fallen. Thus, the ambiguity at the end of *Nouvelle Héloïse* can be read as Rousseau's own unresolved determination of the role of the theorist in political communities.

the people of Clarens. But as spectacle, she also becomes the trace of what is absent, that is, a stable secured community. As a representation, she recalls what has already been lost or what perhaps never was. Like Livy's Lucretia, she is a *pharmakon*: both a poison and a cure.

Julie's decaying body also testifies to Rousseau's concern that the use of spectacle to try to guarantee meaning is itself unreliable. The spectacle is a supplement for a presence that never was and a presence that can never permanently be.[30] Julie's decaying body beneath the veil both reveals and conceals Rousseau's recognition that the "real" is itself mercurial; for Rousseau there is no lasting truth beneath the veil. Claire's prohibition against removing the veil marks Rousseau's fear that men will discover that there is nothing under the veil—and more specifically here, that there is no truth of woman. In Rousseau's gender semiotics, woman has been constructed as a spectacle for the male gaze; she has no autonomous content. Rousseau's insistence on the necessity of distance between men and women is, in part, a protection so that men will not discover that woman, like the veil, is constructed to give the illusion of truth, the feigned presence of reality. The veil, in seeming to mask a truth beneath, itself produces the effect of truth. There is a slippage here between the status of truth and the truth of woman as articulated in the staging of Julie's second death.

Finally, the staging of Julie's death further signals Rousseau's anxieties about the success of a newly founded republic dependent, more than any of the earlier versions of Lucretia's story, on femininity and feminine *virtù*. Unlike Livy's Lucretia and Machiavelli's Lucrezia, Julie is not isolated. In Rousseau's version there is a reliance on matrilineal inheritance; Julie has a female friend, Claire. In fact, Julie marks this as an "exceptional blessing. . . . I am a woman, and yet have known a true friend" (*Eloisa*, 4:247).[31] Also, as already noted, unlike the other Lucretias, Julie does not die before men

30. The staging of Julie's second death recalls Rousseau's ambivalence toward spectacles throughout his work. On the one hand, Rousseau critiques spectacles as inadequate representations: they are not the real. This is Rousseau's own rehearsal of Plato's argument. Yet, simultaneously, Rousseau recognizes the necessity of spectacle for two primary reasons: (1) spectacles have unique access to the imagination, which is the most potent threat to community unity; and (2) spectacles are imperative for orchestrating the appearance of the "real" in a world in which the "real" itself is unstable. The staging of Julie's second death and the burial of her decaying corpse demonstrates both Rousseau's anxiety that the spectacle is not the real (Julie's body begins to decay) and his reliance on spectacle to persuade the imagination (the community is only dissuaded from its belief that Julie is still alive by another spectacle—the display of Julie's corpse).

31. The "and yet have known a friend" suggests the structural exceptionalism of the friendship between Claire and Julie in Rousseau's gender economy.

but in Claire's arms. Wolmar describes the scene to Saint Preux: "I was alarmed at a low, indistinct noise that seemed to come from Julie's room. I listened, and thought I could distinguish the groans of a person in extremity. I ran into the room, threw open the curtain, and there—St. Preux! there I saw them both, those amiable friends, motionless, locked in each other's embrace, the one fainted away, and the other expiring. I cried out, and hastened to prevent or to receive her last sigh: but it was too late! Julie was no more!" (*Eloisa*, 4:264).

Several nights before her death, Julie had invited Claire to stay in her bed so that Claire would not have to worry about her during the night. Yet as Wolmar describes it, "For my part, they turned me out of the room." When he arises early the next morning, "being anxious what might have passed in the night," he finds Julie more animated than the night before, "having borrowed the vivacity of her cousin . . . something had given her a *secret joy* which contributed to it [her appearance] not a little; but of which I could not discover the cause" (*Eloisa*, 4:221).[32]

After this night, Julie designates Claire as her children's mother. She even brings the children into her bedroom for this introduction, announcing to her rather bewildered progeny, "Go, my children, go and throw yourselves at the feet of your mother; this is she whom Providence has given you, depriving you of nothing in taking me." The children take Claire's hand and call her "their good mamma, their second mother" (*Eloisa*, 4:224). Is it unreasonable to suggest that metaphorically Claire and Julie's night together seems to have generated children of whom they agree to share parentage? This scene of matrilineage captures in rather amusing fashion both Rousseau's hope that Claire will fill Julie's role and his patriarchal fear that women do not need men. Despite his insistence that women do not have the generative power of imagination and thus the possibility of autonomous female desire, this vignette seems to suggest otherwise.[33]

32. Emphasis mine. Again, this scene seems to testify to Julie's role as founder rather than Wolmar's. She is clearly the affectionate favorite of *Nouvelle Héloïse*. Wolmar is still seen here as representing the patriarchal and aristocratic order that Rousseau's republic would overcome. For example, it is Wolmar as father-figure (just as it is Julie's father early in *Nouvelle Héloïse* and Lucrèce's father in "La Mort de Lucrèce") who thwarts the young lovers.

This scene is also one of several places where Wolmar is made to look rather foolish. He seems not to understand what is happening, nor is he able to direct the course of events. Finally, the people of Clarens are clearly attached to Julie, so much so that they eagerly hope for her resurrection from the dead, whereas Wolmar worries that he will be accused as a "parricide of a husband, who had buried his wife alive" if he should bury her too quickly.

33. There is much here that parallels Machiavelli's own ambivalence about the role of Fortuna.

What does this "apparitional lesbianism"[34] signal in Rousseau's founding narrative? Most obviously, it marks the fear Western civilization has had for centuries of "women without men"—that is, of women indifferent to male desire. For Rousseau this anxiety is particularly acute. Because his formulation of heterosexuality is about the fulfillment of male desire, which women simply mirror and satisfy, there is no possibility of independent female desire in Rousseau's gender economy (see the following section). In Luce Irigaray's terms, there is no sexual relation, only man's self-affection mediated by the feminine.[35] Women no longer relate to each other except in terms of what they represent of men's desire.

Female homosexuality is quite disruptive to the stability of Rousseau's ideal domestic order. Claire represents not only the refusal of heterosexuality but also the disruption of domestic tranquility. Indeed, she writes to her new fiancé early in *Nouvelle Héloïse*: "When I tell you that my Julie is dearer to me than you, you only laugh, and yet nothing is more true. Julie knows it so well that she is more jealous in your place than you are" (*Eloisa* 1:299). Here the affection between Claire and Julie threatens the newly formed bonds between a man and a woman. Nonetheless, Rousseau's gender semiotics require that Claire identify closely with Julie as the lineage of inheritance for the community, "Clarens," suggests. Julie even goes so far as to suggest that Claire should marry Saint Preux. Thus, Julie tries to inscribe in Claire's heart the morals and manners necessary for the maintenance of the community—among them heterosexuality. After Julie's death, Claire must maintain the *virtù* of femininity in the community. She must assume her role as supplement to male desire, crafting herself as a spectacle without content that satisfies and yet forestalls the extravagance of male narcissism and mediates the failure of male self-transparency (see the following section).

Like the pregnant Lucrezia at the end of *La Mandragola*, the role of Claire testifies to the importance of femininity in the maintenance of Clarens. Julie's death is not sufficient guarantee for men's already flawed masculinity. The "secret" relationship between Julie and Claire, of which Wolmar cannot discover the cause, resonates with Rousseau's insistence that women's power must be covert in order to remain potent. None of the male members of the community are privy to the conversations between

34. Terry Castle's phrase from her book of that title, *The Apparitional Lesbian: Female Homosexuality and Modern Culture* (New York: Columbia University Press, 1993).

35. Luce Irigaray, *The Sex Which Is Not One*, trans. Catherine Porter (Ithaca: Cornell University Press, 1985).

Julie and Claire. So while Julie is presumed to be "recruiting" Claire to heterosexuality, the ghost of lesbianism, of autonomous female desire, haunts Rousseau's political imagination. This anxiety is signaled, in part, by Claire's recalcitrance after Julie's death. She remains the community's most disruptive member. Not only does she refuse to consider marrying Saint Preux, but she also is loathe to love the child she considers responsible for Julie's death.

In his attempt to ameliorate Claire's grief, Wolmar mistakenly resorts to solace through staged imitations; he orders his young daughter, Harriet, to be dressed "as much in imitation of Julie as possible." Although this initially mollifies Claire's distress, it propels her to gluttony and sickness, and Wolmar finally decides "not to try any more projects of this kind as they might affect her *imagination* too much. Sorrow is more easily cured than madness" (*Eloisa*, 4:275; emphasis mine). Thus, in this scene is evident the mistakes men make in appealing to appearances, but also tellingly the power of spectacle and the resulting danger of autonomous female desire—imagination. Indeed, the lesbian is the only woman to whom Rousseau attributes the powers of imagination.[36] Because there is no place in Clarens for autonomous female desire, it must appear as if heterosexuality is imperative for women's "sanity." In some ways, Claire's insanity is a warning to women who do not willingly assume their idealized role as simply supplements to men. That is, through the character of Claire, Rousseau foretells the misery of women who resist their position in his idealized economy of heterosexuality.

II. On Maintaining the Republic

A. Integrating Difference into the Political Community

As just elaborated through the analysis of Julie's death, what most threatens the newly founded republic is narcissism (*amour-propre*) and the empire of public opinion. The dilemma with which Rousseau is confronted is twofold. First, each problem grows out of a "natural" condition. For example, *amour-propre* is a perversion of *amour de soi* (self-love): "Love of oneself is a natural sentiment which inclines every animal to watch over its own preservation, and which, directed in man by reason and modified by pity, produces humanity and virtue" (*Second Discourse*, 222). *Amour-propre* is an

36. See *Letter to D'Alembert*, in which Rousseau insists that women have no imagination.

artificial sentiment, born in society, that inspires each individual to have greater esteem for himself than for anyone else.

The second part of the dilemma is that it is ostensibly to Nature that Rousseau would like to return to resolve the dilemma. Rousseau's quandary, then, becomes how to forestall this corruption into narcissism and into what is profoundly related, the empire of public opinion, but without the possibility of a pristine Nature to which to return.

Other readers of Rousseau have suggested that Rousseau's solution, as a theorist of transparency, is to attempt to eliminate the very obstacle of difference—the other itself. Starobinski has done the most extensive work on this theme:

> What Rousseau is looking for, and what he will never find, is a state of universal Sameness. . . . But since Sameness can only be defined in terms of Self, freedom for Rousseau is above all freedom from Otherness. The only escape is either to make one's own Sameness function as a transcendent absolute, thus eliminating all obstructions by making the world a transparent extension of the self, or to refuse any encounter with the Other by declaring all that is different to be an insurmountable obstacle and withdrawing in alienation from the world.[37]

Nonetheless, despite Starobinski's compelling argument, rather than trying to eliminate difference per se, Rousseau actually reformulates difference in the form of the ideal woman. His conception of politics is dependent on the maintenance of a particular kind of difference—a difference that Derrida calls "the supplement."[38] This supplement, the ideal woman, not only compensates for the failure of Nature while seeming to mimic it, but the femininity of this supplement is integral to Rousseau's conception of politics and political life.

* * *

Rousseau's critique of difference rests in part on his conception of *amour-propre*. With the "discovery" of difference comes the onset of comparison, of jealous rivalries, and of judgments of merit and worth. One compares

37. Jean Starobinski, *Jean Jacques Rousseau: Transparency and Obstruction,* trans. Arthur Goldhammer (Chicago: University of Chicago Press, 1988), xxii.

38. Jacques Derrida, *Of Grammatology,* trans. Gayatri Spivak (Baltimore: Johns Hopkins University Press, 1974).

oneself to another and strives ceaselessly to *appear* different than what one is. The opinion of others based on that appearance becomes more important than who one actually is. Consequently, there is an estrangement from oneself as that self is mediated through its objectification by and for others. Narcissism, thus, inaugurates man's opacity to himself. Rather than regarding himself as the sole spectator to himself, he now regards others as his primary audience. In his quest to have others love him as he loves himself, he allows their idea of him to mediate his view of himself; thus he loses his own self-transparency.

What concerns Rousseau is not only this self-estrangement but also the dependence on others that the concern with others' opinions implies. Men no longer evaluate circumstances, events or people for themselves. Opinions are solidified and seemingly orchestrated by elusive "opinion makers." Although one could argue that these "opinion makers" are the phantasmagoria of Rousseau's paranoia, there is another plausible explanation for Rousseau's critique.

For Rousseau, "public opinion" in the mid-eighteenth century was pernicious, domineering and monolithic. Unlike contemporary thinkers rereading the eighteenth century, such as Jürgen Habermas, who now laud public opinion as the result of "critical public debate" in which there was "the public competition of private arguments as the basis of a consensus over that which was necessary for the general good,"[39] Rousseau worried that the process of public opinion was itself congealed. Rousseau asserts that public opinion becomes a verdict that cannot be violated, that it represents an ideology without politics. Public opinion assumes a kind of authority that cannot be transgressed. And of course, Rousseau feels himself the quintessential victim of its tyranny. In the *Dialogues*, the character "Jean Jacques" argues at length with "Frenchman" about the dangers of treating "Rousseau" with contempt for crimes for which he has not been formally tried and convicted: "Not to dare subject them to the proof that would confirm them makes me presume they would not stand up to that proof. This great principle, the basis and sanction of all justice without which human society would crumble at its foundations, is so sacred, so inviolable in practice, that if everyone in town had seen one man murder another in the public square, the murderer would still not be punished

39. Jürgen Habermas, *The Structural Transformation of the Public Sphere: An Inquiry into a Category of Bourgeois Society*, trans. Thomas Burger (Cambridge: MIT Press, 1989), 105.

without having a hearing first."[40] Rousseau is acutely aware of the way in which public opinion, arrived at through the seemingly democratic process of a contestation of ideas, subsequently assumes a life of its own that cannot be breached; the product of such a debate—dubbed public opinion—assumes an existence independent of those who crafted it.

So, while Rousseau despairs over the obstacles the difference of the other poses, he also simultaneously wants to inaugurate a process that will maintain a certain kind of difference; that is, he wants to minimize one's dependence on the other for self-knowledge without necessarily eliminating that difference or that other. For example, Rousseau argues that if differences are diminished through cabals and associations, the general will itself becomes less general: "The differences being less numerous, they produce a result less general. Finally, when one of these associations becomes so large that it prevails over all the rest, you have no longer the sum of many opinions dissenting in a small degree from each other, but one great dictating dissentient."[41] Consequently, "every citizen should speak his opinion entirely from himself."[42]

Granted, Rousseau does not herald "differences" as John Stuart Mill eventually will for the sake of diversity or because we can learn and benefit from each other's differences. Rather, with his formulation of the general will, Rousseau is trying to avoid the tyranny of the other. His invention of the general will strives to maintain the unity secured by the "empire of public opinion" but without the resulting loss of individual autonomy. What Rousseau attempts to craft is a "public opinion" (i.e., the general will) without either the process of debate or the ossification that process usually entails. The result is a private, political man: "If, when the people sufficiently informed, deliberated, *there was to be no communication among them,* from the grand total of trifling differences the general will would always result and their resolutions always be good."[43] This is Rousseau's asocial political

40. *Rousseau, Judge of Jean-Jacques: Dialogues,* ed. and trans. Judith Bush, Roger D. Masters, and Christopher Kelly (Hanover: University Press of New England, 1990), 1:155. Although I am suspicious of readings of Rousseau that trace a linear trajectory from his work to the French Revolution and the Jacobean Terror, I do think that my reading here of Rousseau's conception of public opinion suggests that the "authoritarian" trajectory from Rousseau to the Terror may not be as straight as some have supposed. In fact, one could argue quite easily that Rousseau's work strives to deflect just such a path.

41. "Whether the General Will Can Err," *Social Contract,* 26.

42. Ibid., 27.

43. Ibid., 26; emphasis mine.

collectivity. It is a way of being common without being political. There is no agora or public forum for the open exchange of ideas. For Rousseau those exchanges are so dangerous, so apt to lead to the "empire of opinion," that he is willing to forgo all social intercourse in the political process. Here, paradoxically, the more "individual" one is, the more "general" is the resulting political will. Thus, it is not surprising that the private sphere is idealized for Rousseau not simply as a retreat from the world of politics but as a haven *for* politics.

While other readers of Rousseau have argued that by confining women to the private sphere Rousseau is creating either a refugee from politics[44] or a complement to politics,[45] the relation Rousseau actually conceives between men and women is integral to politics. Neither a refugee from, nor an aside to politics, sexual difference is instead a haven for politics; the private sphere not only mimics the political relations Rousseau postulates for the public sphere, but the relation between men and women is foundational to Rousseauist politics. Women fulfill two vital functions for politics: (1) they rescue men from narcissism, and (2) they forestall the contagion of public opinion. At the moment when men are becoming totally self-absorbed, woman is invented. For example, when the threat of masturbation looms, the tutor begins the search for Sophie, the ideal woman. And secondly, women disrupt public opinion because they fulfill man's desire to be loved by others in the same way he loves himself. This is possible because in Rousseau's gender semiotics the ideal woman is granted no autonomous desire. She is a mirror without a reciprocal gaze.

The world of domesticity is a place where man can be political without the dangers Rousseau attributes to politics in the public sphere. The domain of women is not one without politics; rather it is a world that enables and preserves Rousseau's asocial formulation of politics. Indeed, it is a world constructed largely to solve the problem(s) of politics.

In important ways, the relationship between men and women is the kind of difference with which Rousseau is the most comfortable. It is a difference that first prevents man's *amour-propre* from becoming consuming,

44. Judith Shklar, *Men and Citizens: A Study of Rousseau's Social Theory* (Cambridge: Cambridge University Press, 1969).

45. See Joan Landes, *Women and the Public Sphere in the Age of the French Revolution* (Ithaca: Cornell University Press, 1988), or Joel Schwartz, *The Sexual Politics of Jean Jacques Rousseau* (Chicago: University of Chicago Press, 1984).

and second, it supplements what completely autonomous man lacks but without his conscious recognition of that insufficiency. The general will fulfills a similar function to the supplementarity of women: it thwarts the *amour-propre* of the citizen (i.e., his particular interests) *and* fills the gap left by a fully autonomous citizen (i.e., his motivation for community and for unity and harmony).

The general will, as Rousseau conceives it, is not arrived at through the lively contestation and discussion of political issues. Rather, what Rousseau wants is a way to act for the public interest by simply consulting oneself.[46] This Rousseau proposes doing by asking each citizen to answer the right question. Rousseau believes citizens neglect the general will often because they have asked themselves the wrong question; instead of asking what is good for the whole, they have asked some permutation of what is good for themselves or their particular faction. However, Rousseau still allows that even when one has tried to answer the right question, one may still be mistaken. But this, he insists, is the beauty of the general will; even when one is mistaken as to what the general will is, the majority will necessarily answer the question correctly, and one will not be forced, unwittingly, to do what is actually against the state's (and thus one's own) best interests. This is an element of Rousseau's conception of being compelled to be free.

Nonetheless, the differences that Rousseau cultivates and jealously guards among men necessitate the *art* of politics: "If there were no different interests, we should scarcely perceive the common interest, which never finds any opposer; everything would go on regularly of itself, and politics be no longer an art."[47] And it is this necessity for art that haunts Rousseau's political philosophy. It is also what makes him insist that women too are by "nature" creatures of artifice.

Rousseau strives to address this need for art, first, with an argument, as noted earlier, in which citizens are crafted to fit the law, rather than the other way around. From his early *Discourse on Political Economy* to his later essay on Corsica, Rousseau urges political leaders to "create men so that they may command them." Rousseau has faith in the citizens primarily because they will be handcrafted: "If it is good to know how to deal with men as they are, it is much better to make them what there is need that

46. And what woman provides in this context is an "other," who when consulted is found to be the "same."

47. "Whether the General Will Can Err," *Social Contract*, 26; Rousseau's note 2.

they should be. The most absolute authority is that which penetrates into man's inmost being.... Make man, therefore, if you would command men."[48]

These are not natural men coming to the public sphere; rather they are creatures denatured and transformed from the republic's inception: "Those who dare to undertake the institution of a people must feel themselves capable, as it were, of changing human nature."[49] Indeed, from the moment of the social compact, man's nature is shown to be impaired. Early in *The Social Contract,* Rousseau asserts that the purpose of the contract is to guarantee that each man shall "obey only himself and remain as free as before."[50] The difficulty, of course, is that it is a *crisis* that is the catalyst for the contract: "Men in the state of nature are arrived at that crisis when the strength of each individual is insufficient to overcome the resistance of the obstacles to this preservation."[51] What does it mean to be as "free as before" if it is a crisis that inaugurates the social contract? Here, the state of nature is shown to be imperfect; the social contract is meant to be a substitute that is more natural than nature but without the flaws of nature: "The fundamental compact substitutes, on the contrary, a moral and legal equality for the physical inequality which nature placed among men."[52]

Yet, even as the social contract is a supplement to nature, the flaws remain. The general will is itself not a natural manifestation but rather the result of political art and artifice. Ideally, the general will (which predates the legislator) artificially returns man to his *amour de soi,* which he has lost through its corruption by *amour-propre.* The general will is independent of natural man, yet it is what will return him to his nature. Nonetheless, the dilemma remains that it is this "nature" that initially created the crisis that necessitated convention.

In his essay, "Postal Politics and the Institution of the Nation," Geoffrey Bennington conceives of the general will as the sending of a letter by the citizen as member of the sovereign to that same citizen as subject.[53] There is thus complete transparency between the sovereign and

48. *A Discourse on Political Economy,* trans. G. D. H. Cole (Chicago: William Benton Publisher, 1952), 372.

49. "Of the Legislator," *Social Contract,* 36.

50. "Of the Social Compact," *Social Contract,* 15.

51. Ibid., 14.

52. "Of Real Property," *Social Contract,* 22.

53. Geoffrey Bennington, "Postal Politics and the Institution of the Nation," *Nation and Narration,* ed. Homi K. Bhabha (New York: Routledge, 1990), 129.

the citizen. The citizen sends himself the law, and in this sending names himself as citizen; this structure is, more generally, Rousseau's ideal of autonomy.

Rousseau's anxiety, however, is that the letter may not always reach its destination. "Politics" is thus the name for the possibility of the failure of autonomy to close this circuit.[54] In other words, if the letter always reached its destination (always being in fact returned to its sender), there would be no need for it to be sent, for it would have always already arrived. Rousseau notes this when he asserts, "A people who never abused the powers of government would never abuse independence; a people who always governed well would have no need to be governed."[55]

The possibility of the failure of the circuit opens the space for politics and suggests, again, the reason why full autonomy can never be achieved. This failure is the ground of differentiation that allows for the fact that "citizens are always in fact bearers of so-called proper names, and are not just isomorphic points."[56] That is, citizens are differentiated with autonomous private wills, not mere place holders in a political forum.

Thus, Rousseau installs the legislator in order to try to guarantee that the general will will always be right. The legislator becomes a "natural" necessity of man's flawed nature, while government, after the death of the legislator, maintains "the link between the people and the sovereign."[57] Again, the very fact that a link is now required contrasts with Rousseau's initial insistence that the relation between the sovereign and the citizen was transparent and would be violated by any mediation.

While other thinkers of the Enlightenment (e.g., Locke) have faith in individuals, Rousseau does not conceive of politics as the aggregate of individual wills. Rather, politics is a supplement to a failed human nature. Rousseau's political formulation is searching in some peculiar way for a guarantee from the necessity of politics; his formulation of the general will is an attempt to safeguard against the contingencies on which Machiavellian politics thrives.[58] The general will is Rousseau's *virtù*, and judgment his

54. Ibid.

55. "Of Democracy," *Social Contract*, 59.

56. Bennington, "Postal Politics," 129.

57. "Of Government in General," *Social Contract*, 54.

58. For Rousseau *virtù* is a sentiment rather than a quality for action. Unlike Machiavelli, Rousseau is less willing to accommodate contingency, so he works to craft citizens once and for all, without sufficient attention to how they will accommodate changing circumstances. Rousseau spends most of his energy trying to figure out how he can forestall change rather than how he will

Fortuna. The general will has a cultivated attention to the common good, while judgment remains in the unstable realm of individual interpretation. Politics, then, is the constant negotiation between the two: "The general will is always right, but the judgment that guides it is not always enlightened."[59] Politics is a seduction, a constant and renewable performance of gaining access to the general will. The general will is a beacon—unchanging, absolute; politics is the messy interrogation and transformation of the self in order to gain access to it.[60] Politics, like the general will, is a compensatory tool for what ought to lack nothing—man's self-transparency.

There is a striking parallel here between the truth-telling of the Fourth Walk in *The Reveries of a Solitary Walker* and Rousseau's formulation of politics. The problem of politics, like the problem of truth-telling, seems to revolve around the complicated Delphic maxim, "Know Thyself"; politics, in part, is about securing the identity of the self—a self that is not natural nor completely mimetic of the law but is liable to culture, particularly in the form of the opinions of others. Rousseau thus tries first to construct a stable self (hence his reliance on the law to craft the citizens) but then recognizes the impossibility of this kind of fixity and the threat its success would pose to the differences necessary for politics; and thus, secondarily, he tries to regulate and channel these contingencies through spectacles.

With truth-telling what is of central concern is one's motivations, although consistently those elude even the self. And in politics there is a similar concern with knowing the self, although here what disrupts the possibility of self-transparency is *amour-propre* and the empire of public opinion. So, although the citizen Rousseau imagines is fabricated to correspond to the contrived and manufactured truth of the general will, danger remains in the form of imagination, which could derail one from the preordained telos. Imagination, enflamed by public opinion, is the catalyst for the corruption of *amour de soi.* Imagination remains outside Rousseau's pedagogical reach and is thus a primary source of disruption. Although he

---

cope with it. Although in his practical treatises (e.g., *Government of Poland*) Rousseau is much closer to Machiavelli in terms of recognizing the need to respond to what is, he still consistently resists the possibility that politics may require continual refashioning of citizens and the general will. Rousseau will permit one initial crafting of the ideal citizen by the founder, but he is profoundly uneasy with Machiavelli's continual adjustments.

59. "Of the Legislator," *Social Contract,* 35.

60. In contrast, consider Hobbes, for whom the contract will not change human nature but only control it. For Rousseau, on the other hand, the social contract is an act of transformation.

can attempt to fashion citizens to the law, he cannot control their private imaginations: "The real world has its limits; the imaginary world is infinite. Unable to enlarge the one, let us restrict the other, for it is from the difference between the two alone that are born all the pains which make us truly unhappy" (*Emile,* 81). This unlimitability of imagination, like Machiavelli's Fortuna, has the power to enflame our desires but not to satisfy them. For Rousseau the infinite is not to be found in the universe but in ourselves. Again, it is our own human capacities that are the source of misery.

As a solution, Rousseau turns to spectacles, which offer the possibility for public reflectiveness without debate. "Good spectacles" offer the potential for reciprocity without contestation. They are an instrument through which Rousseau hopes unity can be maintained. Because of their unique access to imagination, Rousseau concedes to the need for spectacles: "The impression of the word is always weak, and one speaks to the heart far better through the eyes than through the ears" (*Emile,* 321), and again, "The object that is exhibited to the eyes shakes the imagination, arouses curiosity, keeps the mind attentive to what is going to be said" (*Emile,* 322).

Much as Machiavelli laments the effeminacy of Christian rituals as compared with pagan ones, so Rousseau mourns the loss of powerful symbols and their power to inspire: "The august display of royal power impressed the subjects. Marks of dignity—a throne, a scepter, a purple robe, a crown, a diadem—were sacred things for them. These respected signs made the man who was thus adorned venerable to them." He goes on to praise the Romans for whom "everything . . . was display, show, ceremony, and everything made an impression on the hearts of the citizens" (*Emile,* 322). In fact, Rousseau even asserts that one of the most esteemed people in contemporary society is a man in drag (or, at least, partial drag): "Apart from the Pope adorned with his tiara, there can be neither king nor potentate nor man in the world so respected as the Doge of Venice—without power, without authority, but *rendered sacred by his pomp and dressed up in a woman's hairdo under his ducal bonnet*" (*Emile,* 322).

Here is one of Rousseau's most obvious articulations of the links among femininity, spectacle and power. Apparently, part of the Doge's power is derived from his public donning of the artificiality of woman (his woman's hairdo). Rather than making him effeminate, his knowledge of how to make an effective spectacle of himself adds to his authority. It is thus to women as spectacles that Rousseau turns as he seeks to secure his politics. As spectacle, Rousseau's ideal woman seeks to solve the problem of difference and to offer a way to have politics without debilitating dependence.

B. Woman as Supplement: Femininity, Spectacles, and Imagination

With the necessary death of the legislator, who combines the power of both the sovereign and the legislator, is born politics, or what Rousseau calls *government.* Government now mediates between the once transparent relation between the sovereign and the citizen. Government is not the sovereign but the minister to it; yet the fact that the sovereign now needs a minister again signals its flawed nature. Government, then, is itself a supplement to the relation between citizen and sovereign.

By government, Rousseau means everything from the tribuneship, the dictatorship, and the censorship to civil religion. Indeed, the last twenty pages of *The Social Contract* read as if they are the exhausted effusions of a man who realizes his project is coming unraveled and is seeking to secure it with threadbare yarn when what he needs are steel girders. Just before the final book of *The Social Contract,* in a chapter that parallels Book 9 of Plato's *Republic,* Rousseau, like Plato, foretells the "death of the body politic": "The body politic, as well as the human body, begins to die from its birth, and bears within itself the causes of its destruction. . . . The constitution of man is the work of nature; that of the State is the product of art."[61]

Each of the subsequent short, almost aphoristic chapters proposes a way to secure the transparency of the citizen/sovereign and to forestall this dissolution, yet each solution itself raises the specter of the problem it seeks to resolve—the resurgence of private interest over the general will: "Just as the private will continually acts against the general will, so the government makes an unremitted effort against the Sovereign. . . . This innate and inevitable vice tends, from the birth of the body politic, to destroy it, as old age and death do in the human frame."[62]

Each of Rousseau's supplements suggests the failure of the general will (e.g., the tribuneship that prevents mistaken laws, the dictatorship that in emergencies replaces the general will). Each marks the general will as already inadequate to its task. Indeed, Rousseau's argument for the necessity of civil religion seems almost to disregard the general will altogether:

61. "The Death of the Body Politic," *Social Contract,* 79.
62. "Of the Abuse of Government and Its Propensity to Degenerate," *Social Contract,* 76.

"It is of consequence to the State that each of its citizens should have a religion which will dispose him to love his duties. . . . There is therefore a purely civil profession of faith, the articles of which it is the business of the Sovereign to arrange, not precisely as dogmas of religion, but as sentiments of sociability *without which it is impossible to be either a good citizen or a faithful subject*."[63]

It is striking that by the end of *The Social Contract* Rousseau is adamant that *without* the artifice of civil religion, community is quite impossible. In fact, he proclaims that anyone who initially adheres to the dogmas of a specific civil religion and then chooses to disregard them should be put to death: "For he has committed the greatest of all crimes: he has lied in the face of the law."[64] It is alarming that a thinker who has so persuasively elaborated the danger of public opinion ends by seeking security (in his panic) in a nondialogic subscription to the law.

Nonetheless, this is not Rousseau's last resolution to the difficulty of community in the face of the resurgence of the private interest/*amour-propre*. He develops another alternative in his formulation of woman and femininity.[65] In other words, Rousseau's ideal woman,[66] like the social contract, and like the general will and civil religion, is invented at the moment when Nature has failed. Just as the general will is an abstract idea—a conception of unity that does not exist among men—so "woman" is an idea designed to secure community. Like the general will, she is meant to guarantee what men seem repeatedly unable to secure for themselves—unity.

In order to fulfill this function, Rousseau's ideal woman is emptied of any independent subjectivity. Crafted as "sameness," she reflects only the needs and demands of men, while nonetheless skillfully masquerading as difference. As supplement, "woman" is the image and representation of man's self-presence. That is, as the spectacle of difference, she supplements male insufficiency and forestalls the desire for the reinscription of either narcissism (i.e., masturbation) or the empire of public opinion (i.e., tyranny).

Nonetheless, as Jacques Derrida notes, supplements are always

63. "Of Civil Religion," *Social Contract*, 23–24; emphasis mine.

64. Ibid.

65. It is noteworthy that Rousseau is believed to have been writing *The Social Contract* and *Emile* concurrently.

66. Here I am referring to the "civilized" woman of *Nouvelle Héloïse* and *Emile*, not to the largely ungendered female of *The Second Discourse*.

dangerous, in part, because they call attention to the deficiency and infirmity of that which they supplement.[67] The supplement further runs the risk of making one forget the vicariousness of its own function, and thus itself mistakenly passing for the plentitude of that which it only supplements. Thus, we witness Rousseau's fear that women may actually be the strong, while they were intended only to supplement the strong.

Rousseau's ideal women are both the product of imagination, having been conjured by imagination, *and* as spectacles, are designed to regulate imagination. Indeed, for Rousseau, woman is primarily invoked through imagination rather than through the body. He even insists that desire is not a matter of the body but rather of imagination. Consider, for example, Saint Preux's sexual frenzy precipitated simply by the inflammation of his imagination while in Julie's room. Upon entering the room, he exclaims, "I am in the sanctuary of all my heart adores." And what he adores and what arouses him in Julie's absence are the very artifices she uses to fan his imagination—her perfume; "the scattered parts of [her] dress present to my ardent imagination those of [her] body that they conceal"; her "headdress which sets off the large blond curls it *pretends* to cover," her corset, including the whalebone, "oh voluptuous sight!" (*Eloisa,* 1:243). Thus for Rousseau imagination, not the body, can also be the primary antagonist.[68] In fact, in several instances it is the body that protects and preserves the self from the vagaries of imagination. For example, while the imagination is the catalyst for masturbation, physical activity can constrain the danger: "It is by exercising his body with hard labor that I restrain the activity of imagination that is carrying him away. When the arms work hard, the imagination rests" (*Emile,* 320).

In a parallel vein, Rousseau seeks to replace woman's very materiality with men's created representations. Just as Brutus in Livy's story of the rape of Lucretia tries to replace a real woman with a representation by substituting Mother Earth for his own mother, so Rousseau tries to replace "real women" with more compliant imaginary models. For example, Sophie is an idea for Emile long before she is a corporeality. In fact, the idea of Sophie is in many respects more important than her materiality. She must

67. Derrida, *Of Grammatology,* 144.

68. Consider further the example Rousseau gives in *Letter to D'Alembert* of the naked dancing of Spartan women: "It is the *imagination* which scandalizes the eye in revealing to it what it sees not only as naked but as something that ought to be concealed" (243; emphasis mine). Apparently, it is not the body itself that ignites desire but one's imagining that it ought to be dressed.

correspond to the idea Emile has of her rather than vice versa: "It is unimportant whether the object I depict for him is imaginary; it suffices that it make him disgusted with those that could tempt him. . . . And what is true love itself if it is not chimera, lie and illusion? We love the image we make for ourselves far more than we love the object to which we apply it. If we saw what we love exactly as it is, there would be no more love in the world" (*Emile,* 329). The purpose of this imaginary model is to attach Emile to everything resembling it and to estrange him from everything not resembling it. Rousseau wants the experience of the representation to replace any knowledge acquired from "real women."

Similarly, Rousseau's citizen is himself conjured through imagination: "The moral person which constitutes the State [is] a creature of the imagination, because it is not a man, he may wish to enjoy the rights of a citizen without being disposed to fulfill the duties of a subject."[69] Here, however, Rousseau grants to the moral person a measure of autonomy denied to his ideal women. While the moral person of the state may still maintain some subjectivity independent of the general will, Rousseau's ideal women offer no such resistance.

* * *

Because imagination is the source both of cohesion and of discord to his unified political community, Rousseau equivocates about the role of spectacles in his republic. He wants to discount all "bad" spectacles while using "good" ones to regulate the well-ordered republic.[70] His ambivalence is registered further in his conflicting evaluations of women.[71] On the one

69. "Of the Sovereign," *Social Contract,* 18.

70. Part of the difficulty of Rousseau's *Letter to D'Alembert* is its equivocation between being a critique of theatre specifically versus a critique of spectacles in general. As a critique of spectacles in general, Rousseau attempts to follow Plato's critique of imitation in *The Republic*. Nonetheless, the *Letter* finally succeeds only as a critique of the institution of theatre and of "bad spectacles," not of spectacles more generally. Indeed, Rousseau expresses his willingness to debate the effect of the *content* of plays but not the impact of the *institution* of theatre. For example, Richard Fralin notes in his book, *Rousseau and Representation: A Study of the Development of His Concept of Political Institutions* (New York: Columbia University Press, 1978), that Rousseau's critique of the institution of theatre stemmed, in part, from his belief that the aristocracy advocated theatre as a way to turn the people away from critique of the government. In other words, Rousseau is only opposed to theatre, not to spectacles more generally, as his praise and advocacy (even in the *Letter to D'Alembert*) for festivals, dances and so forth suggests.

71. This distinction between "good" and "bad" spectacles, like the distinction between good and bad women, means, in part, that Rousseau will deploy spectacle (and women) when it serves a specific political purpose, and malign it (and them) for philosophical rather than political reasons when it threatens "justice" or "goodness." Generally, as far as Rousseau can determine,

hand, Rousseau's ideal woman is the perfect spectacle, fashioned to be looked at without a dangerous reciprocal gaze. On the other hand, like theatre, the fallen woman hastens the demise of the republic.

In *The Letter to D'Alembert* Rousseau equates the rise of theatre with the corruption of women. He criticizes the theatre for further "extend[ing] the empire of the fair sex" (47). Since so many plays are about love, which is "the realm of women," the plays serve only to enlarge women's power. Nonetheless, the primary motivation for Rousseau's discomfort with women in theatre is not with their power itself, but with how public, how manifest that power is. He asserts: "The ancients had, in general, a very great respect for women; but they showed this respect by refraining from exposing them to public judgment, and thought to honor their modesty by keeping quiet about their other virtues" (*D'Alembert*, 48).

Keeping women's "power" covert is imperative for men's potency. It is not so much that Rousseau wants to deny women's power as that he wants to disguise men's lack of power. For example, in the *Letter to D'Alembert* Rousseau applauds the exile of Manilius for kissing his wife in front of his daughter. For Rousseau, Manilius's kiss exposes male vulnerability and thus endangers his authority. Since love is about seduction, "however love is depicted, it seduces or it is not love" (*D'Alembert*, 55). When Manilius kisses his wife he is displaying his seduction by a woman, jeopardizing his supremacy and inadvertently risking the inflammation of his daughter's desires.

A woman's goodness, like a spectacle, is secured by her being seen to be good. A bad woman is not one who has fallen from her nature but one who does not know how to make a spectacle of herself. Consider Rousseau's attempt in the *Letter to D'Alembert* to establish women's goodness as "natural": "Is it not nature which adorns young women with those features so sweet and which a little shame renders even more touching? Is it not nature which puts the timid and tender glance in their eyes which is resisted with such difficulty? Is it not nature which gives their complexion more lustre and their skin more delicacy so that a modest blush can be better provided?" (*D'Alembert*, 87). Yet, Rousseau's use of the interrogative suggests his uncertainty. Indeed, he immediately asserts that even without

---

theatre serves no good purpose in a good town such as Geneva, although as he notes in the Second Preface to *Nouvelle Héloïse*, public theatres are necessary in corrupt times, much as femininity in the form of the ideal woman is necessary when men's nature has failed.

nature what guarantees women's goodness is the sight of them in their "natural" occupations: "Even if it could be denied that a special sentiment of chasteness was natural to women, would it be any less true that in society their lot *ought* to be a domestic and retired life, and that they *ought* to be raised in principles appropriate to it? Is there a *sight* in the world so touching, so respectable, as that of a mother surrounded by her children, directing the work of her domestics, procuring a happy life for her husband and prudently governing the home?" (*D'Alembert,* 87).

Here it is the *sight* of a woman in her domesticity that helps to guarantee what she *ought* to be. Seeing women fulfilling their role validates its naturalness; in this instance, the spectacle of woman serves to maintain the "natural order." Like Lucretia being found at her spinning while her compatriots are cavorting in luxury, Rousseau's virtuous women, as "good spectacles," counter and replace the lure of "bad spectacles." That is, the virtuous woman, unlike contemporary theatre, "moderates rather than promotes men's penchants" (*D'Alembert,* 17).

The ideal woman is also an antidote to the isolation of the theatre: "The social relationship of the sexes is an admirable thing. This partnership produces a moral person of which the woman is the eye and the man is the arm, but they have such a dependence on one another that the woman learns from the man what must be seen and the man learns from the woman what must be done" (*Emile,* 377). Oddly, here woman is both the spectacle and the eye—both the object of the gaze and that which looks. Joined with her, man becomes one moral person, no longer isolated but not exactly dependent. "The woman learns from the man what must be seen," and then creates it in herself as spectacle. Rousseau's women create themselves as spectacles in order to give back to man what he needs. They are men's needs masquerading as difference. And "man learns from the woman what must be done," which is, again, only her re-presentation of what he wants.

As an ideal, woman is constructed to be looked at, and as spectacle she represents not simply a collection of images but the social relation between men and women:

> By the very law of nature women are at the mercy of men's judgments. . . . It is not enough that they be estimable, they must be esteemed. It is not enough for them to be pretty, they must please. It is not enough for them to be temperate; they must be recognized as

> such. Their honor is not only in their conduct but in their reputation.... When a man acts well, he depends only on himself and can brave public judgment; but when a woman acts well, she has accomplished only half of her task, and what is thought of her is no less important to her than what she actually is.... Opinion is the grave of virtue among men and its throne among women. (*Emile,* 364)

So while elsewhere Rousseau is profoundly critical of the demeaning power of the gaze, here he proposes three relations to it that are fundamentally different than elsewhere in his work: First, he begins to articulate a notion of spectacle that understands, in Machiavellian style, that in some circumstances being attentive to being looked at can be not only politically expedient but also powerful. That is, for woman being looked at is the throne of her *virtù*; her *virtù* is exemplified in her ability to create herself as spectacle. A woman's *virtù* requires being attentive to the contingency of the gaze. Only when she is looked at is her *virtù* manifest and maintained. In fact, her *virtù* demands learning how to read men and adjusting her presentation of self accordingly. This is Rousseau's reformulation of *virtù* from a martial virtue (hence, masculine) to a domestic one (thus, feminine). *Virtù,* as that which inaugurates politics, is now ascribed to women. Just as Julie's *virtù* was exemplified in the spectacle of her death, so Rousseau suggests that the ideal woman will know how to make a spectacle of herself that will reproduce Rousseau's ideal of an asocial political collectivity.

Second, Rousseau acknowledges not only the controlling power of being looked at (i.e., that which men exercise over women), but also the power of representation, of signs themselves. Here is a recognition that *seeming to be* can be as important as being. Although Rousseau wants women to be what they seem and, as discussed in the previous chapter, is concerned about this potential slippage between the referent (woman) and the sign (her appearance), here, in his construction of femininity is a theory of representation unconstrained by notions of authenticity. Again, Rousseau recognizes the *effects* of man's imagination—what women *appear to be* is as important as what they *are.*

Third, Rousseau develops a conception of power in which looking does not necessarily entail the degradation of being looked at; that is, men presumably can look at women without the fear of a reciprocal gaze. Rousseau fashions a reciprocal gaze that is actually a guaranteed mirror. In other words, women, as spectacles, do not look back with autonomous female desire; rather, as spectacles invested only with male desire, they can only return the male gaze, as itself, to itself. Male narcissism is thus satisfied without the obstacle of an other who also wants approval.

The formulation of female *virtù* as spectacle, however, creates the possibility for simulation; that is, the possibility remains that women will appear to be chaste while in fact being corrupt; will appear to be estimable while being improper. This is the genesis, perhaps, of Rousseau's paranoia. The specularity of woman is a kind of Frankenstein's monster. Attempting to solve the problem of imagination, Rousseau has not only exposed the insufficiency of male desire but also marked the inherence of female duplicity. While imagination, which spectacles are designed to regulate, is infinite, the real world has limits (*Emile,* 81). Again, imagination is much like women, whom the law of nature "gives more facility to excite the desires than man to satisfy them" (*Emile,* 360).

Hoping to secure one category, Rousseau has simultaneously destabilized another. Yet, Rousseau seeks to solve this problem by insisting that women themselves have no imagination: "But that celestial flame which warms and sets fire to the soul, that genius which consumes and devours, that burning eloquence, those sublime transports which carry their raptures to the depths of hearts, will always lack in the writings of women; their works are cold and pretty as they are; they may contain wit as you please; never a soul; they are a hundred times more sensible than passionate. They do not know how to describe nor feel even love" (*D'Alembert,* 103). Rousseau does not want women to feel, only to perform. Yet, ironically, it is women whom Rousseau needs to attribute here as possessing more sense. Because women lack imagination, they cannot achieve what men can and thus are not "genuine difference"; they have neither autonomy nor independent will. Women can only imitate what men have projected onto them. They can only "consent," not "want."

Indeed, in *Emile* Rousseau asserts that rape no longer exists: "Rapes are hardly ever spoken of anymore, since they are so little necessary and men no longer believe in them. . . . If fewer acts of rape are cited in our day, this is surely not because men are more temperate but because they are less credulous, and such a complaint, which previously would have persuaded simple peoples, in our days would succeed only in attracting the laughter of mockers" (*Emile,* 360). Although Rousseau concedes in a footnote that occasionally there may actually be such a disparity in age and strength between a man and a woman as to make rape a possibility, he insists that "*real rape* is not only the most brutal of all acts but the one most contrary to its end" (*Emile,* 359; my emphasis). And, he contends, men have discovered that "their pleasures depend more on the will of the fair sex than they had believed, [thus] men have captivated that will by attention for which the fair sex has amply compensated them" (*Emile,* 360).

Rousseau seems to be saying two things, here. First, men's sexual pleasure is increased if they do not rape women but actually gain their consent; and second, that in some way all sex is rape, that is, "theatrical rape" as opposed to what he calls "real rape." A woman does not consent to sex, rather she "consents to let him be the stronger." Woman yields but "with what skill she needs to get stolen from her what she is burning to give!" (*Emile,* 384). What is "sweetest" for man "in his victory is the doubt whether it is weakness which yields to strength or the will which surrenders" (*Emile,* 360). "Real rape" is when he takes from her what she did not want to give; mutual intercourse is when she *pretends* that she did not want to give what he has taken. In this scenario there is no autonomous female desire, "only man's self affection mediated by the feminine."[72] For Rousseau's men pleasure can never be found except in relation to the same; that is, to a "sameness" masked as "difference." Nonetheless, the illusion of consent remains pivotal because it implies difference, another autonomous "I," without marking the subordination of that difference.

Rousseau needs woman as difference in order to limit man's narcissism, but not as a difference that would encourage man to alienate himself from himself. That is, woman must endlessly repeat as her own desires what are actually man's, in order that man not suffer the threat another's will would pose to his subjectivity. The confrontation with difference ignites man to seek the other's approval and to try to appear as something he is not. Woman, instead, mirrors himself back to him, and this confrontation with sameness masquerading as difference does not alarm his inadequacies but rather confirms his identity. In other words, man looks at woman and she does not look back.

All of Rousseau's advice to Sophie in Book 5, for example, is about how she should conduct herself as a spectacle, not as a subject. A few nights after Emile and Sophie are married, Rousseau learns that Sophie has made Emile spend the night in a separate bed. Although Rousseau has advised Sophie to learn how to manage their pleasure together, he wants

72. Irigaray, *The Sex Which Is Not One,* 77.

to ensure that she properly understand why and how this is to be done: "It will cost you some painful privations, but you will reign over him if you know how to reign over yourself. . . . Let him view you as reserved, not whimsical. Take care that in managing his love you do not make him doubt your own. Make yourself cherished by your favors and respected by your refusals" (*Emile*, 478–79). In other words, Sophie must not exercise an independent will ("be whimsical") or contribute to Emile's male anxiety ("not make him doubt your [love]"). Everything she does must be to maintain his pleasure and his security. When she mistakenly tries to assert her own autonomous subjectivity, she is chided by the tutor and reminded that her primary responsibility is to govern Emile's desires.

However, if woman is not afforded an autonomous subjectivity, the issue of consent is further complicated by the difficulty of determining when her consent has been given. Because part of what ignites desire is the imagination's inflammation by obstacles—"Obstacles set before the eyes serve only to excite the imagination more" (*D'Alembert*, 134)—the difficulty becomes determining what are obstacles calculated to enflame desire and what are obstacles of genuine resistance. Thus, Rousseau must teach men how to read spectacles, how to discern "truth" from "appearance." Of course, in this instance, what men want is the *appearance* of resistance that is actually veiled consent. Thus, gaining consent, like gaining access to the general will, is about following the correct procedure, asking the right question. For example, Rousseau dismisses what women say as a way to determine consent. Modesty prohibits women from saying "yes," so men must learn to read their "silent consent" (*Emile*, 85).

The primary distinction is *men's* behavior: between "audacity" and "insolence and brutality." The former he attributes to "man's vocation . . . receiving its laws from love." The latter he ascribes to "a soul without morals, without refinement, incapable of either love or decency." So what determines whether a woman means "yes" is dependent upon the man's approach. Thus, a man must learn how "to give witness to his desires without displeasing, to make them attractive, to act in such a way that they be shared, to enslave the sentiments before attacking the person." But even here the man is implored to gain consent, not permission, for his desires. Indeed, since woman has no autonomous will, she cannot give permission but only accede to his desires. Woman is not positioned as an authority dispensing her favors; rather, she is, again, only a mirror reflecting men's desires. No effort is even made to determine if she has her own desires;

the only effort is to make male desires amendable, somehow "civilized" before he "attacks her person." Because Rousseau's women are not afforded any independent subjectivity or even imagination, they are presumed to consent if a man's approach is relatively decorous.

There is an interesting correspondence here to Rousseau's suggestions for gaining access to the general will. Just as to secure a woman's consent one must take the correct approach (i.e., be "civilized"), so in order to gain access to the general will, one must ask the correct question (i.e., what is in the interest of the common good). Moreover, just as women have been denied what would make them protest men's sexual advances (autonomous female desire), so too is the general will produced through the stripping of what would make citizens dissonant (the primacy of private interests). The point is succinctly summarized in *The Social Contract*: "The more these natural powers are annihilated, the more august and permanent are those which he acquires, the more solid and perfect is the institution; so that if each citizen is nothing and can do nothing but when combined with all the other citizens, and the force acquired by the whole from this combination is equal or superior to the sum of all the natural forces of all these individuals, it may be said that legislation is at the highest point of perfection which human talents can attain."[73] In other words, this newly acquired "nature" will have no conception of a private interest; it will only be able to understand itself as part of a collectivity.

Yet what is rather odd about the "nature" Rousseau now gives his citizens is that it seems to contradict one of his central critiques of eighteenth-century Parisian society—men's reliance on the opinions of others and their consequent lack of independence. This paradox suggests several things: first, that the catalyst for man's decline was not society but the failure of man's nature itself. "Nature" was never what guaranteed goodness; rather, goodness has always been the result of cultivation. Second, this "artificial nature" is equal if not superior to the original; the supplementary powers augment instinct with justice. Perfection is cultivated, not natural, although even this cultivated perfection is haunted by the instability of man's nature. Although the citizen is crafted, indeed imagined to correspond to the sovereign in transparent reciprocity (as the metaphor of the letter sent that has always already arrived elaborated), even this imaginary citizen fails to maintain his self-transparency. Consequently, by

73. "Of the Legislator," *Social Contract*, 36.

the end of *The Social Contract,* Rousseau is seeking for tools to supplement what was expected to be perfect—that is, without need of mediation, autonomous, and transparent to itself.

Woman too is imagined as an ideal supplement. When man's self-transparency is interrupted (i.e., by masturbation or the empire of public opinion), when his self-love (*amour de soi*) fails to protect his self-presence, "woman" becomes necessary. Self-love being natural but distorted into *amour-propre,* femininity is added as an image or representation. In that sense, woman is not natural. She diverts the immediate presence of man to himself into representation and imagination. She is a kind of technique, a sort of artificial and artful ruse to make man present to himself when he is actually absent. She is a violence done to the natural destiny of *amour de soi.*

Yet, as Derrida insists, supplements are not only "bizarre," but dangerous.[74] And Rousseau's anxiety of woman's danger is foreshadowed both in the character of Claire at the end of *Nouvelle Héloïse* and in Sophie in *Les Solitaires,* the unfinished sequel to *Emile,* in which Sophie becomes pregnant with another man's baby. Indeed, Rousseau's fear throughout his work is that the weak (women) are actually the strong, and that men cannot be protected from this knowledge.

Although Rousseau crafts women to supplement what men lack, he worries that women are not merely supplement but are themselves the fullness of nature. Thus each supplement must be disguised, as manifested in his metaphor of veiling and his insistence that women's power be kept covert. Similarly, although Rousseau conceives the social contract, the general will, and civil religion as supplements for the failure of the laws of nature, he seeks to disguise the fact that the laws of nature are lacking, insisting that his artifices are merely natural substitutes.

Thus, Rousseau's texts themselves become rather elaborate artifices to mask that supplements are necessary, that nature is not perfect and that goodness is cultivated. Rousseau works simultaneously to find supplements for the shifting foundations his genealogy continually reveals and to veil the fact that there *are* both shifting foundations and necessary supplements. Indeed, Rousseau works nobly to smooth over the instabilities and failures that his own project exposes.

74. Derrida, *Of Grammatology.*

7

Concluding Remarks

At the origin of republics is a myth, a fable, a story. The very fiber of the origin is available for contestation. Indeed, how is it possible to secure a republic with a myth? As story, the narrative of the rape of Lucretia calls into question the very possibility of an original essence, of a fixed immutable anchor, of foundation itself. And this question crystallizes the dilemma that haunts the founding of republics. By what authority is the republic founded? To what does it appeal before it constitutes itself as legitimate? At the founding must be both a guaranteed foundation *and* the possibility for politics, for political action. Politics is imperative because as the inaugural force of the republic it articulates and enacts the spirit that will animate that which it brings into existence. Thus, the origin must have authority but not so much determinacy that politics is itself forestalled.

And it is a story, a fable, a myth that seems most adequately to fulfill both requirements. If at the origin is a story rather than the Law or Nature, then, the origin is itself politicized, cultivated, a place of possibility. Simultaneously, if the story is one that is endlessly repeated and rehearsed, even in its permutations, it acquires some necessary authority as it frames the constitutive elements of the republic.

I. The Mythical Origin

As this book has shown, storytelling is itself a form of politics. The story is a nonfoundational politics that is still both legitimate and authoritative. The story of the rape of Lucretia has an authority that demonstrates the possibility of politics in a world devoid of traditional, foundational guarantees. Consider again, in this regard, Machiavelli's retelling of the origin story in *La Mandragola*. The story is a reconfiguration of Roman authority.

Machiavelli's rewriting allows for the possibility of political action without the tyranny of Roman authority or universals. Yet Machiavelli maintains in some form both Roman authority and its innovation. His compromise is echoed later by Hannah Arendt when she asserts about the American founding that its authority was the "authority of reconstitution itself; an authority inherent in its own performances."[1] Republican authority must be exercised in a way that further politicizes the people rather than in a way that renders them quiescent.[2] And that is exactly what Machiavelli's rendition of the founding in *La Mandragola* does.

Machiavelli's revision demonstrates the capacity for the founding to be amended and augmented. Set in contemporary Renaissance Italy rather than in ancient Rome, the play sets the beginning, the possibility for founding, in the present. "Foundation is, as it were, continuous foundation."[3] The maintenance of Roman antiquity is achieved through an augmentation that takes place by way of translation.[4] Machiavelli maintains the authority of Rome through a rendition, a translation of a traditional story—Livy's account of the rape of Lucretia.

The return to the origin story of the rape of Lucretia does not necessarily signal the recurrence of violence but often, as in both Machiavelli and Rousseau's versions, a return to the *spirit* of origins, to the human capacity to originate. The origin story, as performative, is marked by all the features characteristic of action as Hannah Arendt describes it. Performative utterances necessarily take place in concert and require for their success the presence of spectators in order to achieve their purpose, which is to bring into being something that did not exist before.[5] For example, the political aspect of a "performative utterance" is shown in Rousseau's formulation for gaining access to the general will in *The Social Contract*. Each member, by asking himself the correct question (i.e., what serves the common good), secures the unity of the community. Here the performative utterance brings something (unity) into existence, although admittedly Rousseau tries to minimize the reliance of this process on one's fellow spectators.

In this regard, it is noteworthy that the story of the rape of Lucretia

1. Hannah Arendt, *On Revolution* (New York: Viking Press, 1963).

2. Hanna Pitkin, *Fortune Is a Woman: Gender and Politics in the Thought of Niccolo Machiavelli* (Berkeley: University of California Press, 1984), 88.

3. Leo Strauss, *Thoughts on Machiavelli* (Chicago: University of Chicago Press, 1978), 44.

4. Jacques Derrida, "Deconstruction in America: An Interview with Jacques Derrida," *Critical Exchange* 17 (1985): 24–25.

5. Hannah Arendt, *The Human Condition* (Chicago: University of Chicago Press, 1958).

is itself theatrical. Both Machiavelli and Rousseau enact their founding narratives as drama. Both as text and as performance, drama is a medium that is significantly more dependent on reception and audience response than is a more traditional political treatise. Drama is a more interactive medium. Even Rousseau's reformulation of the founding in *Nouvelle Héloïse,* an epistolary romance, stages within itself action dependent on response and reception in the exchange of letters. Rousseau's revision is also a manifestation of his desire to orchestrate audience response; spectators have become too dangerous in Rousseau's political semiotics. Nonetheless, what is significant about this theatrical origin for both Rousseau and Machiavelli is that it structurally enacts what is pivotal to the maintenance of the polity—the reliance of each citizen on the other.

This is not to suggest, however, that this "performative utterance" does not bring with it its own set of quandaries. Foremost, for both Machiavelli and Rousseau, the "performative" raises the specter of the potential unreliability of the other upon whom each depends for the preservation of the community. If politics depends on the interaction and interdependence of citizens, then each political actor wants the assurance that the other is a stable entity able to fulfill in the future what he indicates today—that he says what he means and means what he says. Arendt calls this "the power of stabilization inherent in the faculty of making promises."[6]

For Machiavelli, this stability is ephemeral, and politics itself is about the contestation of meaning. Thus, for Machiavelli politics is about manipulating appearances in order to achieve the desired end. Machiavelli embraces the dilemma of the instability of each to the other and articulates a politics that assumes the mediation of appearances and adjusts itself accordingly. As argued here, this antagonism and reconciliation is personified in Machiavelli's articulation of the relation between *virtù* and Fortuna. Machiavelli is the realist who recognizes the "real" as the realm of appearances; the stability of promises is premised on the orchestration of appearance.

Rousseau, on the other hand, laments the nontransparency of each to the other as well as of each to himself, and he tries to construct a politics that is not dependent on the stabilization of promises or on the transparency of others. Instead, Rousseau tries to cultivate a citizen fully autonomous and transparent to himself, although his project too founders on the

6. Ibid., 243.

instability of that very self on whom Rousseau would depend. Thus, Rousseau's response to the instability of political life is to try to formulate an asocial political collectivity, augmented by supplements hidden from view.

II. The Insurgence of Gender at the Origin

This book as a genealogical project is "concerned with the insurrection of knowledges that are opposed primarily . . . to the effects of the centralizing powers that are linked to the institution and functioning of an organized . . . discourse."[7] Genealogies have the potential to illuminate what has been marginalized, what has been produced as an effect. Specifically, in this instance, the story of the rape of Lucretia is an *effect* of a canonical republican trajectory as it tries to achieve and maintain integrity. The story can be seen as an effect of the centralizing discourses of republican formulations of fraternity, of *virtù* and even of politics itself. As an insurgent knowledge, the story of the rape of Lucretia marks the failure of this particular tradition of republican politics to vanquish the feminine; the retellings articulate the inability, finally, for politics to be only about a stable and secured masculinity.

Femininity is an effect produced as the republican tradition strives for certainty, stability and foundation. It is also simultaneously what is forgotten, banished and unaccounted for. In every system, whether linguistic, cultural or political, there is a moment or place, as Jacques Derrida points out, that the system cannot account for. Femininity is this "moment" or "place" in the republican tradition, because recognition of its constitutive importance would also be a recognition of masculinity's dependence, an acknowledgment of the reliance of *virtù* on *fortuna,* of fraternity on sexual violence, and so forth. This reliance must remain masked or at least pressed to the margins in order for male power to remain dominant—indeed, sometimes for male power even to remain potent.

As Bonnie Honig eloquently argues: "[Fable] is an act of memory and de-reification meant to capture and thereby reenable the revolutionary spirit that is the vitality of republican politics. . . . *And the effect of this fable is the same as all legitimating fables: to prohibit further inquiry into the origins of the system*

7. Michel Foucault, "Two Lectures," in *Power/Knowledge: Selected Interviews and Other Writings 1972–1977,* trans. Colin Gordon (New York: Pantheon Books, 1980), 84.

and protect its center of illegitimacy from the scrutiny of prying eyes."[8] It is this prohibition against investigating into the origins that the genealogical approach trespasses.

This book has examined not only "the revolutionary spirit" of the story of the rape of Lucretia but also what is masked and denied in the articulation of the tale, "protected from the scrutiny of prying eyes"—that is, the dependence of *virtù,* fraternity and politics itself on constructions of femininity and notions of ideal womanhood. Thus, the origin becomes both a place of memory and of forgetting. It is the construction of a memory that strives to forget what it does not want to acknowledge and indeed *cannot* acknowledge as it struggles to secure its foundations. In other words, it is a memory designed to ignite political action even as it aims to occlude femininity.

Both Machiavelli and Rousseau manifestly regard women as having a veiled role in politics. Both perceive women's role as most powerful and thus most dangerous when hidden or secret. Machiavelli, on the one hand, when discussing women's role in conspiracies, insists they cannot be trusted because they are the most likely to break the trust of the compact; women are prone to betrayal. Yet on the other hand, Machiavelli celebrates the seductive duplicity of Lucrezia's *virtù* in *La Mandragola.* Likewise, Rousseau assigns women a hidden or secret agency; for example, in "Essai sur les Evénements Importants Dont Les Femmes Ont éte la Cause Secrette" (*Oeuvres Complètes,* Vol. 2), he laments the historical failure to recognize the influence that women have had on events. Women have often mediated events through their husbands and fathers. Instead of bemoaning the role women have played, Rousseau occasionally applauds this role. Yet he too worries about their covert power.

For Machiavelli, men and women are natural sexual antagonists, just as are *virtù* and *fortuna*. Machiavelli lists women among the state's enemies[9] as well as likening his enemies to women.[10] Nevertheless, ultimately he celebrates this sexual antagonism, if not femininity itself. For Machiavelli

8. Bonnie Honig, "Declarations of Independence: Arendt and Derrida on the Problem of Founding a Republic," in *Rhetorical Republic: Governing Representations in American Politics,* ed. Frederick Dolan and Thomas Dumm (Amherst: University of Massachusetts Press, 1993), 216; emphasis mine.

9. See *Discourses,* 3:26, "How States Are Ruined on Account of Women."

10. Ibid., 3:36.

there is a need to understand how struggle with the enemy (political) can aggrandize oneself and ensure one's own success. Indeed, throughout Book 2 of *The Discourses* he details "How Rome Became Great by Ruining Her Enemies." Rome was able to become powerful through struggle partially, as Machiavelli elaborates, because she fought *without* annihilating or completely impoverishing the conquered country. In a parallel vein, as demonstrated through my exegesis of *La Mandragola,* antagonism with *fortuna*, with femininity, enriches male *virtù*. Women serve as worthy enemies who augment men's *virtù*; contestation and struggle with women both teaches men and empowers them. Thus, Machiavelli grants women, as personified by Fortuna, some autonomous power. Fortuna (chance) does, after all, still control half men's actions.

For Rousseau, on the other hand, woman is not an enemy (unless untamed) but an ideal complement. Nonetheless, Rousseau maintains the necessity of resistance (feigned, of course) so that men will still believe in their own power. The ideal woman must compensate for a lack man has. For Machiavelli the threat women pose is that they may weaken male strength, male *virtù*. For Rousseau, the hazard is that the weak (women) may become, or really are, the strong. Indeed, for Rousseau, women jeopardize male sexual potency as well as identity itself. Rousseau thus wants distance from women, not in order to prevent contamination, but so that men will not discover their reliance on them. Machiavelli's misogyny, on the other hand, stems more from his disdain for weakness, from his concern that the strong may be enervated by engagement with the enemy. Although Machiavelli grants women some autonomous power, he is still confident, in ways that Rousseau is not, of men's superiority.

Nonetheless, for both theorists, sexual relations are conceived entirely in terms of producing an increase in the forces of men. For Machiavelli, the maximization of male forces does not require the annihilation of female forces, only engagement with them; and for Rousseau, the maximization of male forces seems to necessitate the denial of the very possibility of autonomous female power. Indeed, this conception of sexual difference personifies each theorist's formulation of power. For Machiavelli, power is embedded in the plurality and contestation inherent in community. Machiavelli is confident in the ability of male *virtù* to mark its distinctiveness in the world, to give its signature to matter. For Rousseau, on the other hand, community embodies not plurality but otherness, and the threat of usurpation of one's own uniqueness. *Virtù* has become a sentiment for Rousseau, no longer sufficient for impressing one's will on the world; individual male distinctiveness must be preserved by the mediation of femininity. Thus, antagonism is feigned, as the strong (women) concede their power for the preservation of the public good and the social order.

III. Repetition(s) at the Origin

As a genealogy, this project began with a set of questions that sought, not to recover the root or the basis for sexual violence or of misogyny in the republican tradition, but rather to explore the ways in which the story of the rape of Lucretia, as told first by Livy and then repeated in the tradition of political theory by Machiavelli and Rousseau, conceives sexual difference, produces republican citizens and formulates political action in each thinker's oeuvre. This book has focused on how sexual difference, citizenship and politics are constructed, in part, through the articulation and repetition of the story of the rape of Lucretia in the republican tradition.

I have not looked to the story of the rape of Lucretia in order to find the essence of, or to trace the "progress" of, republicanism; rather, I have deployed this story as a way to examine how the republican tradition produces its conceptions of sexual difference, citizenship and politics in and through this story. The story has been so productive for this project because as an origin story, it reveals that at the origin there is *not* a timeless and essential secret but rather "the secret that the [origin] has no essence or that its essence has been fabricated in a piecemeal fashion."[11] At the very beginning of the republic is dissension and disparity. The origin story is itself revealed as unstable. As each distinct rendition of the story establishes, the origin is polyvalent.

Nonetheless, it cannot be denied or overlooked that it is the same story, the story of the rape of Lucretia, even if in different incarnations, that is repeated at the origin. Thus, the question of why it is to this particular story that these republican theorists return must finally be taken in hand. Without constructing a metanarrative about republics, I do want to gesture toward some possible reasons for this repetition. Primarily, the story of the rape of Lucretia is so compelling for republican theorists because it not only tells the story of the founding, but it metaphorically reenacts it. The

11. Michel Foucault, "Nietzsche, Genealogy and History," in *The Foucault Reader*, ed. Paul Rabinow (New York: Pantheon Books, 1984), 78.

three most significant features of the story—its violence, its concern with issues of paternity, and the perceived indeterminacy of the crime itself—rehearse the features salient to founding a republic.

First, the violence of the rape recalls the violence of all political beginnings. Yet the violence of Lucretia's rape is a violence not committed by the republicans themselves but merely recollected by them. Republicans do not rape Lucretia; they only witness the spectacle of her violation. The violence of the story, as demonstrated in its various versions, gestures toward the violence of foundings without necessarily reenacting it. For each of these republican theorists, the violence of the founding was something they wanted to mark but not recommend. In fact, each thinker has an ambiguous relation to the question of whether a violent deed can (or is even necessary to) regenerate a community; hence they simultaneously point to and resist the power of violence.

Moreover, the violence of this story, which is a spectacle to republican citizens, signals the importance of vision to republican citizenry. As spectators of the violence done to Lucretia but not direct participants in it, these first republican citizens are recalled not only to their manhood but to their republicanism. The spectacle is what creates a bond among men. Thus, despite each of these three thinkers' different presentations of the story, the privileging of spectacle signals the importance of a founding violence without the potential for the contagion of vengeance. The *narration* of the rape and suicide of Lucretia offers violence without the fear of reprisal. The violence of Lucretia's rape is recollected but not mimicked.

As spectacle, this narrative violence occurs in an arena (for Machiavelli and Rousseau in theatre) where self-conscious evaluation is possible. Theatre, like ritual, provides a structure that allows these thinkers to approach and investigate the paradox of violence safely. The spectacle stems the tide of reciprocal violence and redirects it into "proper channels": the renewal of masculinity as well as of the republic. And each narration of the story explores whether spectacles of politically directed events are sufficient to change the political landscape.

Second, the story of the rape of Lucretia is overtly concerned with issues of paternity and patriarchy. Because Lucretia's rape violates not only her chastity but also her father's and husband's claim to her as well as to her (their) progeny, the story (again, even in its various revisions) implicitly addresses the relation between patriarchy and republicanism. The founding of republics marks the transition from political power garnered through patriarchal privilege to political power forged through fraternal camaraderie. Although each theorist formulates the juxtaposition in slightly different ways, the relation between patriarchy and republicanism is pivotal to each. Themes of paternity (in terms of relations between men and women) as well as the relations between fathers and sons occupied Livy, Machiavelli and Rousseau. Importantly, the tension between these two forms of rule also prefigures how each thinker manages the public/private split in his newly imagined republic. This aspect of the story offers a conduit through which each thinker develops his conception of the role of masculinity and femininity in political life.

In addition, particularly for Machiavelli and Rousseau, questions of paternity are featured in their conception of the relation of the present to the past. Issues of lineage helped to mark the republican desire for continuity with the past, with tradition, as well as a desire for autonomy and freedom from that authority. By focusing on paternity with its concomitant concern with issues of certainty, of authenticity and imitation, these republican thinkers address questions of how to render the past into the present.

Finally, what makes the story of Lucretia specifically potent for these specific republican thinkers, and why they seem to need to retell the tale, is the perceived indeterminacy of the crime itself. This indeterminacy dovetails with the republican conception of founding as a restoration of boundaries that have become blurred or indistinct. The indeterminacy of the crime is threefold. First, there is the rather obvious he-said, she-said aspect of accusations of rape. Issues of speech, of truth-telling and lying, as well as of perspective are embedded in the crime itself, at least from the perspective of both Machiavelli and Rousseau. For them the indeterminacy of the crime provides, in part, the very space for politics.

In addition, the indeterminacy of the crime marks it as a crime not of divine intervention but of human making. This is not a crime of fate or destiny but of human emotions and desires. Oddly, this feature of the crime restores for republican theorists their sense of the potency of human agency. Human actors make their own destiny in the story these republican thinkers tell. Even Lucretia, who is clearly not a beneficiary of the narrative, is in each version given some agency either in the narration of her violation or in the meaning of her seduction. These thinkers exploit the perception that political modes of thought have usurped the relationship to power that religious or mythological modes traditionally held.

Finally, the indeterminacy of the crime also rests on its blurring of the public/private distinction. Rape is a private crime that in this instance has public, political consequences. This aspect of the story—the way in which Lucretia's rape achieves political significance—is reminiscent of what happens under tyranny. Political power encroaches on private freedoms. Here is a rather Aristotelian view that the private sphere is a microcosm of the public sphere. Again, while each theorist will create a different link between the two spheres, the constitution of the two spheres is pivotal to each one's conception of political life. There is a recognition that republican political power does not exist solely in the relation between the state and the citizen, but that power also asserts itself through imposing interpretative grids on the human body.

Finally, I want to say one last thing about the repetitions themselves. Early in this book I argued that the repetition of the story marks a repression that fails, that the story of the rape of Lucretia is a symptom of what republican thinkers could not finally deny: the role of the feminine in the founding of the republic. Most of this book has been concerned with detailing how this denial was repeatedly attempted and how it repeatedly failed. Now I want to add a more general claim to those detailed observations about how the story acted as a symptom in each theorist's work. More generally, the repetitions of the story demonstrate the uneasy relationship between political theory and storytelling.

In a recent essay on narrative, Philip Abbott details four difficulties that political theorists have with storytelling:[12] (1) no matter how directly a story is related to a theory or a part of a theory, its impact can be challenged by the offering of another story. The number of counter stories is limitless. In other words, because the Lucretia story makes its point anecdotally, it is unsecured by science or fact and is thus forever subject to subversion by yet another tale of the "real" relation between sexual violence and political foundings. (2) The story itself is subject to reinterpretations and alterations. Nothing, perhaps, makes this point more cogently than the repetitions of the Lucretia story themselves. Each theorist challenges the theory of the previous storytellers/theorists by offering a counter version of the tale. (3) The story itself is theory embedded in ways potentially independent of, or at odds with, the theorist's own project. The fit between the story and the theory can never be complete or perfect; as

12. Philip Abbott, "Storytelling and Political Theory," in *Memory, Identity, Community: The Idea of Narrative in the Human Sciences,* ed. Lewis Hinchman and Sandra Hinchman (Albany: State University of New York Press, 1997), 281–306.

Amy Guttman notes, "[Narratives] can rarely clinch the case for a particular position."[13] (4) Since the relationship between the story and the theory is broadly analogical, the "point" of the story must be made to fit the "point" of the theory. Telling the story commits the theorist to this process without the assurance that it will be successful; that is, there is uncertainty as to whether the interpretation and reception of the story will correspond to the theorist's intended point. There is no guarantee that audiences will even understand or recognize that the story of Lucretia has something to say about the foundings of republics.

The repetitions of the story of the rape of Lucretia are, in part, a manifestation of the attempt by these republican theorists to try, finally, to get this founding narrative right, to have it adequately tell the story of the founding. The repetitions mark both the ambition, the investment in the possibilities of storytelling for political theory, and the story's perceived failure to render the founding satisfactorily from the perspective of the next generation of republican theorists. The repetitions demonstrate how seductive storytelling is to republican theorists as well as how precarious it can be to their project.

Storytelling is seductive from the perspective of these republican theorists because they believe that these narratives enlarge reality, that they expand our notion of ourselves and of what is possible. Moreover, their reproduction of these stories is not imitative but creative of reality. Storytelling is for each of these theorists a practice of critical understanding: "Storytelling both situates our theories in the experiences from which they came and engages an audience in a different kind of critical thinking than argument does. A story can represent a dilemma as contingent and unprecedented and position its audience to think from within that dilemma. It invites [a] kind of situated critical thinking."[14]

Furthermore, Machiavelli's and Rousseau's reliance on storytelling also parallels their conception of republican political power. Power, for both, is "not an individual property but a possibility of plurality that springs up between men when they act together and vanishes the moment they disperse."[15] Under conditions of plurality, one acts always in situations where contingencies cannot be mastered. Like storytelling, one of the

13. Amy Guttman, "Moral Philosophy and Political Problems," *Political Theory* 10 (1982): 38.

14. Lisa Disch, *Hannah Arendt and the Limits of Philosophy* (Ithaca: Cornell University Press, 1994), 110.

15. Arendt, *Human Condition*, 200.

consequences of this kind of power is that an act will take on meanings in the eyes of others that the actor did not intend or anticipate.[16] Another consequence is that it will have unforeseen and unwanted results: much like the relation the political theorist has to his storytelling. Like republican political power, storytelling serves not to resolve questions but to unsettle them and to inspire spontaneous critical thinking.

The repetitions of the story of Lucretia thus work on multiple levels. First, there is the content of the tale itself, which metaphorically reenacts the founding of the republic. Second, there is the expression of the uneasy relation political theory has with storytelling. And finally, there is the relation the contingencies of storytelling itself has with Machiavelli's and Rousseau's conception of republican political power.

IV. Not an Origin Story: Feminist Repetitions

Finally, there remains the question of the significance of yet another repetition of the Lucretia story; that is, what is the meaning of my own retellings of the story? Why have I, a republican feminist thinker, retold this tale? In some ways, I have done so for reasons that parallel those of Machiavelli and Rousseau. Like Machiavelli, I have retold the tale in part to establish my legitimacy inside the tradition of political theory. Just as Machiavelli explicated the work of Livy as a way to legitimize his reinterpretation of Roman authority, so I have retold the tale of Lucretia as a way to validate my feminist reevaluations of the tradition. Also, like Rousseau, who retold and remade the myth as a way to comment on his contemporary world, I have retold the tale as a way to lay open to view some of the republican history of the relationship between sexual violence and political foundings.

Specifically, my ambition has been twofold: first, through this retelling I have sought to demonstrate the power of narrative for politics; and second, I have simultaneously endeavored to dispel some of the power of this particular narrative of sexual violence and political founding. On the first count, in the ways I have detailed, I applaud storytelling for the kind of critical thinking it makes possible; I do not have a suspicious view of storytelling. That is, I do not imagine that narrative constitutes only an escape, a consolation or a diversion from reality; nor do I conceive of it as

16. Disch, *Hannah Arendt and the Limits of Philosophy*, 81.

an opiate—a distortion imposed from without as an instrument of power and manipulation. Rather, my view has more in common with that of Paul Ricoeur, who conceived of narrative as enlarging reality and expanding our notion of ourselves and of what is possible.

Nonetheless, I have simultaneously endeavored to dispel some of the mythic power of this particular narrative of sexual violence and political founding. I have sought to demonstrate that this story is an effect of other political forces and have thus attempted to lessen its power as a explanatory model. By an "effect" I mean two things: first, the story is an effect in the sense that it marks the attempt to deny the role of the feminine in the constitution of the political; and, second, it is an effect in the sense that the story has always been recollected and narrated from the perspective of its beneficiaries: male republican citizens.

My retelling of the story exemplifies a counter mythical thrust in its treatment and analysis of the victim. My retelling parallels the perspective from which the stories of Joseph and others are told in the Old Testament. As René Girard notes, unlike other mythological texts, these biblical stories take the perspective of the innocent scapegoat. For example, when Joseph is in Egypt, everyone believes that he has betrayed his adoptive father, Potiphar, and committed an action analogous to the incest of Oedipus. The biblical text, unlike the Oedipus myth, disbelieves the accusations, recognizing in it, as Girard argues, "the kind of story that is expected from a community, that, for a number of reasons, happens to be disturbed and is mimetically, i.e., unconsciously, looking for scapegoat relief."[17]

The Joseph story, like many other biblical stories, is told from the perspective of the victim rather than from that of the persecutors; it is told from the perspective of Joseph. Similarly, my retellings of the stories of Lucretia have been an effort to repeat the tale with particular attention to the perspective of the victim. The republican theorists who had previously rendered Lucretia's story did not, and perhaps could not, comprehend the role of her sacrificial act in their narrative of political founding. In order for the story to function as a founding narrative, a certain kind of scapegoating as well as misunderstanding of the significance of Lucretia was required. She served as a substitute for the male members of the community and was offered up by them as such. Her sacrifice served to protect

17. René Girard, "Mimesis and Violence," in *The Girard Reader*, ed. James G. Williams (New York: Crossroad Herder Books, 1996), 17.

the community from its own violence. This is often called a *scapegoat effect.* Yet a scapegoat effect that can be acknowledged as such is no longer effective. Among my purposes has been to dispel the power of this story to rationalize the relation between sexual violence and political foundings, to disable Lucretia from functioning simply as a scapegoat in the transition to a republican founding.

In another register, Hannah Arendt calls this attempt to dismantle traditional formulations "thinking without banisters." By this she means thinking without traditional concepts that are no longer adequate to the phenomena they purport to explain. She calls banisters "categories and formulas that are deeply ingrained in our mind but whose basis of experience has long been forgotten and whose plausibility resides in their intellectual consistency rather than in their adequacy to actual events."[18] It has seemed to me that the myth of Lucretia is of such an age—the myth is no longer adequate to explain the founding of republics, but its juxtaposition of sexual violence and political founding has become almost a force of habit—an "intellectual consistency" rather than an experiential one.

It has also become important to try to unravel some of the logic of the Lucretia narrative, not because it is now being specifically retold as a foundational politics for budding republics, but because its logic of sexual violence and political foundings is still quite influential. Indeed, international attention recently focused on the use of rape as an element of political foundings in the 1990s when the United Nations commission and various human rights groups revealed that ethnic Serb paramilitary groups had systemically tolerated or encouraged the raping of Bosnian Muslim women. Rape was also employed by Hutu troops against Tutsi women in the genocidal campaign Hutu leaders conducted in Rwanda in 1994. In 1998 women who identified with secular culture in Algeria accused desperate rebels fighting in the name of the Islamic revolution of kidnapping them and making them sex slaves. In Indonesia, reports are surfacing that suggest that members of the security forces may have been among the men who raped ethnic Chinese women during rioting in May of 1998.[19]

Significantly, some analysts believe that the fast pace of international communication today may be a factor in the rapid recurrence of the use

18. Quoted in Disch, *Hannah Arendt and the Limits of Philosophy*, 144. Originally in Arendt, "Personal Responsibility under Dictatorship," 1964 Library of Congress, MSS Box 76, 27.

19. Barbara Crossette, "An Old Scourge of War Becomes Its Latest Crime," *New York Times*, 14 June 1998, A-1.

of rape as a tactic in such widely separate parts of the world. And if that is true, it is also evident that rapid international communication has played a role in stirring international outrage. Thus, again, both the sexual violence and the narratives of this violence have assumed a certain kind of logic and power. Of course, the specificity of each of these instances of sexual violation requires detailed analysis. The usefulness of this project for understanding the proliferation of these crimes remains primarily a methodological one: it points to the importance of thinking about the ways in which these atrocities have been narrated on the world stage and how the construction of each story has created or forestalled the possibility of a certain kind of political response. Consider, in this regard, two examples. First, there are the reports from the Kareta Feminist Group in Bosnia that pornography was being made of the rapes of Muslim women.[20] Perversely, visually narrating the rape (from the perspective of the prosecutors) was part of the political potency of the crime. The spectacle of rape apparently created a bond among some Serbian men. The sexualization of violence was a source of manhood. The pornography was also intended to demonstrate the effeminacy of Muslim men. There were multiple reports of the Serbian desire to show that Muslim men could not protect their own women and therefore the next generation of Muslims. This logic is similar to that operative in Livy's account of the rape of Lucretia.

Consider also a visual image from the *New York Times,* which appeared as the banner photo in April of 1994. The photo is of a dead woman sprawled on the sidewalk as Serbian men dressed in military uniform and walking in military formation literally step over her on their way, presumably, "to battle." Here the iconography visually articulates a founding initiated "over her dead body." Again, as in Livy's version, it is a woman's body that seems to ignite political action, even as the materiality of her body is neglected and forgotten. How this photo is interpreted by Western eyes remains unclear, however. One could argue that the display helped to spur outrage at human rights violations and encouraged the eventual prosecution of Serbian war crimes. On the other hand, this display might also be read in ways that parallel Rousseau's own rendition of the Lucretia story. This is a woman already fallen—she is a Third World woman after all, and presumably Muslim. And although the sacrifice of her virtue will enable

20. Catharine MacKinnon, "Turning Rape into Pornography," in *Mass Rape: The War Against Women in Bosnia-Herzegovina,* ed. Alexandra Stiglmayer (Lincoln: University of Nebraska Press, 1994).

republican renewal, there is no place yet carved out for her in the new republic. Like Julie, she too must die.

While one would not want to claim that these narratives of sexual violence tell the entire story of contemporary foundings, they do demonstrate the still-mythic power of the sexual violation of women in political foundings. They also demonstrate that the representation of this violence is still part of its political force. I hope that through this genealogical history I have offered some tools for better understanding this logic and for dispelling its power.

V. One Last Story: Relating Republican and Feminist Theory

Perhaps the best way to conclude a book concerned with the political power of storytelling is to tell yet another story. In *A Room of One's Own,* Virginia Woolf offers an apology because she cannot fulfill what is imagined as the first duty of a lecturer: "to hand you after an hour's discourse a nugget of pure truth to wrap up between the pages of your notebooks and keep on the mantlepiece forever."[21] Perhaps this book too should end with just such an apology, for there is no final nugget explaining once and for all why there is this relationship between sexual violence and political founding. However, such an apology, like Woolf's, would be disingenuous.

Instead of a "nugget of truth," Woolf offers the story of how she came to the conclusion that what is needed for a woman to write fiction is money and a room of her own. She narrates a story because, as she herself notes, she wants to give the audience "the chance of drawing their own conclusion as they observe the limitations, the prejudices, the idiosyncrasies of the speaker." Woolf suggests that the most productive way to think through a social question or problem is to situate it in the context of the beliefs that give rise to it. As Lisa Disch notes: "This means telling the story of a situation in a way that makes explicit the disposition of the author and relates as many of its constituent perspectives as possible. Storytelling is more truth than fact, because it communicates one's own critical understanding in a way that invites discussion from rival perspectives."[22] Thus, this book has tried to think through the republican history

21. Virginia Woolf, *A Room of One's Own* (1929; reprint, New York: Harcourt Brace Jovanovich, 1981), 4.

22. Disch, *Hannah Arendt and the Limits of Philosophy,* 140. For reminding me of Woolf's own relation to storytelling I am indebted to Disch's analysis.

of the relation between sexual violence and political founding by telling the story from several constituent perspectives. I have tried not only to illuminate Machiavelli's and Rousseau's critical understanding of the juxtaposition through their versions of the Lucretia story, but to offer as well a critical understanding of the story from a feminist perspective.

So with both Woolf's apology and Machiavelli's and Rousseau's storytelling in mind, I will conclude with a story as a way to articulate the relation I have sought to create between feminist political thought and republican theory generally.

* * *

In her recent collection of fairy tales, A. S. Byatt tells the story of "The Eldest Princess."[23] In this story, a King and Queen have three daughters. One day the sky is no longer blue but green. The witches and wizards of the kingdom recommend a quest to fetch a single silver bird in order to restore the sky's color. Per custom, the eldest princess is sent on a quest. She, however, is quite conscious of the pattern these stories most often take. She is "by nature a reading, not a traveling princess" and consequently foresees what usually happened in stories with a quest: "The two elder sisters (or brothers) set out very confidently, failed in one way or another, were turned to stone or imprisoned in vaults, or cast into magic sleep, until rescued by the third royal person, who did everything well, restores the first and second (persons) and fulfilled the Quest" (47).

The eldest princess realizes she is caught in a pattern she knows and suspects that she has no power to break it and that eventually she is going to meet a test, fail and "spend seven years as a stone." With this depressing knowledge, she sits down on the side of the road and hears a voice crying out for help. It is a wounded scorpion. The story proceeds with the Princess deciding not to travel the straight road in an attempt to fulfill the quest but rather, taking the advice of the scorpion, to seek the counsel of a wise old woman who will be able to heal the wounded creature.

On her journey to the wise woman, the eldest princess helps not only the wounded scorpion but also an injured toad and a nearly crushed cockroach. They each in turn help her to avoid various hazards, including the Siren whistle of the Fowler and the ax of the brawny Woodcutter. They also "help her find a variety of nuts and herbs and berries and wild mushrooms she would never have found for herself" (57).

23. A. S. Byatt, *The Djinn in the Nightingale's Eye* (New York: Random House, 1994), 47. References in the text are to this work.

Finally the entourage arrives at the "Last House," where the old woman lives. The old woman has a "sharp face covered with intricate fine lines like a spider's web woven of her history." When the Princess enters the house "everywhere there [are] eyes, catching the light, blinking and shining. Eyes on the mantelpiece, in the clock, behind the plates on the shelves, jet-black eyes, glass green eyes, huge yellow eyes, amber eyes, even rose-pink eyes" (63). The old woman heals the scorpion, the toad and the cockroach by asking them "to tell the story of their hurts" while she applies ointments and drops. For her part, the eldest princess feels "she ha[s] come home to where she [is] free." The story ends with the old woman narrating the stories of the other two princesses, or at least, as she says, "their possible stories" (67).

* * *

If one imagines the eldest princess as a feminist theorist, one recognizes her critique of the heroics of the mandatory quest. Like Sheldon Wolin's political theorist, the eldest princess is more interested in a journey than a quest. A quest, as A. S. Byatt details it, has only one correct way of succeeding; a journey, on the other hand, allows for the possibility that there is more than one way to reach its not-well-defined destination. The feminist political theorist, like the eldest princess, is less concerned with getting everything right than with learning interesting things along the way. For the feminist political theorist of this project, the quest is the equivalent of locating the foundation of republican theory. Going off the straight path is following the multiple incarnations of the story of the rape of Lucretia. The quest requires following the straight road with all of the creatures of chaos held back at the road's edge. The journey, on the other hand, necessitates travel among these denied and neglected creatures on the side of the road. The journey is concerned with making visible what has historically been invisible from the thoroughfare.

The journey is also the effort to articulate what has been unspeakable in the vernacular of political discourse. It is an attempt to tell a different story, to recognize the pattern but not to rehearse it. Because she is schooled in the tradition, the eldest princess, like the feminist theorist of this book, recognizes the pattern of the quest narrative even as she renounces it and seeks to find an alternative. Thus, the alternative she finds is itself always in some partial relation to what has been abandoned. The story of the rape of Lucretia bears some important relation to the quest, even as it comments on the limitations of that ambition. The multiple versions of the story of the rape of Lucretia manifest the inability for there to be, finally, one version of the republican founding, even as each version attempts to enact just such a foundation. The variety and multiplicity of stories suggest the loss of a foundational politics, of a quest that could once and for all inaugurate an everlasting republic.

Instead, the journey of this book has shown how with the assistance of the scorpion, the toad and the cockroach, a feminist political theorist can better understand not only the scorpion, the toad and the cockroach, but also the liabilities of her own narrative horizon. Just as the scorpion, toad and cockroach assist the eldest princess, so Livy, Machiavelli and Rousseau enable the feminist political theorist to survey the terrain of republican thinking, to "find things she never would have found for herself." It is interesting to note that while these creatures may be wounded from the perspective of much feminist theory, their injuries are healed by the stories they tell of how they acquired them. Isn't it interesting to note that in the stories (plays, novels, etc.) that Machiavelli and Rousseau tell one finds their most developed female characters as well as their most interesting formulations of masculinity and femininity?

While the retellings of the stories of the rape of Lucretia have sought in one way to exhaust the foundational power of this myth, the retellings have also simultaneously reinscribed the power of storytelling itself. When the eldest princess arrives at the Last House, the home of the wise woman (perhaps, in the iconography of this book, Lucretia herself or another almost mythic woman: a senior feminist political theorist), she is surrounded by multiple pairs of eyes. From the viewpoint of the retellings of this book, the multiple eyes remind us of the multiple perspectives from which every event can be narrated and that, at the end, there are only more stories—or, as the old woman asserts, at least "possible stories."

What this book has attempted to do has been to exhaust any residual power of the story of the rape of Lucretia as well as to celebrate the power of storytelling for politics. On the one hand, my retellings have sought to demystify the justifying juxtaposition of sexual violence and political foundings. Rather than a narrative that explains twentieth-century sexual violence as part of a centuries-old trajectory of sexual violence and political foundings, my retelling of these stories has sought to dismantle the explanatory and exculpatory power of that history. Nonetheless, these retellings have also uncovered how politically powerful and potentially democratic storytelling can be to the founding and creating of political spaces.

The rape of Lucretia was not retold by Machiavelli and Rousseau as a moral tale of horror but was retold in a way that returned agency to political actors. Neither, then, endorses violence, political or sexual, but rather each argues that the alternative to violence is not the prescription of moral categories but rather reformulations that inject citizenship and politics with notions of agency, of action and of community, back into political life. And here lies the most important, if seemingly obvious, contribution of this genealogical history: the stories that we tell matter; they shape the political world in which we live. Stories are, in part, the metaphors, the filaments, that establish the ties among seemingly disparate elements of a world. Stories do not merely reflect the world, they help to create it. Thus, the kind of political world that is possible depends, in no small part, on the kind of stories we narrate about where we have been and how we came to be who we are.

BIBLIOGRAPHY

Abbott, Frank Frost. "The Theatre as a Factor in Roman Politics under the Republic." *Transactions of the American Philological Association* 38 (1907): 49–56.

Abbott, Philip. "Storytelling and Political Theory." In *Memory, Identity, Community: The Idea of Narrative in the Human Sciences,* ed. Lewis Hinchman and Sandra Hinchman, 281–306. Albany: State University of New York Press, 1997.

Andrews, Richard. *Scripts and Scenarios: The Performance of Comedy in Renaissance Italy*. Cambridge: Cambridge University Press, 1993.

Archambault, Paul. "The Analogy of the Body in Renaissance Political Literature." *Bibliothèque d'Humanisme et Renaissance* 29 (1967): 21–53.

Arendt, Hannah. *The Human Condition*. Chicago: University of Chicago Press, 1958.

———. "Truth and Politics." In *Between Past and Future: Eight Exercises in Political Thought*. New York: Penguin Books, 1961.

———. "What Is Authority?" In *Between Past and Future: Eight Exercises in Political Thought*. New York: Penguin Books, 1961.

———. *On Revolution*. New York: Viking Press, 1963.

Aristotle. *The Poetics*. Trans. S. H. Butcher. New York: Dover Publications, 1951.

———. *The Politics*. Trans. Ernest Barker. Oxford: Oxford University Press, 1958.

Ascoli, Albert Russell, and Victoria Kahn, eds. *Machiavelli and the Discourse of Literature*. Ithaca: Cornell University Press, 1993.

Augustine, Saint. *The City of God*. Trans. Marcus Dods. New York: Modern Library, 1950.

Bal, Mieke. "The Rape of Narrative and the Narrative of Rape: Speech Acts and Body Language in Judges." In *Literature and the Body: Essays on Populations and Persons*. Ed. Elaine Scarry. Baltimore: Johns Hopkins University Press, 1988.

Barish, Jonas. *The Anti-Theatrical Prejudice*. Berkeley and Los Angeles: University of California Press, 1981.

Baron, Hans. *The Crisis of the Early Italian Renaissance*. Princeton: Princeton University Press, 1956.

Baudrillard, Jean. *Simulations*. Trans. Paul Foss, Paul Patton, and Philip Beitchman. New York: Semiotexte, 1983.

———. *Seduction*. Trans. Brian Singer. New York: St. Martin's Press, 1990.

Behuniak-Long, Susan. "The Significance of Lucrezia in Machiavelli's *La Mandragola*." *Review of Politics* (Spring 1989): 264–80.

Bennington, Geoffrey. "Postal Politics and the Institution of the Nation." In *Nation and Narration*. Ed. Homi K. Bhabha. New York: Routledge, 1990.

Berman, Marshall. *The Politics of Authenticity: Radical Individualism and the Emergence of Modern Society*. New York: Atheneum, 1970.

Binns, J. W. "Women or Transvestites on the Elizabethan Stage? An Oxford Controversy." *The Sixteenth Century Journal* 5 (October 1974): 95–120.

Boccaccio, Giovanni. *The Decameron*. Trans. G. H. McWilliams. London: Penguin Books, 1972.

Bock, Gisela, Quentin Skinner, and Maurizio Viroli, eds. *Machiavelli and Republicanism*. Cambridge: Cambridge University Press, 1990.

Bok, Sissela. *Lying: Moral Choice in Public and Private Life*. New York: Vintage Books, 1989.

Bondanella, Peter, and Mark Musa, ed. and trans. *The Portable Machiavelli*. New York: Penguin Books, 1979.

Boswell, John. *Christianity, Social Tolerance and Homosexuality*. Chicago: University of Chicago Press, 1980.

Braidotti, Rosi. *Patterns of Discourse: A Study of Women in Contemporary Philosophy*. Cambridge, UK: Polity, 1991.

Brennan, Teresa. *The Interpretation of the Flesh: Freud and Femininity*. New York: Routledge, 1992.

Brint, Michael. *Tragedy and Denial: The Politics of Difference in Western Political Thought*. Boulder: Westview Press, 1991.

Bronfen, Elisabeth. *Over Her Dead Body: Death, Femininity and the Aesthetic*. New York: Routledge, 1992.

Brown, Norman O. *Love's Body*. New York: Vintage Books, 1966.

Brown, Wendy. *Manhood and Politics: A Feminist Reading in Political Theory*. Totowa, N.J.: Rowman and Littlefield, 1988.

Burckhardt, Jacob. *The Civilization of the Renaissance in Italy*, Vol. 1. Trans. S. G. Middlemore. New York: Harper and Row, 1958.

Burgin, Victor. *Formations of Fantasy*. Ed. James Donald and Cora Kaplan. New York: Routledge, 1989.

Burke, Peter. *The Italian Renaissance: Culture and Society in Italy*. Princeton: Princeton University Press, 1986.

Butters, Humfrey. "Good Government and Limitations of Power in the Writings of Niccolo Machiavelli." *History of Political Thought* 7 (Winter 1986): 411–18.

Byatt, A. S. *The Djinn in the Nightingale's Eye*. New York: Random House, 1994.

Case, Sue-Ellen, ed. *Performing Feminisms: Feminist Critical Theory and Theatre*. Baltimore: Johns Hopkins University Press, 1990.

Cassirer, Ernst. *The Philosophy of the Enlightenment*. Trans. Fritz C. Koelln and James Pettegrove. Princeton: Princeton University Press, 1951.

Castiglione, Baldesar. *The Book of the Courtier*. Trans. Charles Singleton. New York: Anchor Books, 1959.

Castle, Terry. *The Apparitional Lesbian: Female Homosexuality and Modern Culture*. New York: Columbia University Press, 1993.

Cicero, Marcus Tullius. *De Oratore*. Trans. J. S. Watson. London: Henry G. Bohn, 1855.

Coleman, Patrick. *Rousseau's Political Imagination: Rule and Representation in the Lettre à d'Alembert*. Geneva: Librairie Droz S.A., 1984.

Cope, Jackson. *Secret Sharers in Italian Comedy: From Machiavelli to Goldoni*. Durham: Duke University Press, 1996.

Cowie, Elizabeth. "Woman as Sign." *M/F* 1 (1978): 49–63.

Cranston, Maurice. *Jean-Jacques: The Early Life and Work of Jean-Jacques Rousseau (1712–1754)*. London: Penguin Books, 1983.

Crocker, Lester. "The Priority of Justice or Law." *Yale French Studies* 28 (Fall–Winter 1961–62): 34–42.

Cropper, Elizabeth. "The Beauty of Woman: Problems in the Rhetoric of Renaissance Portraiture." In *Rewriting the Renaissance: The Discourses of Sexual Difference in Early Modern Europe,* ed. Margaret Ferguson, Maureen Quilligan, and Nancy Vickers. Chicago: University of Chicago Press, 1986.

Crossette, Barbara. "An Old Scourge of War Becomes Its Latest Crime." *New York Times,* 14 June 1998, A-1.

Daedalus: Journal of the American Academy of Arts and Sciences 107. Special Issue, "Rousseau for Our Time" (Summer 1978).

Darnton, Robert. "Readers Respond to Rousseau: The Fabrication of Romantic Sensitivity." In *The Great Cat Massacre and Other Episodes in French Cultural History*. New York: Basic Books, 1983.

Debord, Guy. *The Society of the Spectacle*. Detroit: Black and Red, 1983.

Derrida, Jacques. *Of Grammatology*. Trans. Gayatri Spivak. Baltimore: Johns Hopkins University Press, 1974.

———. "Deconstruction in America: An Interview with Jacques Derrida." *Critical Exchange* 17 (1985): 24–25.

Diderot, Denis. *The Paradox of Acting*. Trans. W. H. Pollack. New York: Hill and Wang, 1957.

Dionysius of Halicarnassus. *The Roman Antiquities,* Vol. 2. Trans. Earnest Cary. Cambridge: Harvard University Press, 1961.

Disch, Lisa. 1994. *Hannah Arendt and the Limits of Philosophy*. Ithaca: Cornell University Press.

Di Stefano, Christine. *Configurations of Masculinity: A Feminist Perspective on Modern Political Theory*. Ithaca: Cornell University Press, 1991.

Donaldson, Ian. *The Rapes of Lucretia: A Myth and Its Transformations*. Oxford: Clarendon Press, 1982.

Duncan, Carol. "Happy Mothers and Other New Ideas in Eighteenth-Century French Art." In *Feminism and Art History: Questioning the Litany*. Ed. Norma Broude and Mary Garrard. New York: Harper and Row, 1982.

Earl, Donald. *The Moral and Political Tradition of Rome*. Ithaca: Cornell University Press, 1967.

Eco, Umberto. *Travels in Hyper-reality: Essays*. Trans. William Weaver. New York: Harcourt Brace Jovanovich, 1986.

Edgerton Jr., Samuel Y. *The Renaissance Rediscovery of Linear Perspective*. New York: Harper and Row, 1975.

Eldar, Dan. "Glory and the Boundaries of Public Morality in Machiavelli's Thought," *History of Political Thought* 7 (Winter 1986): 419–38.

Elshtain, Jean Bethke. *Public Man/Private Woman: Women in Social and Political Thought*. Princeton: Princeton University Press, 1981.

———. *Meditations on Modern Political Thought: Masculine/Feminine Themes from Luther to Arendt*. University Park: Penn State University Press, 1986.

Erlanger, Rachel. *Lucrezia Borgia: A Biography*. New York: Hawthorn Books, 1978.

Euben, J. Peter. *The Tragedy of Political Theory: The Road Not Taken*. Princeton: Princeton University Press, 1990.

Fedden, Henry Romilly. *Suicide: A Social and Historical Study*. New York: Benjamin Bloom, 1938; reissued 1972.

Ferroni, Guilio. "Transformation and Adaptation in Machiavelli's *Mandragola*." In *Machiavelli and the Discourse of Literature*, ed. Albert Russell Ascoli and Victoria Kahn, 81–112. Ithaca: Cornell University Press, 1993.

Flaumenhaft, Mera J. "The Comic Remedy: Machiavelli's *Mandragola*." *Interpretation: A Journal of Political Philosophy* 7 (May 1978): 33–74.

Fleisher, Martin. "Trust and Deceit in Machiavelli's Comedies." *Journal of the History of Ideas* 27 (1966):365–80.

Forrester, John. "Rape, Seduction and Psychoanalysis." In *Rape: An Historical and Social Enquiry*, ed. Sylvanna Tomaselli and Roy Porter, 57–83. Oxford: Basil Blackwell, 1989.

Foucault, Michel. *Discipline and Punish: The Birth of the Prison*. Trans. Alan Sheridan. New York: Random House, 1977.

———. *The History of Sexuality: An Introduction*. Trans. Robert Hurley. New York: Vintage Books, 1978.

———. *Power/Knowledge: Selected Interviews and Other Writings 1972–1977*. Trans. Colin Gordon. New York: Pantheon Books, 1980.

———. "Nietzsche, Genealogy and History." In *The Foucault Reader*. Ed. Paul Rabinow. New York: Pantheon Books, 1984.

Fralin, Richard. *Rousseau and Representation: A Study of the Development of His Concept of Political Institutions*. New York: Columbia University Press, 1978.

Freccero, Carla. "Practicing Queer Philology with Marguerite de Navarre: Nationalism and the Castigation of Desire." In *Queering the Renaissance*. ed. Jonathan Goldberg. Durham: Duke University Press, 1994.

Freud, Sigmund. *Totem and Taboo: Some Points of Agreement Between the Mental Lives of Savages and Neurotics*. London: Routledge, 1961.

Garver, Eugene. *Machiavelli and the History of Prudence*. Madison: University of Wisconsin Press, 1987.

Gilbert, Felix. "The Humanist Concept of the Prince and *The Prince* of Machiavelli." *Journal of Modern History* 11 (December 1939): 449–83.

Girard, René. "Mimesis and Violence." In *The Girard Reader*, ed. James G. Williams, 9–19. New York: Crossroad Herder Books, 1996.

Goodman, Dena. *The Republic of Letters: A Cultural History of the French Enlightenment*. Ithaca: Cornell University Press, 1994.

Gordon, Daniel. "Philosophy, Sociology and Gender in the Enlightenment Conception of Public Opinion." *French Historical Studies* 17 (Fall 1992): 882–911.

Graham, Ruth. "Rousseau's Sexism Revolutionized." In *Woman in the 18th Century and Other Essays*. Ed. Paul Fritz and Richard Morton. Toronto: Hakkert and Co., 1976.

Grazia, Sebastain de. *Machiavelli in Hell*. Princeton: Princeton University Press, 1989.

Greenblatt, Stephen. *Renaissance Self-Fashioning: From More to Shakespeare*. Chicago: University of Chicago Press, 1980.

———. "Fiction and Friction." In *Reconstructing Individualism: Autonomy, Individuality, and the Self in Western Thought*. Ed. Thomas Heller, Morton Sosna, and David Wellbery. Stanford: Stanford University Press, 1986.

Guttman, Amy. "Moral Philosophy and Political Problems." *Political Theory* 10 (1982): 33–47.

Habermas, Jürgen. *The Structural Transformation of the Public Sphere: An Inquiry into a Category of Bourgeois Society*. Trans. Thomas Burger. Cambridge: MIT Press, 1989.

Hallett, Judith P. *Fathers and Daughters in Roman Society: Women and the Elite Family*. Princeton: Princeton University Press, 1984.

Hariman, Robert. "Composing Modernity in Machiavelli's *Prince*." *Journal of the History of Ideas* 50 (January 1989): 3–29.

Hartsock, Nancy. "The Erotic Dimension and the Homeric Ideal." In *Money, Sex and Power: Toward a Feminist Historical Materialism*. New York: Longman, 1983.

Hemker, Julie. "Rape and the Founding of Rome." *Helios* 12 (Spring 1985): 41–48.

Hermassi, Karen. *Polity and Theatre in Historical Perspective*. Berkeley: University of California Press, 1977.

Herrick, Marvin T. *Comic Theory in the Sixteenth Century*. Urbana: University of Illinois Press, 1950.

Higgins, Lynn, and Brenda Silver, eds. *Rape and Representation*. New York: Columbia University Press, 1991.

Higonnet, Margaret. "Speaking Silences: Women's Suicide." In *The Female Body in Western Culture*. Ed. Susan Suleiman. Cambridge: Harvard University Press, 1986.

Honig, Bonnie. "Toward an Agonistic Feminism: Hannah Arendt and the Politics of Identity." In *Feminists Theorize the Political*. Ed. Judith Butler and Joan M. Scott. New York: Routledge, 1992.

———. "Declarations of Independence: Arendt and Derrida on the Problem of Founding a Republic." In *Rhetorical Republic: Governing Representations in American Politics*. Ed. Frederick Dolan and Thomas Dumm. Amherst: University of Massachusetts Press, 1993.

———. *Political Theory and the Displacement of Politics*. Ithaca: Cornell University Press, 1993.

Irigaray, Luce. *The Sex Which Is Not One*. Trans. Catherine Porter. Ithaca: Cornell University Press, 1985.

Jacobs, Mary. "The Phallic Woman." In *Reading Woman: Essays in Feminist Criticism*. New York: Columbia University Press, 1986.

Jacobson, Norman. *Pride and Solace: The Functions and Limits of Political Theory*. New York: Methuen, 1978.

Jed, Stephanie. *Chaste Thinking: The Rape of Lucretia and the Birth of Humanism*. Bloomington: Indiana University Press, 1989.

———. "The Scene of Tyranny: Violence and the Humanist Tradition." In *The Violence of Representation*. Ed. Nancy Armstrong and Leonard Tennehouse. New York: Routledge, 1989.

Johnson, Marion. *The Borgias*. New York: Henry Holt and Co., 1981.

Joplin, Patricia. "Ritual Work on Human Flesh: Livy's Lucretia and the Rape of the Body Politic." *Helios* 17 (Spring 1990): 51–70.

Jordan, Constance. *Renaissance Feminism: Literary Texts and Political Models*. Ithaca: Cornell University Press, 1990.

Kahn, Victoria. "Humanism and the Resistance to Theory." In *Rhetoric, Prudence and Skepticism in the Renaissance*. Ithaca: Cornell University Press, 1985.

———. "Virtù and the Example of Agathocles in Machiavelli's *Prince.*" *Representations* (Winter 1986): 63–83.

Kelly, Joan. "Did Women Have a Renaissance?" In *Becoming Visible: Women in European History*. Ed. Renate Bridenthal and Claudia Koonz. Boston: Houghton Mifflin, 1977.

———. "The Doubled Vision of Feminist Theory." In *Women, History, and Theory*. Chicago: University of Chicago Press, 1984.

Kennard, Joseph Spencer. *The Italian Theatre: From Its Beginning to the Close of the Seventeenth Century*. New York: Benjamin Bloom, 1932.

Keohane, Nannerl. "But for Her Sex . . . the Domestication of Sophie." In *Jean Jacques Rousseau*. Ed. Harold Bloom. New York: Chelsea House Publishing, 1988.

Klapisch-Zuber, Christine. *Women, Family and Ritual in Renaissance Italy*. Chicago: University of Chicago Press, 1985.

Kofman, Sarah. "Rousseau's Phallocratic Ends." In *Hypatia* 3 (Winter 1989): 119–36.

———. *Freud and Fiction*. Trans. Sarah Wykes. Boston: Northeastern University, 1991.

Kraus, Christina S. "Initium Turbandi Omnia a Femina Ortum Est: Fabia Minor and the Election of 367 B.C." *Phoenix* 45 (1991): 314–25.

Landes, Joan. *Women and the Public Sphere in the Age of the French Revolution*. Ithaca: Cornell University Press, 1988.

Lange, Lynda. "Women and the General Will." In *Rousseau, Nature and History*. Ed. Asher Horowitz. Toronto: University of Toronto, 1987.

Laquer, Thomas. *Making Sex: Body and Gender from the Greeks to Freud*. Cambridge: Harvard University Press, 1990.

L'Hoir, Franceso Santoro. *The Rhetoric of Gender Terms: 'Man', 'Woman' and the Portrayal of Character in Latin Prose*. Leiden: E. J. Brill, 1992.

Levene, D. S. *Religion in Livy*. Leiden: E. J. Brill, 1993.

Lintott, Andrew. "Roman Historians." In *The Roman World*. Ed. John Boardman, Jasper Griffin, and Oswyn Murray. Oxford: Oxford University Press, 1986.

Livy, Titus. *The Early History of Rome*. Trans. Aubrey de Selincourt. New York: Penguin Books, 1978.

———. *Rome and Italy*. Books 6–10 of *The History of Rome from Its Foundations*. Trans. Betty Radice. New York: Penguin Books, 1982.

Loraux, Nicole. *Tragic Ways of Killing a Woman*. Trans. Anthony Forster. Cambridge: Harvard University Press, 1987.

Lovejoy, Arthur. "The Supposed Primitivism of Rousseau's *Discourse on Inequality*." *Modern Philology* 21 (1923): 165–86.

Machiavelli, Niccolo. *The Comedies of Machiavelli*. Ed. and trans. David Sices and James B. Atkinson. Hanover: University Press of New England, 1985.

———. *The Discourses*. Trans. Leslie J. Walker, S.J. London: Penguin Books, 1970.

———. *Florentine Histories*. Trans. Laura Banfield and Harvey C. Mansfield Jr. Princeton: Princeton University Press, 1988.

———. *The Letters of Machiavelli*. Ed. and trans. Allan Gilbert. Chicago: University of Chicago Press, 1988.

———. *The Literary Works of Machiavelli*. Ed. J. R. Hale. London: Oxford University Press, 1967.

———. *Lust and Liberty: The Poetry of Machiavelli*. Trans. Joseph Tusiani. New York: Obolensky Press, 1963.

———. *Machiavelli: The Chief Works and Others*, Vols. 1–3. Trans. Allan Gilbert. Durham: Duke University Press, 1989.

———. *The Prince*. Trans. Peter Bondanella and Mark Musa. Oxford: Oxford University Press, 1984.

———. *The Prince and the Discourses*. Trans. Luigi Ricci. New York: Modern Library, 1950.

MacKinnon, Catharine. "Turning Rape into Pornography." In *Mass Rape: The War Against Women in Bosnia-Herzegovina*, ed. Alexandra Stiglmayer, 73–81. Lincoln: University of Nebraska Press, 1994.

Mansfield, Harvey J. *Machiavelli's New Modes and Orders: A Study of the Discourses on Livy*. Ithaca: Cornell University Press, 1979.

Marks, Elaine, and Isabelle de Courtivron, eds. *New French Feminisms: An Anthology*. Amherst: University of Massachusetts Press, 1980.

Marshall, David. "Rousseau and the State of Theatre." *Representations* 13 (Winter 1986): 84–114.

Martinez, Ronald L. "The Pharmacy of Machiavelli: Roman Lucretia in *Mandragola*." In *Renaissance Drama as Cultural History: Essays from Renaissance Drama 1977–1987*. Ed. Mary Beth Rose. Evanston: Northwestern University Press, 1990.

McManners, John. *Death and the Enlightenment: Changing Attitudes to Death Among Christians and Unbelievers in Eighteenth-Century France*. Oxford: Clarendon Press, 1981.

Mead, William. "*La Nouvelle Héloïse* and the Public of 1761." *Yale French Studies* 28 (Fall–Winter 1961–62): 13–19.

Merleau-Ponty, Maurice. "A Note on Machiavelli." In *Signs*. Trans. Richard C. McCleary. Evanston: Northwestern University Press, 1964.

Migiel, Marilyn, and Juliana Schiesari. *Refiguring Woman: Perspectives on Gender and the Italian Renaissance*. Ithaca: Cornell University Press, 1991.

Miles, Gary B. "The Cycle of Roman History in Livy's First Pentad." *American Journal of Philology* 107 (Spring 1986): 1–33.

———. "Maiores, Conditores, and Livy's Perspective on the Past." *Transactions of the American Philological Association* 118 (1988): 185–208.

———. *Livy: Reconstructing Early Rome*. Ithaca: Cornell University Press, 1995.

Mittman, Barbra. *Spectators on the Paris Stage in the Seventeenth and Eighteenth Century*. Ann Arbor: UMI Research Press, 1984.

Montesquieu, Charles Louis de Secondat. *The Spirit of the Laws*. Trans. Thomas Nugent. Berkeley: University of California, 1977.

Morford, Mark, and Robert Lenardon. *Classical Mythology*. New York: Longman, 1985.

Morrison, Toni. "Unspeakable Things Unspoken: The Afro-American Presence in American Literature." *Michigan Quarterly Review* 28 (Winter 1989): 1–34.

Mosher, Michael. "The Judgmental Gaze of European Women: Gender, Sexuality, and the Critique of Republican Rule." *Political Theory* 22 (February 1994): 25–44.

Najemy, John. *Between Friends: Discourses of Power and Desire in the Machiavelli-Vettori Letters of 1513–1515*. Princeton: Princeton University Press, 1993.

Nietzsche, Frederick. *Daybreak: Thoughts on the Prejudices of Morality*. Trans. R. J. Hollingdale. Cambridge: Cambridge University Press, 1982.

O'Brien, Mary. "The Dialectics of Reproduction." In *The Politics of Reproduction*. Boston: Routledge, 1981.

———. "The Root of the Mandrake: Machiavelli and Manliness." In *Reproducing the World: Essays in Feminist Theory*. San Francisco: Westview Press, 1989.

Ogilvie, Robert M. *A Commentary on Livy: Books 1–5*. Oxford: Clarendon Press, 1965.

Okin, Susan. *Women in Western Political Thought*. Princeton: Princeton University Press, 1979.

Pais, Ettore. *Ancient Legends of Roman History*. Trans. Mario Cosenza. New York: Dodd, Mead and Co., 1905.

Pangle, Thomas. "A Critique of the Leading Interpretations of the Political Theory Informing the Founding." In *The Spirit of Modern Republicanism: The Moral Vision of the American Founders and the Philosophy of Locke*. Chicago: University of Chicago Press, 1988.

Pateman, Carole. *The Sexual Contract*. Stanford: Stanford University Press, 1988.

Pitkin, Hanna. *Fortune Is a Woman: Gender and Politics in the Thought of Niccolo Machiavelli*. Berkeley: University of California Press, 1984.

Platt, Michael. "*The Rape of Lucrèce* and the Republic for Which It Stands." *Centennial Review* 19 (Spring 1975): 59–79.

Pocock, J. G. A. *The Machiavellian Moment: Florentine Political Thought and the Atlantic Republic Tradition*. Princeton: Princeton University Press, 1975.

Radcliff-Umstead, Douglas. *The Birth of Modern Comedy in Renaissance Italy*. Chicago: University of Chicago Press, 1969.

Rahe, Paul. *Republics Ancient and Modern: Classical Republicanism and the American Revolution*. Chapel Hill: University of North Carolina Press, 1992.

Rebhorn, Wayne. *Foxes and Lions: Machiavelli's Confidence Men*. Ithaca: Cornell University Press, 1988.

Rich, Adrienne. "Conditions for Work: The Common World of Women." In *On Lies, Secrets, and Silence: Selected Prose*. New York: Norton, 1979.

Ricoeur, Paul. *Freud and Philosophy*. Trans. Denis Savage. New Haven: Yale University Press, 1970.

———. *The Philosophy of Paul Ricoeur: An Anthology of His Work*. Ed. Charles Reagan and David Stewart. Boston: Beacon Press, 1978.

Ridolfi, Roberto. *The Life of Machiavelli*. Trans. Cecil Grayson. Chicago: University of Chicago Press, 1963.

Rousseau, Jean-Jacques. *Jean-Jacques Rousseau Oeuvres Complètes*, Vol. 2. Edition Publiée sous la Direction de Bernard Gagnebin et Marcel Raymond. Paris: Bibliothèque de La Plèiade, 1964.

———. *Citizen of Geneva: Selections from the Letters of Jean Jacques Rousseau*. Trans. Charles William Hendel. New York: Oxford University Press, 1937.

———. *The Confessions*. Trans. J. M. Cohen. New York: Penguin Books, 1953.

———. *Considerations on the Government of Poland*. Trans. Frederick Watkins. Madison: University of Wisconsin Press, 1986.

———. *A Discourse on Political Economy*. Trans. G. D. H. Cole. Chicago: William Benton Publisher, 1952.

———. *Eloisa, or a Series of Original Letters*. Trans. William Kenrick. 1803; Oxford: Woodstock Books, 1989.

———. *Emile, or On Education*. Trans. Allan Bloom. New York: Basic Books, 1979.

———. *The First and Second Discourses*. Trans. Roger D. and Judith R. Masters. New York: St. Martin's Press, 1964.

———. *Letter to D'Alembert on the Theatre in Politics and Art*. Trans. Allan Bloom. Ithaca: Cornell University Press, 1960.

———. *The Miscellaneous Works of Mr. J. J. Rousseau*, Vols. 1–5. New York: B. Franklin, 1972.

———. *The Reveries of a Solitary Walker*. Trans. Charles E. Butterworth. New York: Harper and Row, 1979.

———. *Rousseau, Judge of Jean-Jacques: Dialogues*, Vol. 1. Ed. and trans. Judith Bush, Roger D. Masters, and Christopher Kelly. Hanover: University Press of New England, 1990.

———. *The Social Contract: An Eighteenth-Century Translation Completely Revised*. New York: Hafner Press, 1947.

Rubin, Gayle. "The Traffic in Women." In *Toward an Anthropology of Women*. Ed. Rayna R. Reiter. New York: New Monthly Review Press, 1995.

Saxonhouse, Arlene. *Women in the History of Political Thought: Ancient Greece to Machiavelli*. New York: Praeger Publishers, 1985.

Schwartz, Joel. *The Sexual Politics of Jean Jacques Rousseau*. Chicago: University of Chicago Press, 1984.

Scott, Joan Wallach. *Gender and the Politics of History*. New York: Columbia University Press, 1988.

Sedgwick, Eve Kosofsky. *Between Men: English Literature and Male Homosocial Desire*. New York: Columbia University Press, 1985.

Sennett, Richard. *The Fall of Public Man*. New York: W. W. Norton, 1974.

Serres, Michael. *Rome: The Book of Foundations*. Trans. Felicia McCarren. Stanford: Stanford University Press, 1991.

Shklar, Judith. "Rousseau's Two Models: Sparta and the Age of Gold." *Political Science Quarterly* 81 (March 1966): 25–51.

———. *Men and Citizens: A Study of Rousseau's Social Theory*. Cambridge: Cambridge University Press, 1969.

———. "Jean Jacques Rousseau and Equality." *Daedalus* 107 (Summer 1978): 24.

Silverman, Kaja. *Male Subjectivity at the Margins*. New York: Routledge, 1992.

Skinner, Quentin. *The Foundations of Modern Political Thought*. Cambridge: Cambridge University Press, 1978.

———. *Machiavelli*. New York: Hill and Wang, 1981.

Smith, Bruce James. *Politics and Remembrance: Republican Themes in Machiavelli, Burke and Tocqueville*. Princeton: Princeton University Press, 1985.

Spivak, Gayatri. "Can the Subaltern Speak?" In *Marxism and the Interpretation of Culture*. Urbana: University of Illinois Press, 1988.

Stallybrass, Peter. "Patriarchal Territories: The Body Enclosed." In *Rewriting the Renaissance: The Discourses of Sexual Difference in Early Modern Europe*. Ed. Margaret

Ferguson, Maureen Quilligan, and Nancy Vickers. Chicago: University of Chicago Press, 1986.

Starobinski, Jean. *Jean Jacques Rousseau: Transparency and Obstruction.* Trans. Arthur Goldhammer. Chicago: University of Chicago Press, 1988.

———. *Blessings in Disguise; or, The Morality of Evil.* Trans. Arthur Goldhammer. Cambridge: Harvard University Press, 1993.

Strauss, Leo. *Thoughts on Machiavelli.* Chicago: University of Chicago Press, 1978.

Strong, Roy. *Splendour at Court: Renaissance Spectacle and the Theatre of Power.* Boston: Houghton Mifflin, 1973.

Strong, Tracy. *Jean-Jacques Rousseau: The Politics of the Ordinary.* Thousand Oaks, Calif.: Sage Publications, 1994.

Sullivan, Vickie. "Machiavelli's Momentary Machiavellian Moment: A Reconsideration of Pocock's Treatment of the Discourses." *Political Theory* 20 (May 1992): 309–18.

Sumberg, Theodore. "*La Mandragola*: An Interpretation." *Journal of Politics* 23 (1961): 320–40.

Tanner, Tony. "Julie and La Maison Paternelle: Another Look at Rousseau's *La Nouvelle Héloïse.*" In *Jean Jacques Rousseau.* Ed. Harold Bloom. New York: Chelsea House Publishers, 1988.

Tomaselli, Sylvanna, and Roy Porter, eds. *Rape: An Historical and Social Enquiry.* Oxford: Basil Blackwell, 1989.

Ullman, B. L. "The Postmortem Adventures of Livy." In *Studies in the Italian Renaissance.* Rome: Edizioni di Storia e Letteratura, 1973.

Walsh, P. G. *Livy: His Historical Aims and Methods.* Cambridge: Cambridge University Press, 1970.

Wolin, Sheldon. *Politics and Vision: Continuity and Innovation in Western Political Thought.* Boston: Little, Brown, 1960.

Wood, Neal. "Machiavelli's Concept of *Virtù* Reconsidered." *Political Studies* 15 (1967): 159–72.

———. "The Value of Asocial Sociability: Contributions of Machiavelli, Sidney and Montesquieu." In *Machiavelli and the Nature of Political Thought.* Ed. Martin Fleisher. New York: Atheneum, 1972.

Woolf, Virginia. *A Room of One's Own.* 1929. Reprint, New York: Harcourt Brace Jovanovich, 1981.

Yale French Studies 28. "Special Issue on Jean-Jacques Rousseau" (Fall–Winter 1961–62). New Haven: Yale University Press.

Yates, Frances A. *The Art of Memory.* Chicago: University of Chicago Press, 1966.

Zeitlin, Froma. "Playing the Other: Theater, Theatricality and the Feminine in Greek Drama." *Representations* 11 (Summer 1985): 63–95.

Zirelli, Linda M. "Machiavelli's Sisters: Women and 'the Conversation' of Political Theory." *Political Theory* 19 (May 1991): 252–76.

———. "Resignifying the Woman Question in Political Theory." In *Signifying Woman: Culture and Chaos in Rousseau, Burke, and Mill.* Ithaca: Cornell University Press, 1994.

INDEX

Abbot, Philip, 164
Ab Urbe Condita (Livy), 23
adultery, 82–83
amour-propre. See narcissism
appearances, 1, 91
Arendt, Hannah, 8–9, 84, 89, 156, 168
Augustine, Saint, 4, 36, 52
  Machiavelli's criticism of, 66–68
  on suicide, 67 n. 39
authority
  republican, 156
  spectacle and, 141–42

Bal, Mieke, 30
Baudrillard, Jean, 91
Bennington, Geoffrey, 138–39
Boccaccio, Giovanni, 4
Borgia, Lucretia, 4
Bronfen, Elisabeth, 128
Brown, Norman O., 5–6
Brutus, 26, 28–29
burials, Roman, 36–37
Byatt, A. S., 171–72

Christianity, Machiavelli's defense of, 84
Cicero
  definition of comedy, 54
  story of Sabine women, 42
  use of memory by, 47–48
citizenship, 2
  performative, 12
  republics and, 10
The City of God (Augustine), 67
Collatinus, 28, 107
comedy
  imitation and, 54–55
  Machiavelli's use of, 55–57
  theory of laughter and, 57–58
common good, 1, 7, 11
The Confessions (Rousseau), 105–6
corruption, Rousseau's use of, 107–10

De Clamatio Lucretia (Salutati), 72–76
Derrida, Jacques, 133, 143–44, 153, 158
Diderot, Denis, 120
Disch, Lisa, 170

The Early History of Rome (Livy), 24–25
Emile (Rousseau), 123, 147, 149–50

fatum, 39–40, 114
femininity, 3, 18, 158
  founding of republics and, 3
  Latin forms of, 33 n. 25
  in Livy's republic, 36
feminist political theory, 14–20, 173
festivals, 102. *See also* spectacles; theatre
fortuna, 13, 39–40, 114
Foucault, Michel, 114
fraternity, 10, 33
Freud, Sigmund, 5

gazing, power of, 11–12, 148–49
Geertz, Clifford, 12
gender
  grammar of, 18–19
  in republics, 3
general will, Rousseau and, 135, 137, 139–40
Girard, Rene, 167
government, Rousseau and, 142
Guttman, Amy, 165

Habermas, Jürgen, 134
Herodotus, 40
homosexuality, 32–33, 32 n. 22
Honig, Bonnie, 158–59

imitation, comedy and, 54–55
individuality, Rousseau and, 125
Irigaray, Luce, 6, 18–19

Jed, Stephanie, 72, 73
Joseph story, 167–68

La Mandragola (Machiavelli)
  as comedy, 59–64

frontispiece of, 83
interplay of serious and comedic in, 78–80
as political edification, 80
story of, 155–56
use of mandrake in, 80–81
La Mort de Lucrèce (Rousseau), 104–5
laughter
as pretext for deeper meaning, 55
theory of, 57–58
legislators, Rousseau and, 139
lesbianism, Rousseau and, 131–32
Letter to D'Alembert (Rousseau), 123, 146–57
Livy, Titus, 4, 23–24
conception of history, 40–44
concept of *fortuna/fatum*, 40
as historical dramatist, 44–49
use of repetition and, 23–24
Lucomo, 34
Lucretia, rape of. *See also De Clamatio Lucretia* (Salutati); *Early History of Rome* (Livy); *La Mandragola* (Machiavelli); *La Mort de Lucrèce* (Rousseau)
historical accounts of, 4–5
Livy's story of, 21, 23–25
Machiavelli's rewriting of, 84–85
Machiavelli's view of, 82–83, 86–87
multiple levels of repetition in story of, 161–66
reasons for death of, 30–35
republican theorists and, 161–64
Rousseau and, 106–8
suicide and, 38–39

Machiavelli, Niccolò, 1, 4, 10
choice of comedy versus tragedy, 56–57
conception of politics, 69–71
criticism of Saint Augustine's interpretation of rape of Lucretia, 60–66
defense of Christianity by, 84
interpretation of the rape of Lucretia by, 60–66
men/women as sexual antagonists and, 96
nature of people and, 88–89
performance and, 13
as political thinker, 62–63
rape of Lucretia as drama for, 155–57
as realist, 58
reconfiguration of Roman authority by, 89
role of women in politics and, 159–60
role of women in ruin of the state and, 71–72
and Salutati's version of Lucretia story, 74–76
use of comic theater by, 55–57
use of force by, 85–86
use of seduction as metaphor for political action, 91–93
use of theatre by, 51–54
view of comedic and serious, 77–80
view of rape of Lucretia, 86–87
view of violence, 85
view on political actors and control over events, 95–96
mandrake, 80–81, 89–91
Marshall, David, 101
Marx, Karl, 112 n. 23
masculinity, 15, 18
memory, 47–48
Merleau-Ponty, Maurice, 70
Miles, Gary, 41
Mill, John Stuart, 135
mnemotechnics, 48

narcissism, Rousseau and, 132–34
Nouvelle Héloïse (Rousseau), 102–3, 111
Julie's death, 129–30
overview of, 117–19
social association in, 121–22

O'Brien, Mary, 27
Ogilvie, Robert, 46

paradox, Rousseau and, 99–100
Pateman, Carole, 27
paternity, 27, 162–63
patriarchal power, 27–28
patriarchy, 162–63
performance, 1
performative citizenship, 12
Pitikin, Hanna, 64, 84
Pocock, J. G. A., 7
political action
identity and, 8
seduction as metaphor for, 91–93
political actors, control over events by, 95
political foundings
Livy's conception of, 40–44
rape and, 162, 168–69
violence and, 9

INDEX

political identity, 8
political theory, feminist, 14–20, 173
politics
  Machiavelli's view of, 96
  in republics, 2
  role of women in, 159 60
  Rousseau and art of, 137–38
  Rousseau's conception of, 139–40
  theatricality of, 12–13
power
  Foucault's conception of, 114
  patriarchal, 27–28
public opinion, Rousseau and, 132–36

rape. *See also* Lucretia, rape of; sexual violence
  political foundings and, 162, 168–69
  Rousseau and, 149–50
realism, Machiavelli and, 58
recollection, as seduction, 93–94
Remus, 25–26
repetition
  Livy's use of, 23–24
  multiple levels of, in Lucretia story, 161–66
representation, problem of, 10
republican specularity, 11
republican theorists, rape of Lucretia story and, 161–64
republics
  actors in, 1
  citizenship and, 10
  founding of, 7–8
  gender and, 3
  maintaining stability in, 1
  politics in, 2
  public life and, 1
  relation between original and repetion in, 2–3
  tradition in, 2
  "we" and, 9–10
reputation, 1
Rhea Silva (Vestal Virgin), 23, 25–26
Rich, Adrienne, 6
Ricoeur, Paul, 2
rituals. *See* spectacles
Romulus, 25–26
Rousseau, Jean-Jacques, 5, 8
  aristocracy and, 112 n. 24
  art of politics and, 137–38
  authenticity and falsity, 13
  chance and, 114
  conception of politics for, 139–40
  corruption and, 107–9
  gender, 131
  general will and, 137, 139–40
  good versus bad women and, 146–47
  government and, 142
  ideal woman for, 143–44
  individuality and, 125
  law and founding of republic, 119–21
  legislators and, 124, 139
  lesbianism and, 131–32
  men's nature's and, 126
  narcissism and, 125, 132–34
  paradox and, 99–100
  passion and, 102
  possibility of ideal community for, 127
  public opinion and, 132–36
  rape and, 149–50
  rape of Lucretia as drama for, 155–57
  religion and, 143
  role of women for, 136, 159–60
  spectacle and, 128–29, 150–51
  theatre and, 100, 101, 145 n. 70, 146
  virtue for, 101
  women as legislators and, 119–23
Rubin, Gayle, 27

Sabine women
  Cicero's account of, 42–43
  Livy's staging of, 49
Salutati, Coluccio, 4, 52, 59, 72–76
seduction
  Machiavelli's view of, 91–93
  remembrance as, 93–94
  Rousseau and, 101–2
Serres, Michael, 49
Sextus, 27, 107
  in Rousseau's account, 111–13
sexual violence, 24, 43–44. *See also* rape
The Social Contract (Rousseau), 122–23, 138, 142
Sophie, Rousseau's interpretation of, 13–14
spectacles
  authority and, 141–42
  Machiavelli's use of, 93–94
  Rousseau and, 101–2, 128–29, 141–42, 145 n. 70, 145 n. 71
  violence and, 162
specularity, republican, 9–11
speech, 1

Starobinski, Jean, 133
storytelling, 155, 164–66, 170
Strong, Tracy, 100
suicide, 38, 67 n. 39, 118 n. 3
supplements, 133, 143–44, 153

Tanaquil, 34
theater
  in Livy's history, 47
  Machiavelli's use of, 51–54
  for Rousseau, 145 n. 70
  Rousseau's criticism of, 146
  in Rousseau's descriptions, 101
  Rousseau's renunciation of, 100
theatrical power, 12–13
Thucydides, 40
tradition, 2
tragedy, 56
truth
  Machiavelli and, 13
  Rousseau and, 13
truth-telling, 13, 140
Tullia, 34

Vestal Virgin (Rhea Silva), rape of, 23, 25–26
violence, 9. *See also* rape; sexual violence
  Machiavelli's view of, 85
  political foundings and, 9, 162
virtù, 3
  female versus male, 35–36
  Rousseau and, 101, 148–49, 160–61
Voltaire, 5, 120

"we," and republics, 9–10
Wolin, Sheldon, 15–16, 17, 172–73
Woolf, Virginia, 170